THE WHEEL OF EMPIRE

THE WHEEL OF EMPIRE

*A Study of the Imperial Idea
in Some Late Nineteenth and Early
Twentieth-Century Fiction*

ALAN SANDISON

*Bound in the wheel of Empire, one by one,
The chain-gangs of the East . . .*

KIPLING: 'The Exiles' Line'

MACMILLAN
London · Melbourne · Toronto

ST MARTIN'S PRESS
New York
1967

MACMILLAN AND COMPANY LIMITED
Little Essex Street London WC2
also Bombay Calcutta Madras Melbourne

THE MACMILLAN COMPANY OF CANADA LIMITED
70 Bond Street Toronto 2

ST MARTIN'S PRESS INC
175 Fifth Avenue New York NY 10010

Library of Congress catalog card no. 67–13850

Printed in Great Britain by Richard Clay (The Chaucer Press), Ltd.,
Bungay, Suffolk

Contents

Acknowledgement

PARTS of Chapter Four have appeared in my essay 'Rudyard Kipling: The Artist and the Politician', published in *Kipling's Mind and Art*, edited by Professor Andrew Rutherford. I would like to thank the editor and the publishers — Messrs. Oliver & Boyd — for their kind permission to make use of this material here.

A. S.

Introduction

THE following study is an attempt to discover the nature and function of the imperial idea in the work of some late Victorian novelists and short-story writers. These are, principally, Rider Haggard, Rudyard Kipling, Joseph Conrad and John Buchan. Of varied literary ability, all of these men had come to maturity and published works before the end of the nineteenth century, and all, at one time or another, had lived, worked and written within the context of empire in its hey-day; Haggard as Master of the High Court of the Transvaal, Kipling as a journalist in India, Conrad as an officer of the Merchant Marine in the Far East and Buchan as one of Lord Milner's 'young men' in the work of reconstruction following the Boer War.

I will try to show that, for example, Kipling's relation to the imperial idea is far from a simple matter of jingo politics, that to view it at all from a political point of view is misleading and obstructive, and that the real nature of the idea for him is much more profound and much more central to his artistic vision than has been suggested. To Conrad and Buchan, empire is likewise far more than either an exotic backdrop or a forcing-ground for upper-class ideals, and must be regarded as of major significance in their creative vision too. Haggard's case offers an interesting contrast. Though he writes a great deal about the imperial milieu, the tensions of his art have no moral connection with the tensions of the imperial idea: indeed, they are inimical to the latter whose dramatic form is, in fact, made to negate some of the idea's basic premises. Perhaps this is the more surprising in that Haggard is the only one of these four writers deeply responsive to current evolutionary argument, which, according to popular notions of the relationship between empire and writer, should have cast him in the role of an exponent of political Darwinism. As the study will show, however, this is not the nature of Haggard's response to evolutionary theory, nor does it explain the place of empire in his stories. Even more emphatically neither pure nor impure Darwinism provides the dynamic which informs the imperial idea embodied in the work of the other writers to be discussed here.

For writers like Haggard, Kipling and Buchan the traditional assumption has always been that action in their work was principally directed towards promulgating an imperial ideal. Speaking for the inheritors of a vast political *savoir-faire* they, the reading goes, confidently sponsored the alien government of less experienced breeds. Equipped with a sturdy faith in man's ability to mould nature to his will, intuitive confidence in the irresistibility of empirical method — whether the problem was physical or moral — and a rather conservative idea of progress firmly based on a British ideological patent which had received its imprimatur from Father Time himself, they set out to plough the profits of their political heritage back into the virgin lands of empire.

Almost the exact opposite is, in fact, the case. With the altogether significant exception of Haggard, the basis of action in these writers' work is not primarily political but moral. A 'practical' objective may be conceived to justify action and so predicate a world susceptible to human control, but, in fact, achievement and reality lie in the *process* of action itself since it alone can secure man his identity and integrity. Thus the imperial idea becomes not an end in itself but a major expression of the problems of self-consciousness.

As for Haggard, adhering to a quite different cosmology, action is still pragmatic, man's existence being guaranteed by a transcendental power. His confidence in such a system is, however, extremely frail and his handling of the idea of empire comes to reflect his deepening fear that humanity in all its racial compartments, primitive and sophisticated alike, might yet turn out to be the helpless subject of a vast mechanistic process, ungoverned and ungovernable.

Two distinct ideas of nature are implicit in this and these will, of course, require investigation if the true function of the theme of empire in these works is to be appreciated. In general, little reference is made to works which do not in some way illustrate the nature of these authors' literary relationship to the imperial idea. But just because the action associated with the imperial idea in these books is significant, indeed organic, to the whole of each author's corpus, the end-product may be hoped to further the appreciation of his total achievement.

CHAPTER ONE

The Paradox of Empire

For it is man's nature to change his Dialect from century to century; he cannot help it though he would.

THOMAS CARLYLE

THAT the British Empire was put together in a fit of absence of mind is one of those self-gratifying national convictions which are virtually imperishable. It is, after all, a reassurance that we were not in the game for anything so squalid as money.

Of course, as an explanation of the origins of the empire it is valueless — but then, to a considerable extent, so is the theory that the dynamic was an economic one.

Certainly with Chamberlain's arrival at the Colonial Office in 1895 there came support for the view that more formal control was necessary if British merchants operating in West Africa were to maintain and enlarge their commercial footholds. Instead of commerce bringing the prerequisite of peace it had all too often discomfited its propagandists by spreading unrest and anarchy among the chiefdoms of the hinterland. Moreover, to develop these West African holdings a thoroughgoing policy of Government investment was required together with adequate administration.

Because he [Chamberlain] was the first Colonial Secretary to believe in the need for developing tropical Africa as a state enterprise, he set a new value on the possession of territory. He was too late to add much of it to the empire; but he inspired the beginnings of its modern administration and development.[1]

But how and why, if, as the authors of *Africa and the Victorians* show, the Governments of the earlier period were averse to the extension of British sovereignty, did it come about that, for instance, Egypt, the Sudan and so much of Central, East and West Africa should by 1895 have passed under British rule?

The succinct answer is to be found in Robinson and Gallagher's book: the Victorian empire — which is the concern of this chapter — was not acquired for its intrinsic value, but because Africa's relationship to British strategy in Europe, the Mediterranean and the East had altered.

The prime source of British expansion in these years was, in fact, what might be called Mediterranean policy. The crumbling of Turkey as a bastion against the threat of Russian encroachment, the vulnerability of the shortest route to India, the uncertainties of the Egyptian situation, the movements in the balance of power and the effect on this of Germany's emergence — these were the principal factors motivating Britain's decision to assume the role of an occupying Power. And nothing, it seems, expands like this sort of expansion; once it had been decided to take command in Egypt it was necessary to see to its defence — hence the Sudan and hence Uganda. South of the Zambezi, where the focal point was, of course, the Cape, the pattern of events followed a similar pattern. The integrity of this route to India was of such importance that it had to be maintained 'at all hazards and irrespective of costs' — even of subduing the potentially-hostile republics inland.

Britain's Ministers, then, were reluctant imperialists at this formative stage. As late as 1881 the Colonial Secretary, requested to intervene to settle the state of near-chaos in Lagos and its hinterland which was crippling trade, could reply:

Her Majesty's Government, whilst ready to promote by any friendly means the settlement of these long-standing dissensions which . . . seriously affect the prosperity of Lagos, could not approve any measures involving direct interference with the inland tribes. Such a course would not fail to involve the Colonial Government in dangerous complications, and would entail on this country an extension of responsibilities which Her Majesty's Government are not prepared to undertake.[2]

A similar rebuff had met the humanitarians and philanthropists who had been trying for decades to get the British Government to use Zanzibar as a base from which to pacify and develop the interior. In 1884 a disappointed Kimberley recorded with some feeling that 'the cabinet do not want more niggers' and reluctantly abandoned his scheme for the assimilation of Zululand.

But if Britain's Victorian empire grew out of her statesmen's reactions to problems of international strategy what about the mood of the country at large in relation to this subject of Empire?

While it is true to say that there was always a fairly strong anti-imperialist body of vocal opinion in the country and also that Britain was never so jingoistic as later generations of commentators in the period between the wars liked to assume, it would neverthe-less be wrong to minimise the upsurge of strong imperialist feeling that occurred in the last thirty years of the nineteenth century.

The fact that statesmen of the late Victorian era turn out to be very reluctant and defensive imperialists seems to put them rather at odds with the common conception of nineteenth-century Britain as an extremely confident and assertive nation whose imperial fer-vour was simply the vulgar but logical culmination of her insular self-regard. This apparent paradox is a very real factor in any discussion of the mental climate in which the empire took shape.

Undoubtedly the materialism of the early years of the century bred a brash self-confidence. With a criterion of success based on material aggrandisement anything else at this time would have been surprising. Britain was producing more and more: her markets appeared as insatiable as her resources to deal with them inex-haustible. Such power, such rewards and such an image were irresis-tible. 'There is', wrote Carlyle, 'a new theology, with a Hell which means "Failing to make money".'[3]

Certainly current Benthamite teaching did little to oppose the trend. To the contrary it encouraged and lent countenance to the aspirations of the fairly well-off middle-class population.

Factory owners, shopkeepers, wholesale merchants, and bankers translated the gospel of utility into 'efficiency', and the creed of progress into 'push'. Empiricism encouraged their insistence on 'hard facts'. The economic man, selfishly intent on material gain, was the object of their emulation.[4]

Uncultured and unsophisticated such a man might admit to being, but his virtues were also such as placed this materialist world at his feet. What was required of him there was hard work, a practical expertise and a down-to-earth ability to produce. And these quali-ties he possessed in abundance.[5]

To give further sanction to his moral self-satisfaction he could avail himself of the sustaining force of the pervasive Puritan ethic. The Reverend George Croly had assured the nation at large that it was perfectly entitled to

a justified and hallowed feeling that our preservation had been the special act of providence; that a succession of silent miracles have been wrought for our safeguard . . . I have no conceivable doubts that England has been privileged with the extraordinary success, power, and grandeur of the last three centuries, solely for the purpose of sustaining true religion in the world.

Protestantism was in fact the saviour of England. Cromwell, for instance, had no sooner replaced the Popery-dabbling Government of Charles I with his stern Puritan régime than

England was instantly lifted on her feet as by a miracle. All her battles were victories; France and Spain bowed before her. All her adventures were conquests; she laid the foundation of her colonial empire, and of that still more illustrious commercial empire.[6]

But if the English by this adherence to the true religion had become the elect of God they could by no means rest on their laurels: hard work was enjoined not so much for the material rewards which it might bring as for the fulfilment of a duty owed to God.

The one perfect eternal proprietor is the Maker who created them: the temporary better or worse proprietor is he whom the Maker has sent on that mission; he who the best hitherto can educe from said lands the beneficent gifts the Maker endowed them with; or, which is but another definition of the same person, he who leads hitherto the manfullest life on that bit of soil, doing, better than another yet found can do, the Eternal Purpose and Supreme Will there.[7]

And it is the 'Saxon British' who are fulfilling this role at this time, though if 'a manfuller class of cultivators' comes along they will be declared the inheritors.

If a nation or a race refuses to enact the divine ordination to trade, preferring to remain, like Carlyle's 'niggers', 'up to the ears in pumpkin', or like his even more obdurate Chinaman who 'quietly refuses' to recognise the virtues of commercial intercourse with the West, their offence is not simply against common sense but a violation of the will of God. With a righteous indignation, therefore, Carlyle recommended that 'our friends of China' would best be brought to book if the argument over their refusal to trade were carried out in cannon-shot.

The materialistic creed and its by-products did not, however, go unopposed. Carlyle himself was among the first to spell out what the new industrialism meant in human terms, anticipating Marx in his denunciations:

Supply-and-demand is not the one Law of Nature: Cash payment is not the sole nexus of man with man, — how far from it.[8]

Implicit here is a recognition of the loneliness which man found in this society 'where each isolated regardless of his neighbour, turned against his neighbour, clutches what he could get, and cries "Mine"'.[9] J. S. Mill was quite explicit about the position of the intellectual:

In our age and country, every person with any mental power at all, who both thinks for himself and has a conscience, must feel himself to a very great degree alone.[10]

Inevitably Romanticism and Idealism grew in stature in the shadow of Benthamite materialism; students of the late thirties showed a distinct trend in their desertion of Utilitarianism in favour of Scott, Carlyle and the Romantic poets, while the Oxford Movement 'passionately attacked liberalism of every sort in the name of the fathers of the Church and the dogma of the Middle Ages'.[11]

Bentham had drawn attention to the pernicious influence exerted by honour-and-glory ideals, but as Carlyle pointed out in his notorious essay, *The Nigger Question*, pumpkins are not the sole requisite for human well-being, and an increasing reaction to the absence of a more noble middle-class morality can clearly be seen. Confident the age might be, but it had become 'mercenary, venal, and unheroic' Lecky decided,[12] and William Johnston in *England as it is* (1851) agreed that the period was 'essentially unheroic . . . more prolific of prudence than of elevated feeling'.[13] Renan complained that

Very few act with a view to immortal fame . . . Everyone wants to enjoy his own glory; they eat it in the green blade, and do not gather the sheaves after death.[14]

Some went further in their reaction against their unheroic age. Charles Bradlaugh published in the sixties his attack on the materialists' (and particularly the Christian materialists') mean-spiritedness.

Poverty of spirit is no virtue. Honesty of spirit, manliness of spirit, bold, uncompromising determined resistance to wrong and assertion of right, should be taught in lieu of that poverty of spirit which allows the proud and haughty to trample upon, and oppress the highest human rights.[15]

A few years earlier in 'Maud', Tennyson had given a more disquieting version of the same theme on the eve of war with Russia,

> I awake to the higher aims
> Of a land that has lost for a little her lust of gold,
> And love of a peace that was full of wrongs and shames,
> Horrible, hateful, monstrous, not to be told.

Whether we look in the works of Carlyle, in *Tom Brown's Schooldays*, in Charles Kingsley's pathological tirades or in Ruskin's or Macaulay's essays we repeatedly come upon the same theme. What it could amount to W. E. Houghton points out in *The Victorian Frame of Mind*:

... nationalism and racism, sanctioned by Old Testament Puritanism and social Darwinism, created an atmosphere in which the normal control of the beast in man could be seriously weakened.[16]

The imperial ideology of the late nineteenth-century contrived to represent both the materialist–Puritan ethic and the reaction against its failure to give a fuller emotional satisfaction. To those in the latter category the empire could be seen as a vast metaphysical unity immeasurably greater than the sum of human effort and calculation which went into its construction. Lord Rosebery's speeches furnish evidence in plenty of the ecstasy which such a vision could induce.

How marvellous it all is! Built not by saints and angels but the work of men's hands; cemented with men's honest blood and with a world of tears, welded by the best brains of centuries past; not without the taint and reproach incidental to all human work, but constructed on the whole with pure and splendid purpose. Human and yet not wholly human, for the most heedless and the most cynical must see the finger of the Divine. Growing as trees grow, while others slept; fed by the faults of others;

reaching with the ripple of a resistless tide over tracts and islands and continents, until our little Britain woke up to find herself the foster-mother of nations and the source of united empires. Do we not hail in this less the energy and fortune of a race than the supreme direction of the Almighty?[17]

Lord Curzon habitually struck a more sober note though none the less confident:

Your task is to fight for the right, to abhor the imperfect, the unjust or the mean ... to care nothing for flattery, or applause or odium or abuse ... but to remember that the Almighty has placed your hand on the greatest of His ploughs, in whose furrows the nations of the future are germinating and taking shape, to drive the blade a little forward in your time, and to feel that somewhere among those millions you have left a little justice or happiness or prosperity, a sense of manliness or moral dignity, a spring of patriotism, a dawn of intellectual enlightenment, or a stirring of duty where it did not before exist — that is enough, that is the Englishman's justification in India.

What Croly had hinted Fowell Buxton made explicit: the nation had also a divine mission to bring 'the knowledge of the true God to the uttermost ends of the earth'.

The British Empire has been signally blessed by Providence; and her eminence, her strength, her wealth, her prosperity, her intellectual, her moral and her religious advantages, are so many reasons for peculiar obedience to the laws of Him who guides the destiny of nations. These were given for some higher purpose than commercial prosperity and military renown. 'It is not to be doubted that this country has been invested with wealth and power, with art and knowledge, with the sway of distant lands and the mastery of restless waters, for some great and important purpose in the government of the world. Can we suppose otherwise that it is our office to carry civilisation and humanity, peace and good government, and, above all, the knowledge of the true God, to the uttermost ends of the earth?'[18]

The invocation of might in support of right became, of course, much less oblique as the century progressed; a crude insistence on it formed the basis of the jingoists' creed, prompting such addresses as the following by a county Lord-Lieutenant to a distinguished gathering of men and women:

Neither you nor I believe in these perpetual appeals to Providence in the wrong place and at the wrong time. Neither do we believe in these continual quotations from Scripture. We do not believe, either you or I or anybody else here, in the man who holds the Bible in one hand and the Mauser rifle in the other. (Cheers) And another bit of advice I should like to give you is this — if you meet a gentleman, a somewhat aged gentleman, whose name begins with a K, anywhere down Pretoria way, I ask you to make him sing Psalms out of the wrong side of his mouth, — (cheers) — and as to his cant, drive it down his throat with a dose of lyddite — (cheers) — and three inches of bayonet to keep it there. (Prolonged cheers)

But it was quite acceptable for Britain to take the Bible in one hand and a Mauser in the other, when a nation

not only blocks but menaces the way of advancing and Christianising civilisation — be it in South Africa or elsewhere; Britain's sword should then flash with a divine commission as swiftly as when heaven's own lightning leaps from the cloud. Seldom does God place a quite clear and definite issue before either a man or a nation.[19]

Jingoism only became widely manifest towards the close of Queen Victoria's reign but commentators saw it as visibly on the increase from the mid-years of the century.

The Spirit of Jingoism is no new thing; it is always with us; but it has become much more intense during the last half-century.[20]

Cecil Rhodes testified to finding his guiding principles expressed for him in Ruskin's Inaugural Address at Oxford in 1870 when England's inescapable duty was defined as being

To found colonies as fast and as far as she is able, formed of her most energetic and worthiest men; seizing every piece of fruitful waste ground she can set her foot on, and there teaching these her colonists that their chief virtue is to be fidelity to their country, and that their first aim is to be to advance the power of England by land and sea; and that, though they live on a distant plot of ground, they are no more to consider themselves therefore disfranchised from their native land than the sailors of her fleets do, because they float on distant waves . . .

Even Gladstone considered that the sentiment of empire 'may be called innate in every Briton. If there are exceptions, they are like those of men born blind or lame among us. It is part of our patrimony: born with our birth, dying only with our death . . .'[21]

A few years later a 'large and influential audience' at the Royal Colonial Institute cheered the speaker, who concluded his address with the words, 'I hope the day is not far distant when we shall see the Union Jack flying permanently in the centre of Africa'. In an earlier passage he had elaborated the prospects:

> Now this country of Africa ... is a country which I hope some day will belong to England, a country of which the races, many of them, have very many good points. There are many of them who, I believe, have a great deal of pith in them, especially the women because they are forced to be industrious.

A fellow-member in the ensuing discussion evoked companionable laughter when he remarked, 'I believe there is truth in the Yankee saying that "A country which will grow niggers will grow better things".'[22]

By the time of the second Jubilee Beatrice Webb could write in her diary

> June 25th Imperialism in the air — all classes drunk with sightseeing and hysterical loyalty.

Cobden had early recognised the great allure of colonisation 'with all its dazzling appeal to the passions of the people', and the failure of a wider enfranchisement to condemn the policy. As a reviewer expressed it, 'The tone of Empire is to be heard everywhere now, strong, clear and unmistakable, and it has grown and spread and obtained its mastery during the reign of household suffrage.'

The working classes were certainly not indifferent to the greatness which a discerning Providence had thrust upon them. In the words of Joyce Cary's Sargy Gollup:

> I aint complaining — it's a duty laid down upon us by God — but the Pax Britannia takes a bit of keeping up — with 'arf the world full of savages and 'arf the other 'arf getting in the way.[23]

Immense enthusiasm, in fact, was the response when Lord Rosebery addressed the seventeenth Trades Union Congress in 1884 in these words:

> Do these emigrants belong to the upper classes, or mainly to the middle class? No, they are almost entirely belonging to the working classes. ('Hear, Hear', and cheers). It is you who send forth these thousands to these distant countries. They are your brothers, your children, your

B

kinsfolk, your friends, and what I have to ask you today is this — Do you wish that these kinsfolk and these friends of yours shall remain permanently associated with the fortunes of the Empire, or whether they shall wander away to nations, however akin, who are not under the dominion of the British Crown? ... Nothing can be done, indeed, in this matter without the impulse that comes from the popular will both here and in the colonies. I would ask you then to give this impulse and to prove yourselves by embracing this vast and elevating question not merely Britons, keenly watching and canvassing every question that arises within these islands, not merely representatives discussing sectional subjects, but as bright participators of the Empire, which, either at home or in India, or in the colonies, offers a variety of guarantees and opportunities to her workers, the working men of all classes, which can be offered by no other country in the world. (Loud cheers)[24]

With the advent of the new journalism in the last decade of the century designed to play on the cruder emotional reactions of the populace in general, and the commercially fruitful field of the lower classes in particular, the mood achieved a new momentum. R. C. K. Ensor wrote of the nineties:

Whole classes or strata of society were, in some degree, tasting power for the first time; and as they pushed their way out of the inarticulate and into the articulate part of the community a kind of upstart arrogance became vocal with them.[25]

Harmsworth saw the possibilities in the situation. As an associate expressed it:

We realised that one of the great forces, almost untapped, at the disposal of the Press was the depth and volume of public interest in imperial questions.[26]

In 1896 the *Daily Mail* made its appearance, dedicated to

the supremacy and the greatness of the British Empire ... The Daily Mail is the embodiment and mouthpiece of the Imperial Idea. Those who launched this journal had one definite aim in view ... to be the articulate voice of British progress and domination. We believe in England.[27]

No one, of course, would wish to imply that in the upsurge of feeling all was ignoble. Curzon's farewell message quoted on page 7, if it makes some large assumptions nevertheless expresses his sincere and honourable belief that in empire 'we have found not merely the key to glory and wealth, but the call to duty, and the

means of service to mankind'.[28] Another farewell speech — Lord
Milner's at Johannesburg on 31 March 1905 — records a devotion
to the highest ideals which is altogether admirable.[29] Even those
like Lord Lytton who were quite prepared to see war and conquest
as potent agents of civilisation were very far from being hypocrites
whose cant was, in Hobhouse's words, 'more corrupting than the
unblushing denial of right'. It is not at all difficult to perceive the
grounds of Pandit Nehru's conviction that there was something of
a religious temper about the attitude of the British towards their
imperial responsibilities.

The point made at the beginning of this section that there also
existed at this time a vocal anti-imperialist sentiment should likewise be emphasised. J. A. Hobson publicised his contempt
widely, Ramsay MacDonald condemned the degrading of national
pride to 'a consciousness of racial superiority'.[30] Beatrice Webb,
sharing the objections of most of the Fabians to the Boer War, wrote
of 'the unpleasant background to one's private life' arising from 'the
horrible consciousness that we have as a nation shown ourselves to
be unscrupulous in methods, vulgar in manners, as well as in-
efficient'.[31] Seeley, who had done much to recommend the idea of
empire in more or less intellectual quarters found it necessary to
remind people of the dangers and responsibilities inherent in it.
Even Kipling's Aunt Georgie, in defiance of the mob surging
around her home celebrating the end of the war, hung a black
banner from her window with the inscription 'We have killed and
taken possession'. In fact, throughout the duration of the imperial
'movement' there was a deep-seated uneasiness at the role adopted
by Britain. Raghavan Iyer writes:

The similarities with the Roman Empire, actual and alleged, cannot
do as much credit to the British Empire as its overriding dissimilarity in
one crucial respect — the sense of guilt and the desire for atonement.
There was a gnawing doubt from the first that could not be quelled by
the passion for fanfare and pride in grandeur that reached their climax
under Curzon. As the Oxford classicist, Edwyn Bevan, noticed at the
time, the vulgar revelry in vastitude of conquest and even the plea of
national self-interest could never satisfy the British rulers as a justification
of their Indian empire.[32]

It is not intended, by all this, to burden the Puritan conscience
with the entire responsibility for late nineteenth-century racialism

and imperial bellicosity. In passing one might note, however, that the conventional vehicle for the expression of 'conscience', in a general sense, was more than a little compromised. Archbishop Alexander, Primate of All Ireland, was not the only influential churchman to find the 'oratorio of the cannonade' sublime, though not all of them deserted the Prince of Peace for the Lord God of Battles in highly contentious verse.[33]

As for the new scientific advances in evolutionary studies, they were even less likely to be interpreted as a creed in favour of gutless-ness.[34] Sir Charles Dilke was quite explicit:

> Natural selection is being conducted by nature in New Zealand on a grander scale than any we have contemplated, for the object of it here is man. In America, in Australia, the white man shoots or poisons his red or black fellow, and exterminates him through the workings of superior knowledge; but in New Zealand it is peacefully, and without any extra-ordinary advantages that the Pakéha beats his Maori brother.[35]

It seemed quite self-evident to those who adopted such views that Britain was at the top of this new Great Chain of Being. 'We are the first race in the world,' Rhodes proclaimed to W. T. Stead;[36] Chamberlain with a characteristic modification announced his belief that 'the British race is the greatest of governing races the world has ever seen'.[37] Though in more generous moments Germany and the United States might both be admitted to the charmed circle, John Buchan could still write, as late as 1916:

> We call ourselves insular, but the truth is that we are the only race on earth that can produce men capable of getting inside the skin of remote people. Perhaps the Scots are better than the English, but we're all a thousand per cent better than anybody else.[38]

When to these racialist sentiments was added the military fervour of men with Sir Garnet Wolseley's turn of mind, the outlook became even more alarming:

> All other pleasures pale before the intense, the maddening delight of leading men into the midst of an enemy, or to the assault of some well-defended place. That rapturous enjoyment takes man out of himself to the forgetfulness of all earthly considerations.[39]

Glorification of war, though perhaps in less personal terms than these of the 'modern major-general', was widespread: impressive authorities such as Hegel, Spencer and Renan, were all cited as evidence for its defence.

In all this, however, there were commentators even at the time who could acknowledge both the credit and the debit side of the imperial passion, who were able to strike some sort of balance between the conflicting emotions which empire released in the Sons of the Blood. Sir Winston Churchill, for example:

What enterprise that an enlightened community may attempt is more noble and more profitable than the reclamation from barbarism of fertile regions and large populations? To give peace to warring tribes, to administer justice where all was violence, to strike the chains off the slave, to draw the richness from the soil, to plant the earliest seeds of commerce and learning, to increase in whole peoples their capacities for pleasure and diminish their chances of pain — what more beautiful ideal or more valuable reward can inspire human effort? The act is virtuous, the exercise invigorating, and the result often extremely profitable. Yet as the mind turns from the wonderful cloudland of aspiration to the ugly scaffolding of attempt and achievement, a succession of opposite ideas arise. Industrious races are displayed stinted and starved for the sake of an expensive Imperialism which they can only enjoy if they are well fed. Wild peoples, ignorant of their barbarism, callous of suffering, careless of life but tenacious of liberty, are seen to resist with fury the philanthropic invaders, and to perish in thousands before they are convinced of their mistake. The inevitable gap between conquest and dominion becomes filled with the figures of the greedy trader, the inopportune missionary, the ambitious soldier, and the lying speculator, who disquiet the minds of the conquered and excite the sordid appetites of the conquerors. And as the eye of thought rests on these sinister features, it hardly seems possible for us to believe that any fair prospect is approached by so foul a path.[40]

Any examination of the self-confidence of the Victorian Age, however cursory, would be markedly incomplete without reference to that most influential institution, the English public school. Not only did it express in its Victorian conception much of the quality of the age's aspirations together with its complacent and at times arrogant assumptions but it also links these with the physical fact of empire by a process which could almost be described as the codification of the imperial ideology.

When Dr. Arnold undertook the office of headmaster at Rugby in 1828, he described the principles of his régime thus:

What we must look for here is, 1st, religious and moral principles; 2nd, gentlemanly conduct; 3rd, intellectual ability.[41]

The true end-product of the system was, however, not at all easy to define. Lionel Trilling in his book on Matthew Arnold offers us the alternatives of looking for it in 'the synthesis of piety and intelligence' which distinguished Arthur Stanley, or in the frustrated and maimed life of Arthur Hugh Clough. Perhaps, he suggests, it even found authentic expression in the life of William Hodson of Hodson's Horse. Hodson, greatly admired by Arnold at Rugby,

was earnest and hard-working; he was principled: he refused to admit into an asylum for the children of English soldiers 'the slightest dash of color;' he rose to prominence but became involved in a matter of peculation of regimental funds and then in a matter of illegally imprisoning a border chief ... he organized an irregular troop during the Mutiny, Hodson's Horse, and served with magnificent courage; he was accused of looting but actually he had only bought at a very low price from his commanding officer a herd of cattle he had captured; and when, at Delhi, the three sons of the king surrendered to him, he snatched up a carbine from a trooper and shot them dead; he felt it right and expedient.[42]

Fitzjames Stephen, despite his dislike of Dr. Arnold and Rugby, nevertheless admired the 'combination of moral and physical force' which his system was capable of producing:

We will venture to say that scores of Major Hodson's contemporaries at Rugby and Trinity were thoroughly equal to him both in mental and physical capacity. Where are they now? They are the leaders of everyday English life — what we may call the non-commissioned officers of English society, ... the clergy, the lawyers, the doctors, the country squires, the junior partners in banks and merchants' offices, men who are in every sense of the word gentlemen though no one would class them with the aristocracy. Take a man of this order at random, throw him into strange circumstances, repose confidence in him, subject him to responsibility, and Major Hodson is the result.[43]

At any rate, about 1870 Tom Brown had become a pattern for schoolboys, and Arnold's teaching had given way to a new code in which manliness, animal spirits and prowess at games figure as the attributes most to be admired in a boy.[44]

Though Arnoldianism was on the wane in the fifties it was not until the sixties and seventies that schoolmasters began, to quote David Newsome, 'to give their official encouragement to organised games and to see in them a great force in "character building"'.[45] Prior to this, Arnold's belief in the educational value of leisure as an individual discovery operated against regimentation of boys into sports-teams. But, to quote Newsome again,

when the majority of patrons of the schools ceased to pin their hopes on godliness and good learning and came to agree with Squire Brown that what really mattered was that their sons should turn out to be brave, helpful, truthful Englishmen . . . .[46]

— when this happened, the public school ideal changed too.

By 1880 or thereabouts [the mania for games] had come to dominate all the schools, including the once studious Shrewsbury . . . . At Harrow the government of the Houses was passing from boys high in studies to those high in athletics; at Rugby where the athlete did not officially rule, he began to do so unofficially as the monitorial system began to decay.[47]

And what we get is an insistence on those virtues already mentioned — firmness of character, strength of will, sense of duty, reserves of fortitude; and those in turn bred satellite codes of behaviour. Men were wanted to rule the empire: men of courage, endurance and fortitude: men who saw their duty clearly and simply: men who could fulfil their responsibilities with fairness, firmness and justice: men who would willingly sacrifice all they had in the interest of their country's cause. The public schools provided the supply.

The Ten Commandments quoted by H. B. Gray[48] conveys a fair impression of what this meant to the pupils in everyday terms:

There is only one God; and the Captain of School is His Prophet.
My school is the best in the world.
Without big muscles, strong will, and proper collars there is no salvation.
I must wash much and in accordance with tradition.
I must speak the truth even to a master, if he believes everything I tell him.
I must play games with all my heart, with all my soul and with all my strength.
To work outside class hours is indecent.
Enthusiasm, except for games, is in bad taste.
I must look up to the older fellows and pour contempt on newcomers.
I must show no emotion and not kiss my mother in public.[49]

Most of the characteristics are there — the worship of athletic prowess, chauvinistic loyalty, sanctified tradition, contempt for the intellectual, the suppression of feeling and sympathy; and the cultivation of a certain hauteur. Some admitted the narrowness of the English public school man's horizon but it was usually heavily qualified by their insistence that he had at least learned to obey and, by consequence, to command, and would come out well in difficult circumstances. Few regretted with the Reverend T. L. Papillon that 'doing so many things well it seems a thousand pities that he was not trained to do them better, and face the problems of race, creed, and government with a more instructed mind'.[50] Ironically, their ultimate service to the empire was to be terribly marred by their general ignorance of, and lack of sympathy for, more intellectual concepts.

Sanders of the River, who no doubt had a way with natives, might have to be replaced by someone who could cope with the aspirations and assertions of a native intelligentsia; it was certainly hard to envisage Sanders himself doing any such thing.[51]

Much earlier, one finds Sir Arthur Gordon, Governor of the Fijis, perceiving the same failure:

'There is', he told the Royal Colonial Institute in 1878, 'not infrequently a want of imagination on the part of the dominant race which prevents any conception by them of matters from a native point of view, and produces a lack of tolerance for laws or usages not in accordance with European modes of thought, which is often not only as injurious as real injustice, but frequently leads up to it. Indeed it is probable that as much real wrong has been inflicted by the conscientious but narrow-minded desire to act in accordance with maxims in themselves generally sound, but not of universal application, as by violence and consequent tyranny.'[52]

One is tempted to speculate that administrative respect for subject races' feelings and aspirations declined in direct ratio to the advent of the new public school man.[53] And with the increasing consciousness of the usefulness of a public school education in the cause of social advancement, the volume of the schools' production and the area of their impact grew enormously.

I mentioned at the beginning of this section the paradox of the imperial statesmen acting reluctantly and defensively while the mood of the nation often appeared brashly assertive and, in a wide variety of senses, expansionist.

In fact, alongside the aggressive self-confidence and complacency there existed a quite antithetical stream of feeling, for the odd thing is that though such basically optimistic attitudes and emotions largely inspired the imperial ideology, the late Victorian empire itself was, as has been indicated, almost entirely defensive in its conception.

That this is the case, however, is not as illogical as it appears: for, at least among the clerisy, underlying the optimism and the confidence — where these were present — there was to be discerned uneasiness and fear which grew as the century progressed. It was not just that from the seventies anxious questions began to be asked in periodicals and reviews as well as in Parliament about alarming signs in Britain's trading position; nor was it simply the disquiet being voiced more openly about the growth of French and German power. Its roots went much further back and much deeper.

As early as 1831 Carlyle was noting that where once 'action . . . was easy, was voluntary, for the divine worth of things lay acknowledged,' now 'doubt storms in . . . through every avenue'. By the seventies Mallock could argue that through the nineteenth century 'man has been curiously changing. Much of his old spontaneity of action has gone from him. He has become a creature looking before and after . . . we have learnt to take to pieces all motives to actions.' And, between these two commentaries, of course, had come Charles Darwin. Work was still an ethical duty but it was also, as Tennyson admitted, the best antidote to doubt. At least some of the astounding energy and activity associated with the Victorians has its explanation here as has much contemporary anti-intellectualism (responsibility for which was not to be placed entirely on the shoulders of the materialists). Even the widespread fear of democracy and universal suffrage can be seen in the same context, as the suspicion grew that underneath the surface there might be found not a sustaining principle or a natural law but disorder and chaos. In a curious way the concepts with which the 'optimists' played — materialism, Puritanism, electoral reform, the public schools even — experienced a transformation so that while they represented

confidence and complacency at its height, they had in them elements which could be read as the symptoms of disillusionment.

One could take as a specific example the distortion of the great
and precious core of Puritanism itself. What Professor Tawney
said in respect of Puritanism in general is particularly applicable to
its Victorian manifestations:

> For it is will — will organised and disciplined and inspired, will
> quiescent in rapt adoration or straining in violent energy, but always
> will — which is the essence of Puritanism.[54]

But now for many, consciously or unconsciously, a change was
taking place. The moral self-sufficiency which nerved the Puritan's
will in the battle to achieve the Great End had always tended to cor-
rode his sense of social solidarity: loneliness was endemic in his
contempt for the world around him and his determination to seek
God in isolation from his fellow men.[55] But with the increasing
uncertainty of this Great End moral self-sufficiency became at
once more important, more necessary in a psychological sense, and
much more difficult to sustain — it became, in fact almost an end
in itself and the means of achieving it was, paradoxically, the will.
It is not, therefore, difficult to see why firmness of character and
strength of will should have become the hall-marks of teaching in
the second half of the century — or of the imperial servant to
whom the tradition had bequeathed those characteristic features,
'a silent sense of duty and a profound conception of personal
responsibility'.[56]

But if character, strength of will, and a moral self-sufficiency were
the demands of the age they were also those of the writers to whom
most attention is given here — writers who saw the integrity of
the self as profoundly menaced as the statesmen did that of the
nation.

Is it too much to see a connection between these attitudes and
movements and political actions? The most direct expression of the
Zeitgeist may be mainly expected from the artist, but it is absurd
to pretend that the politician is immune from it. This is conceded
by Robinson and Gallagher:

> Statesmen did more than respond to pressures and calculate interests;
> their decisions were not mere mechanical choices of expedients. Judge-
> ments and actions in fact were heavily prejudiced by their beliefs about

morals and politics, about the duties of government, the ordering of society and international relations.[57]

and more explicitly,

their solutions and purposes . . . were charged with the experience and beliefs of the society in which they lived and worked.[58]

And that society was an increasingly anxious and troubled one: without intruding far into the field of social psychology it is easy to see — taking one obvious example — that a wide indulgence in frenetic jingoism is not the symbol of an unworried nation.

After what could perhaps be seen as the last and finest flowering of the Puritan ideal in trade and society in the early years of Victoria's reign, British expansion after the 1880s was clearly negative in purpose and achievement.

The early Victorians had been playing from strength. The supremacy they had built in the world had been the work of confidence and faith in the future. The African empire of their successors was the product of fear lest this great heritage should be lost in the time of troubles ahead.[59]

Individual enterprise which had been 'the main engine of expansion' seemed to flag, and the self-confidence which had carried Victorians so far and revealed a world so full of promise also began to wane: fears of subversion and disloyalty took its place encouraged by the various rebellions in India, Ireland and South Africa. Nationalists refused to be assimilated to British purposes; the old faith in influence and moral suasion declined. As a result they turned more often from the technique of informal control to

the orthodoxies of the Indian Raj for dealing with political anomalies and for securing their interests. They were ceasing to be a dynamic force and becoming a static power. They were more and more preoccupied throughout the world to guard what they had won; and they became less able to promote progress, as they lapsed into the cares of consolidation.[60]

A good deal later, Bulteel, the Resident in Joyce Cary's novel *Mister Johnson* has learned to instruct his juniors

No long views — the age for long views ended twenty years ago — and above all, not too much zeal.[61]

The desire no longer to encourage change but to preserve the *status quo* marks the obsession with security and the increasing pessimism; at the same time, with fearful Darwinian sanctions fresh in their minds, there was a horror of standing still:

> It seems to me that the tendency of the time is to throw all power into the hands of the greater empires, and the minor kingdoms — those which are non-progressive — seem to be destined to fall into a secondary and subordinate place.[62]

There is something significant in terms of their world view in the fact that men like Baring and Chamberlain should come to echo Bentham and J. S. Mill in the weight and importance they give to scientific administration. When Dr. MacDonagh talks about 'the gradual introduction of a dynamic for a static concept of administration'[63] he increases this significance: for that the dynamic should be redirected so that the emphasis no longer falls on an expansive imperial policy is a mark of very great change indeed. In the imperial milieu one can certainly see one waxing as the other wanes:

> Step by step, the easy British optimism modulated into an injured resentment and a harsher outlook ... hence (the Victorians) were driven into abandoning creative policy and replacing it by cold administration and control. Prestige became all important. So, too, did insurance.[64]

When we turn to the artists chosen to exemplify the nature of the imperial idea in its literary manifestation, we should not be surprised to find that what characterises the real nature of the relationship is neither a brash, vulgar self-confidence nor an obtuse nationalism. Just as that which came to be regarded as the imperial ideology — 'la mission civilisatrice' with all its pure and impure accretions — had little to do with the actual fact of Empire as it was founded, so the imperial idea in the work of these writers neither represents simply the superficies of political reaction associated with the wider-still-and-wider school nor (informative though it may be on the subject) the source of their creative inspiration. To see it as such would be to accord the imperial idea a creative role in literature which it never possessed in history. It was a means not an end: a medium through which to express the fearfulness and pessimism which underlay political and artistic expression alike, a pessimism which more accurately represents the real character of late Victorian empire-building. In doing so it underlines the fact (elaborated more fully in a later chapter) that in both sectors the real nature of the idea reflects a clear and logical development of the basic nineteenth-century dialectic.

Even at their most imperial these writers are doing something much more than writing to express the idea of empire. The consequences of failing to acknowledge this are exemplified in the widely-held view that Kipling in his imperial stories is reflecting nothing else *but* the superficies of political reaction: a view which seems to me not only to mistake the role of the idea for a creative one but also to misread the tone of Kipling's work and its quality.

In my attempt to define the precise relationship between the empire and these selected writers I hope to make it clear that if the imperial idea is not the source of their inspiration it has all the same a significance for them which goes far beyond the political and offers us direct access to that source. If this interpretation is accepted it may, for example, further the current disposition to see more in Kipling than a literary jingo and banish the notion of John Buchan as the Peter Pan of Milner's 'Kindergarten'.

NOTES

1. Ronald Robinson and John Gallagher, *Africa and the Victorians* (1961), p. 396.
2. Ibid., pp. 39–40.
3. Thomas Carlyle, *Past and Present*, p. 183. All quotations from Carlyle's works are taken from the Centenary Edition, 1896–1901. See Bibliography for date of first publication.
4. Emery Neff, *Carlyle and Mill* (New York, 1926), p. 120.
5. Of the very important part played by utilitarianism in the imperial ideology, Raghavan Iyer in his essay 'Utilitarianism and All That' (*St. Antony's Papers*, no. 8) provides an illuminating description. He defines a number of other constituents, chief of which were the 'Roman element' of peace under law, the 'Semitic element' of racial exclusiveness and destiny, the 'Prussian element' of militancy and firmness, and the 'non-conformist Radical element' of atonement and penance and expiation (p. 20).

6. George Croly, *The Englishman's Polar Star!!*, (Preston, 1828), pp. 44, 47, 15.

7. Thomas Carlyle, 'The Nigger Question', in *Critical and Miscellaneous Essays*, vol. 4, p. 374.

8. Carlyle, *Past and Present*, p. 186.

9. Carlyle, *Sartor Resartus*, p. 185.

10. J. S. Mill, dated 11 May 1865, *Letters*, ed. Hugh Elliot (1910), vol. 2, p. 29.

11. Emery Neff, op. cit., p. 353.

12. W. E. Lecky, *History of Rationalism* (New York, 1903), vol. 2, p. 345.

13. Quoted by W. E. Houghton in *The Victorian Frame of Mind* (New Haven, Conn., 1957), p. 285.

14. Ernest Renan, *Histoire du Peuple d'Israël* (Paris, 1893), vol. 4, p. 329.

15. Quoted by E. Neff, op. cit., p. 369.

16. W. E. Houghton, op. cit., p. 213.

17. Lord Rosebery, Rectorial Address at Glasgow University, 16 Nov. 1910.

18. Lord Curzon. Quoted by Bennett, *The Concept of Empire: Burke to Attlee 1774–1947* (1953), pp. 351, 105.

19. Quoted by J. A. Hobson in *The Psychology of Jingoism* (1901), pp. 33–34, 50.

20. Lord Farrer in *The Contemporary Review*, no. 74 (1898). Throughout the century India had, of course, always been there to serve as a rallying point for sentiment, and contributed much from these earlier years to late-Victorian imperial ideology.

21. 'England's Mission', in *The Nineteenth Century* (Sept. 1878).

22. *Proceedings of the Royal Colonial Institute*, vol. vii (1875–6), pp. 280–90.

23. Joyce Cary, *Mister Johnson* (1952), p. 144.

24. Earl of Rosebery, speech to the seventeenth Trades Union Congress, quoted by G. Bennett, op. cit., pp. 288–91.

25. R. C. K. Ensor, *England 1870–1914* (Oxford, 1936), p. 304.

26. Quoted by W. L. Langer, *The Diplomacy of Imperialism* (1935), p. 84.

27. Ibid., p. 84.

28. G. N. Curzon, 'The True Imperialism', in *Nineteenth Century* (Jan. 1908).

29. See Alfred Milner, *The Nation and the Empire* (1913), *passim*.

30. Quoted by Bennett, op. cit., p. 354.

31. *Our Partnership* (1948), p. 194.

32. 'Utilitarianism and All That', *St. Antony's Papers*, no. 8 (1960), p. 10.

33. He celebrated the opening of the Boer War with a poem to *The Times*:

> They say that war is Hell, the 'great accursed',
> The sin impossible to be forgiven,
> Yet I can look upon it at its worst
> And still find blue in heaven!
>
> And as I note how nobly natures form
> Under the war's red rain, I deem it true
> That He who hath made the earthquake and the storm
> Perchance made battles too.
>
> Thus as the heavens' many-coloured flames
> At sunset, are but dust in rich disguise,
> The ascending earthquake dust of battle frames
> God's picture in the skies.

34. See A. P. Thornton, *The Imperial Idea and its Enemies* (1959), p. 48.

35. Sir Charles Dilke, *Greater Britain* (4th edn., 1869), ch. vi, p. 281.

36. Quoted by C. E. Carrington in *The British Overseas* (Cambridge, 1950), p. 681.

37. Quoted by W. L. Langer, op. cit., p. 92.

38. John Buchan, *Greenmantle* (1956), p. 29.

39. Sir Garnet Wolseley, 'Is a Soldier's Life Worth Living?', *Fortnightly Review*, 1 May 1889, p. 604.

40. Winston S. Churchill, *The River War* (1899), vol. i, pp. 18–19.

41. Quoted by David Newsome, *Godliness and Good Learning* (1961), p. 34.

42. Lionel Trilling, *Matthew Arnold* (1956), p. 72.

43. Fitzjames Stephen, *The Edinburgh Review* (Apr. 1859). Quoted by Lionel Trilling, op. cit., pp. 72–73.

44. David Newsome, op. cit., p. 37.

45. Ibid, p. 81.

46. Ibid, p. 238.

47. E. C. Mack, *Public Schools and British Opinion since 1860* (1941), pp. 123–4.

48. H. B. Gray, *Public Schools and the Empire* (1913), pp. 172–3.

49. The additional assumption, at Eton in particular, that every boy would at one time or another be in some such position as Viceroy of India, resulted in a system 'capable of producing anything from industrious civil servants to megalomaniac noblemen or industrious

noblemen to megalomaniac civil servants'. [Anthony Powell in *The Old School*, ed. Graham Greene (1934) p. 152]

50. Quoted by Bernard Darwin in *The English Public School* (1929), p. 21.

51. A. P. Thornton, op. cit., p. 312.

52. Sir Arthur Gordon in *Proceedings of the Royal Colonial Institute*, vol. x (1878–9).

53. Not that it was ever marked. As early as 1818 Munro could write to Hastings: 'Foreign conquerors have treated the natives with violence, and often with great cruelty, but none has treated them with so much scorn as we.'

54. R. H. Tawney, *Religion and the Rise of Capitalism* (1961), p. 201.

55. Cf. ibid., pp. 228–9.

56. Raghavan Iyer, op. cit., p. 49.

57. Op. cit., p. 20.

58. Ibid., p. 21.

59. Ibid., p. 472.

60. Ibid., p. 470.

61. Joyce Cary, *Mister Johnson*, p. 231.

62. Robinson and Gallagher, op. cit., p. 404 (Chamberlain is being quoted).

63. Oliver MacDonagh, 'The Nineteenth-Century Revolution in Government: A Reappraisal', *The Historical Journal*, no. 1 (1958), p. 60.

64. Robinson and Gallagher, op. cit., p. 288.

CHAPTER TWO

Rider Haggard:
'*Some Call it Evolution . . .*'

*You know, all is development — the principle is perpetually going
on. First there was nothing; then there was something; then — I
forget the next — I think there were shells; then fishes; then we
came — let me see — did we come next? Never mind that; we
came at last, and the next change will be something very superior
to us, something with wings. . . .*

Lady Constance in DISRAELI's *Tancred*

RUDYARD KIPLING's precocious disclosure that

the wildest dreams of Kew are the facts of Khatmandhu
And the crimes of Chatham chaste in Martaban.

was a mortal affront to some of his countrymen's most respectable
prejudices. Notwithstanding, he went on to develop the theme in
various disguises until it became a recognisable part of the Kipling
'voice'. So much so, that a reader coming across a reflection inviting
him to observe how

the customs of mankind on this matter [marriage] vary in different
countries, making morality an affair of latitude, and what is right and
proper in one place, wrong and improper in another.[1]

could easily be forgiven for thinking of Kipling as its author. The
quotation comes, in fact, from a book by a very close friend of his,
Rider Haggard. Yet far from this shared appreciation of the relativity of cultures being allowed as proof of similarity in the works
of these two writers a comparison will show how different was the
source of the awareness in each case and how much more central it
was in Haggard's fiction than in that of Kipling.

There are two words which are quite crucial to the vocabulary of any criticism of Haggard's work, words to which events of his age had added new and troublesome life. They are 'process' and 'purpose'. The first acknowledges Haggard's acute feeling of things being in a state of flux and change, the second relates to his lasting preoccupation with the question of design in nature, with whether or not there was a Providence which ordered events. The interdependence of these notions is obvious: the terms reflect two aspects of the same concern. Given the fact that things were in continuous process, in a state of Becoming, there were for Haggard three possibilities. These were firstly that there *was* a principle of order in the universe and that it was dictated by God; secondly, that there *was* a principle of order in the universe, but its determination was purely mechanical with accident as its first cause; thirdly, that there was *no* order inherent in the universe and chance dominated all. There is, occasionally, the merest hint of an interesting fourth possibility — that what order there is in nature has been put there by man.

It is towards the pessimistic end of this scale that Haggard undoubtedly inclines. More precisely, though the third seems at times to have a certain purchase, it is the second possibility which exercises the most powerful fascination over him: a fascination which, ideologically, owes much to his association with a certain evolutionary doctrine. At the same time, his desire to find justification for supporting the first possibility is inextinguishable and profound.

That his view of reality has a seminal relationship with a particular evolutionary theory is an observation which the following pages will explore more fully, since it seems to me to be of basic importance to an understanding of this novelist's work. What the examination will ultimately show is that for Haggard as for Darwin the crucial issue was the accidental variation from which species developed. Though, as shall be shown, Darwin was well aware of, and indeed troubled by, the moral implications of his theory, it is the novelist Haggard for whom these implications come to be of fundamental concern: hence his preoccupation with the notions of purpose and process. Pursuing this further, it can be shown clearly that Haggard's relationship to the imperial idea, as it emerges in the role assumed by the latter in his fiction, is dictated by an idea of nature rooted in his reaction to the evolutionary doctrine advanced by Charles Darwin.

Describing Darwin's relationship to scientific materialism, Jacques Barzun writes:

> Contrary to popular belief, Darwin's distinctive contribution to this movement is not the theory of evolution as a whole, but a theory which explains evolution by *natural selection from accidental variations*. The entire phrase and not merely the words Natural Selection is important, for the denial of purpose in the universe is carried in the second half of the formula — accidental variation.[2]

Though conceptions like Ayesha, Mea, or the Inkosazana y Zoola with their supernatural attributes and associations may testify to the strength of Haggard's desire to identify a mystery within which the human spirit has an ordained if inscrutable role, his inability to accept the Darwinian denial of purpose was not matched by any real confidence in the obvious alternative. When Ernest in *The Witch's Head*, contemplating the heavenly immortality he believes in, asks Mr. Alston if he shares his belief, he gets little reassurance from the reply:

> 'I don't know. I think it rather presumptuous. Why should you suppose that for you is reserved a bright destiny among the stars more than for these?' And he put out his hand and clasped several of a swarm of flying-ants which were passing at the time. 'Just think how small must be the difference between these ants and us in the eyes of a Power who can produce both. The same breath of life animates both. These have their homes, their government, their colonies, their drones and workers. They enslave and annex, lay up riches, and, to bring the argument to an appropriate conclusion, make peace and war. What then is the difference? We are bigger, walk on two legs, have a larger capacity for suffering, and, we believe, a soul. Is it so great that we should suppose that for us is reserved a heaven, or all the glorious worlds which people space — for these, annihilation? Perhaps we are at the top of the tree of development, and for them may be the future, for us the annihilation. Who knows? There, fly away, and make the most of the present, for nothing else is certain.'[3]

In almost every case pessimistic misgivings undermine his attempt to find consolation in a conjectural Divine Plan too great for man's puny intellect to grasp. Some such design there might be, but the daily lives of human beings so full of suffering and mitigated with so little hope scarcely suggested the will of a beneficent Providence.

Say, my father, why does the Unkulunkulu who sits in the Heavens above allow such things to be done on the earth beneath? I have heard the preaching of the white men, and they say that they know all about Him — that His names are Power and Mercy and Love. Why, then, does He suffer these things to be done — why does He suffer such men as Chaka and Dingaan to torment the people of the earth, and in the end pay them but one death for all the thousands that they have given to others? Because of the wickedness of the peoples, you say; but no, no, that cannot be, for do not the guiltless go with the guilty — ay, do not the innocent children perish by the hundred? Perchance there is another answer, though who am I, my father, that I, in my folly, should strive to search out the way of the Unsearchable? Perchance it is but a part of the great plan, a little piece of that pattern of which I spoke — the pattern on the cup that holds the waters of His wisdom. *Wow !* I do not understand, who am but a wild man, nor have I found more knowledge in the hearts of you tamed white people. You know many things, but of these you do not know: you cannot tell us what we were an hour before birth, nor what we shall be an hour after death, nor why we were born, nor why we die.[4]

It may be that 'out of the confusions of our lives and deaths order shall yet be born',[5] but the voice we are more aware of is that of Lord Devene in his bequest to Robert Ullershaw:

I express the sincere hope that . . . you and Edith will agree to live together in the accustomed, time-hallowed fashion, and if possible, leave children behind you to carry on the race. Not that it is worth carrying on, except, perhaps, for certain qualities of your own, but one must make sacrifices upon the altars of habit and sentiment. For what other possible reason can the populations of the earth be continued? Yet there is one — Nature — (perhaps in the wilderness you have found out what that word means) commands what the good sense of her most cultivated children condemns as entirely useless and undesirable. Perhaps there is some ultimate object in this, though personally I can see none. To me it appears to be nothing more than the blind brutality of things which decrees the continuance, at any rate for a while, of the highly nervous, overbred and unsatisfactory animal called Man. Well sooner or later he will die of his own sufferings, that increase daily as he advances in the scale of progressive degeneracy, which he dignifies by the name of civilisation. Then perhaps Nature (God is your name for it) will enjoy a good laugh over the whole affair, but as human tears will have ceased to fall, what will that matter?[6]

True the book ends with the affirmation that there exists a God who will reward the just and punish the unrighteous but compared with Lord Devene's speech it is perfunctory and without conviction.

In that very troubled book, *Jess*, the wicked Anglo-Boer Frank Muller is the one allowed to reject the idea of purpose, which he proceeds to do with disconcerting force:

> Bah, a God! I snap my fingers at him. Chance is the only god. Chance blows men about like the dead grass, till death comes down like the veldt fire and burns them up.[7]

Compared with this, the saintly asceticism of Robert Ullershaw makes heavy weather of any display of confidence in the Great Design.

> He knew . . . he should not live uselessly, or endure death in vain, that no life not even that of the ant which toiled ceaselessly at his side in the yellow sand, was devoid of purpose or barren of result, that chance or accident did not exist; that every riddle had its answer, and every pang its issue in some new birth; . . .[8]

Though he feared the worst, Haggard's restless urge to penetrate the flux and discover its secret for himself remains to be either the subject or a large part of the subject of practically every book he wrote. Indeed it is in the tension this compulsion sets up together with the scope through which it works, that we find the principal origin of Haggard's exceptional imaginative power and the explanation of his books' triumph over so much astonishingly bad writing.

If the question 'why?' brought little comfort to Haggard the question 'how?' brought him a breadth of vision which many contemporary Victorians lacked; clearly in this respect, too, he owed much to Darwin. J. A. Symonds, talking about the impact of Darwinism 'on a young man in the sixties' (he was born in 1840) acknowledges the nature of his own debt:

> By penetrating our minds with the conviction that all things are in process, that the whole universe is literally Becoming, it has rendered it impossible for us to believe that any one creed or set of opinions possesses finality.[9]

The work of Rider Haggard, who was born some fifteen years later, is a tribute to the strength and persistence of the same influence and to the authenticity of Symonds's observation. His intense awareness of things being in process — in the sense that Symonds used the word — is fundamental to the great majority of his novels; specific examples are almost too numerous to mention:

> It seems to be a law of life that nothing can stand completely still and changeless. All must vary, must progress or retrograde; the very rocks in the bowels of the earth undergo organic alterations, while the eternal hills that cover them increase or are worn away. Much more is this obvious in the case of ephemeral man, of his thoughts, his works and everything wherewith he has to do, he who within the period of a few short years is doomed to appear, wax, wane, and vanish.[10]

Time thus becomes of central significance in the Haggard scheme: time which stretches immeasurably into the past and forward to the infinity of the future. Thus it can contain changes of all magnitude — and offer scope for the most extensive pursuit of a principle of order. Practically all Haggard's major characters richly avail themselves of the opportunity with which they are presented so that not only the cosmically enterprising Ayesha but also sober figures like Allan Quatermain himself lead a stimulatingly fluid existence between past, present and future. A few among them are more precariously balanced than others. Readers of, for example, *The Ghost Kings*, cannot but deprecate the modesty of Rachel Dove's claim to have inherited a little of her Scottish mother's 'foresightedness': she could, one feels, have foretold the future from a bowl of porridge, if her dexterity in other media is anything to go by. One swift survey of a calabash of dew; one penetrating glance into the informative depths of the pond in Dingaan's kraal — and the salient events of the next forty-eight hours are firmly in her possession. And when her aptitude is boosted by the really sophisticated art of that doyenne of clairvoyantes, the Mother of the Trees, she attains the ultimate in a quite remarkable preview of the Day of Judgement.

At a more serious level, it was the awareness of flux and change which gave Haggard his humanity and his humility, and in few places is this better displayed than in his African stories. On occasion he is, of course, to be found subscribing to a belief in Britain's imperial destiny. But there are very few traces of the familiar Victorian paternalism which contact with 'natives' normally elicited — far fewer than one might have expected from a man who had himself run up the flag in Pretoria on the annexation of the Transvaal. His consciousness of 'process', of 'the truth that it is impossible to isolate phenomena from their antecedents and their consequents' gave him a much wider perspective, and his own honesty both to himself and to a scientific accuracy of observation enabled him to escape the vice of racial prejudice to which so many of his contemporaries succumbed.

When one thinks of what someone like Buchan would have made of the white man's presence in *King Solomon's Mines* one can appreciate Haggard's disengagement from the more vulgar presumptions of the imperial idea. In this book, as in every other he wrote on Africa, he repudiates without fuss the whole arrogant notion of the white man's burden. Physically the European remains supernumerary to the great sum of human tribulation which rises clamorously around him. For it is in the lives and destiny of the Zulus themselves that the main current of life in these novels makes itself manifest. The depiction of them caught in its grip is vivid and memorable, but above all it is their *consciousness* of their predicament which ensures that they are not mistaken merely for colourful native background to the derring-do of a band of Victorian hearties. It is this which allows them — the native race — to hold their own in the centre of the stage with the white man who has strayed into their world. The spiritual reality of their existence may be equalled by that of the lives of the intruders, but it certainly is neither surpassed nor put to shame. Indeed it is Haggard's presentation of them as being under the same doom as the Europeans and sensitively aware of the fact that results in the remarkable degree of identification of native and European spiritual life. Thus when Rachel Dove assumes the role of the Zulu's mystical goddess and becomes the Inkosazana y Zoola, her effortless success in the part is not to be attributed to the fact that a plucky English girl, given a few yards of calico, a bunch of feathers and some pins, can hoodwink any number of witless savages: on the contrary, it is due in very large measure to her sharing the idea the role embodies.

In stories like *Marie, Child of Storm, Nada the Lily*, and even in the African parts of *The Witch's Head* the cultural identity is always that of the Zulu, and the point of view as much his as the white man's. Considering the time and the prejudices of the public at home, all sorts of unlikely things happen. The wild Mameena, for example, captivates the white hunter.

Now, Macumazahn . . . the poor black girl has you, the wise, experienced white man, in her net, and I will show you that she can be generous.[11]

and Quatermain admits it:

This beautiful girl with the 'fire in her heart', this woman who was different from all other women I had ever known, seemed to have twisted her slender fingers into my heart strings and to be drawing me towards her.[12]

Natives, whom it is 'the fashion to abuse' or 'to talk of as black dirt which chances to be fashioned to the shape of a man', are revealed as having a genuine social organisation and culture of their own. Though 'the ways of black people are not as the ways of white men', as Ignosi reminds Sir Henry, this does not invalidate their particular moral code which frequently puts him 'above the Christian who for the most part regards the "nigger" as a creature beneath contempt'. Nor is their social organisation exemplified only in their military machine:

An officer learned in Zulu law — which I can assure the reader is a very intricate and well-established law — I suppose that he might be called a kind of attorney-general, rose and stated the case against the prisoner.[13]

His terminology itself signifies his determination to stress the similarity and by doing so to challenge his society's cherished cultural exclusiveness. Whether done with that intention or not, his sly christening of a distinguished Zulu regiment The Greys no doubt sent a *frisson* down many a ramrod Victorian back.

Conversely, he was quite well aware that to compare them in equal terms with the civilised world was not always to flatter the native race, which had, more often than not, frequent cause for regretting its contact with the imperial power.

Still we may wonder what are the thoughts that pass through the mind of some ancient warrior of Chaka's or Dingaan's time, as he suns himself on the ground, for example, where once stood the royal kraal, Duguza, and watches men and women of the Zulu blood passing homeward from the cities and the mines, bemused, some of them, with the white man's smuggled liquor, grotesque with the white man's cast-off garments, hiding perhaps, in their blankets examples of the white man's doubtful photographs.[14]

Sir Henry Curtis takes the decision at the end of *Allan Quatermain* to maintain Zu-Vendis's isolation, for to do otherwise would be to

endow it with the greed, drunkenness, new diseases, gunpowder and general demoralisation which chiefly marks the progress of civilisation amongst unsophisticated peoples.[15]

After his last visit to Zululand Haggard wrote prophetically:

In the case of the Zulus, civilisation has one of its greatest opportunities, for certainly in them there is a spirit which can be led on to higher things. My earnest hope ... is that this opportunity may not continue to be neglected in the years to come. If so, it seems to me that we shall incur a heavy responsibility towards a bewildered people, that we have broken and never tried to mend, and suffer evils to arise of which the effect will not be endured by them alone.[16]

The consequences of being made to recognise that all things are in process, that 'the whole universe is literally Becoming', had been to awaken Symonds to the sophistry of cultural absolutism. Haggard shows a similar awareness, going beyond Symonds to make his relativist position quite explicit. One of the results for him, as has been noted, is that his presentation of the native African is free on the whole from condescension or disparagement, and his appraisal of his own nation's shortcomings much more clear-sighted.

Of the latter's blind devotion to base materialist ends he was particularly conscious — indeed more than most of the 'imperial' writers he was highly sensitive to the strength of the economic factor in the imperial idea — and in *Jess* he bitterly reproaches a heedless Britain complacently wallowing in the mire of profit and loss. 'I have been twice to England now and I know the Englishman,' says the Boer General in this book written to expose the ignoble surrender of the Transvaal to the Boers,

... He knows nothing — nothing. He understands his shop; he is buried in his shop, and can think of nothing else. Sometimes he goes away and starts his shop in other places, and buries himself in it, and makes it a big shop, because he understands shops. But it is all a question

of shops, and if the shops abroad interfere with the shops at home, or if
it is thought that they do, which comes to the same thing, then the shops
at home put an end to the shops abroad. Bah! they talk a great deal there
in England, but, at the bottom of it, it is shop, shop, shop. They talk of
honour, and patriotism too, but they both give way to the shop. And I
tell you this, Frank Muller: it is the shop that has made the English, and
it is the shop that will destroy them.[17]

Absorbed as the country appeared to be in sordid commercial specu-
tion it failed to take the measure of the corruption growing out of
such self-indulgence. To Haggard the callousness and hypocrisy it
entailed were perfectly clear.

The law of the country (Zu-Vendis) is, on the whole, mild and just,
but differs in several respects from our civilised law. For instance, the law
of England is much more severe upon offences against property than
against the person, as becomes a people whose ruling passion is money.
A man may half-kick his wife to death or inflict horrible sufferings upon
his children at a cheaper rate of punishment than he can compound for
the theft of a pair of old boots.[18]

And when Umslopogaas later in the same book is chided for wanting
to return to the war-path, his defence is succinct:

Ay, Macumazahn, mine is a red trade, yet it is better and more honest
than some. Better is it to slay a man in fair fight than to suck out his
heart's blood in buying and selling and usury after your white fashion.
Many a man have I slain yet is there never a one that I should fear to
look in the face again.[19]

More particularly, Haggard, like all of the writers considered
here, found that his contact with those subject races which metropolitan attitudes so decried left him more conscious of affinity than
disparity:

Scratch the polish, and there you have best raw Zulu human nature.
Indeed to anybody who has taken the trouble to study the question, it is
simply absurd to observe how powerless high civilisation has been to do
anything more than veneer that raw material which remains identical
in each case.[20]

Moreover from a writer intensely aware of the evolutionary process, of the present's inheritance from the past, bland self-satisfied
talk of 'civilisation' could elicit little but scorn. Allan Quatermain,

for example, is frequently driven to rebuke his fellow-countrymen for their facile assumptions about the status arrogated to themselves:

> We white people think that we know everything. For instance, we think that we understand human nature. And so we do, as human nature appears to us, with all its trappings and its accessories seen dimly through the glass of our conventions, leaving out those aspects of it which we have forgotten or do not think it polite to mention.

Quatermain, however, has been brought up in a tougher school where human nature was to be studied very much in the rough:

> For most of the years of my life I have handled the raw material, the virgin ore, not the finished ornament that is smelted out of it — if, indeed, it is finished yet, which I greatly doubt. I daresay that a time may come when the perfected generations — if Civilisation, as we understand it, really has a future and any such be allowed to enjoy their hour on the World — will look back to us as crude, half-developed creatures whose only merit was that we handed on the flame of life.[21]

Not only, then, does Haggard insist that in the so-called 'savage' there is to be found a timely reminder of certain easily disdained home-truths, that in him there is to be seen 'naked and forcibly expressed ... those eternal principles which direct our human destiny', he asserts simultaneously complete cultural relativity.

> ... by what exact right do we call people like the Zulus savages? Setting aside the habit of polygamy, which, after all, is common among very highly civilised peoples in the East, they have a social system not unlike our own. They have, or had, their king, their nobles, and their commons. They have an ancient and elaborate law, and a system of morality in some ways as high as our own, and certainly more generally obeyed. They have their priests and their doctors; they are strictly upright, and observe the rites of hospitality.
>
> Where they differ from us mainly is that they do not get drunk until the white man teaches them so to do, they wear less clothing, the climate being more genial, their towns at night are not disgraced by the sights that distinguish ours, they cherish and are never cruel to their children, although they may occasionally put a deformed infant or a twin out of the way, and when they go to war, which is often, they carry out the business with a terrible thoroughness, almost as terrible as that which prevailed in every nation in Europe a few generations ago.
>
> Of course, there remain their witchcraft and the cruelties which result

---

from their almost universal belief in the power and efficiency of magic. Well, since I lived in England I have been reading up this subject, and I find that quite recently similar cruelties were practised throughout Europe ... that is in part of the world which for over a thousand years has enjoyed the advantages of the knowledge and profession of the Christian faith.

Now, let him who is highly cultured take up a stone to throw at the poor, untaught Zulu, which I notice the most dissolute and drunken wretch of a white man is often ready to do, generally because he covets his land, his labour, or whatever else may be his.[22]

One might note in passing the mode of Haggard's observation, for it has something of the exactness of the social anthropologist's. Interestingly, this is also a feature of the work of other Victorian travellers — such as Richard Burton — who showed a similar natural scientific capacity in their descriptive analysis of the imperial environment. Certainly in Haggard's case the point serves once more to bring to mind his affinity with the age of scientific materialism. In his preface to *Nada the Lily* he emphasises the need for the writer 'to forget his civilisation, and think with the mind and speak with the voice of a Zulu of the old régime', and in order that the expression should be authentic he has, he says, carried out a considerable amount of research into areas where his own experience was insufficient. The result is to

make accessible, in a popular shape, incidents of history which are now, for the most part, only to be found in a few scarce works of reference, rarely consulted, except by students . . .

— even if

all the horrors perpetrated by the Zulu tyrants cannot be published in this polite age of melanite and torpedoes.[23]

His scientific interest extends to the close observation of African flora and fauna. He often breaks off in the middle of a story to describe with a particular clarity a species or variety he has just stumbled on:

[we] saw many varieties of water-lilies in full bloom, some of them blue and of exquisite beauty, though few of the flowers were perfect, owing to the prevalence of a white water-maggot with a green head that fed upon them.[24]

Or to describe a herd of wild animals:

> And there, too, is the wild game, following its feeding-grounds in
> great armies, with the spring-buck thrown out before for skirmishers;
> then rank upon rank of long faced blesbuck, marching and wheeling like
> infantry; and last the shining troops of quagga, and the fierce-eyed,
> shaggy vilderbeeste, to take, as it were, the place of the cossack host that
> hangs upon an army's flanks.[25]

Of the more superficial 'Darwinist' ideology as popularly
rendered, there are, naturally, some traces. References are certainly
not lacking, for example, to a nature,

> which will allow of no standing still among her subjects, and has ordained
> that strife of one sort or another shall be the absolute condition of exist-
> ence.[26]

Explicitly this becomes the struggle for survival exemplified by
those among the African natives 'who carry the doctrine of the
survival of the fittest to its extreme'.[27]

Clearly Haggard is deeply moved and perturbed by the implication of current evolutionary theory. It is all the more striking
therefore that, with the idea of empire so heavily involved, it is not
the common vulgarised version of the doctrine as expressed in
Spencer's phrase 'the survival of the fittest' that confronts us.[28]
Far from it, in fact; his preoccupation leads him not to a crude
'Darwinian' imperialism but to something quite incompatible with
it. His portrayal of tribal society is drawn with great compassion
and an attention to detail which in itself contributes a special poignancy to his picture. What we are shown is not simply an imperial
triumph thrown against a bizarre native background but humanity
absorbed with its squalid vices and petty aspirations in its honey-
comb of racial and tribal compartments, struggling blindly with the
incomprehensible and inexorable movement of which it is an
unwilling part.

From all this it is evident that what Haggard sought was that
'process' should not only reveal a link with 'purpose' but that the
link should be of divine handiwork; so that the principle of order
which would emerge — to assume, with divine sanction, the
direction of events — would, in return for his fidelity to its ethic,
allow man a sense of participation in the management of his destiny.

But no salvation was at hand. What remains is the nightmare vision of the human being's helplessness in the face of a totally indifferent universe, where his one and only consolation is to be seen in that other accident denying him foresight by which 'to see the rock trembling to its fall and they [our best-beloved] loitering beneath it; to see them drink of water and know it full of foulest poison; to see them embark upon a ship and be aware that it was doomed to sink but not to be able to warn them or to prevent them'. He again forcefully recalls Kipling in the terms with which he evaluates the consolation —

The Power that limited our perceptions did so in purest mercy, for were it otherwise with us, our race would go mad and perish raving in its terrors.[29]

At best what Haggard manages is a weary and fragile agnosticism which does little to reconcile him to the travail of existence. ('It does not matter; nothing matters, except being born. That is a mistake.'[30]) In a characteristically wistful gesture Haggard prefixes to *Allan and the Ice-Gods* a few lines of verse (by one H. W. Carruth) making short work of the problem which all along preoccupied him:

> A fire mist and a planet,
> A crystal and a shell
> A jelly fish and a Saurian
> And caves where the cave-men dwell;
> Then a sense of law and beauty,
> And a face turned from the clod —
> Some call it Evolution,
> And others call it God.

But for Haggard the two concepts seemed much more likely to be contradictory than complementary.

There is, indeed, something Tennysonian in the tormented state of mind which, despite the strength of his desire, prevents him from achieving any final reconciliation of the doubts which haunt him with his rebellion against a totally mechanistic universe. Stella, in *Stella Fregelius*, makes a passionate, if crude, plea for just such a reconciliation:

I do not believe that so many generations of good men would have fed full upon a husk of lies and have lain down to sleep at last as though satisfied with meat. My heart rises at the thought. I am immortal. I know I am immortal. . . . Yet, O God, help Thou my unbelief. O God, draw and deliver me from this abyss.[31]

Significantly, failure to achieve a real fulfilment is a notable feature in many of his principal characters. Ayesha, searching for Kalli-krates through aeons of time is perhaps the example that comes most readily to mind, but there are many others — like Mea in *The Way of the Spirit*, Lady Ragnall of *The Ivory Child*, *The Ancient Allan* and also, more or less posthumously (almost a way of life in Haggard fiction), of *Allan and the Ice-Gods*, or like Mameena of the triology *Marie*, *Child of Storm* and *Finished*. Indeed so ob-sessed are Haggard's heroines with their responsibilities above and beyond time that in themselves they appear to stand more for the origin than the female of the species. And if there is a conspicuous failure in ultimate consummation, there is, equally, very little held out in the shape of even a passing happiness.

She looked up. 'A happy mind?' she said. 'Who *can* have a happy mind? Nobody who can feel. Supposing', she went on after a pause — 'supposing one puts oneself and one's own little interests and joys and sorrows quite away how is it possible to be happy, when one feels the breath of human misery beating on one's face, and sees the tide of sorrow and suffering creeping up to one's feet? One may be on a rock oneself and out of the path of it, till the spring floods or the hurricane wave comes to sweep one away, or one may be afloat upon it: whichever it is, it is quite impossible, if one has any heart, to be indifferent to it.'[32]

In his inability to subscribe to orthodox Victorian theology he resembles, as he does in so many other respects, his mentor, Dar-win. His appalled response to the immense amount of human suffer-ing with its origins, so often, in senseless internecine strife, expresses an order of sensitivity common to both men. 'I do not deny the Almighty Power,' says one of the characters in *The Witch's Head*,

I only deny the cruelty that is attributed to Him. It may be that, from the accumulated mass of the wrong and bloodshed and agony of this hard world, that Power is building up some high purpose. Out of the bodies of millions of living creatures Nature worked out *her* purpose and made the rocks, but the process must have been unpleasant to the living creatures by whose humble means the great strata were reared up. They lived, to die in billions, that tens of thousands of years afterwards there might be a rock. It may be so with us. Our tears and blood and agony may provide some solid end that now we cannot guess; their volume, which cannot be wasted, for nothing is wasted, may be building up one of the rocks of God's far-off purpose. But that we shall be tortured *here* for a time in order that we may be indefinitely tortured *there* [and he pointed to the stars], that I will never believe. Look at the mist rising from that hollow; so does the reek of the world's misery as an offering to the world's gods. The mist will cease to rise, and fall again in rain, and bring a blessing; but the incense of human suffering rises night and day for so long as the earth shall endure, nor does it fall again in dews of mercy. And yet Christians, who declare that God is love, declare, too, that for the vast majority of their fellow-creatures this process is to continue from millennium to millennium.[33]

It is interesting to put this beside an extract from one of Darwin's letters to Asa Gray with whom he had a long correspondence on the subject of design in nature.

With respect to the theological view of the question. This is always painful to me. I am bewildered. I had no intention to write atheistically. But I own that I cannot see as plainly as others do, and as I should wish to do, evidence of design and beneficence on all sides of us. There seems to me too much misery in the world. I cannot persuade myself that a beneficent and omnipotent God would have designedly created the Ichneumonidae with the express intention of their feeding within the living bodies of Caterpillars, or that a cat should play with mice. Not believing this, I see no necessity in the belief that the eye was expressly designed. On the other hand, I cannot anyhow be contented to view this wonderful universe, and especially the nature of man, and to conclude that everything is the result of brute force. I am inclined to look at everything as resulting from designed laws, with the details, whether good or bad, left to the working out of what we may call chance.[34]

His conclusion is very uncertain, however, and his real position is more accurately reflected in a brief autobiographical comment:

I cannot pretend to throw the least light on such abstruse problems. The mystery of the beginning of all things is insoluble by us; and I for one must be content to remain an Agnostic.[35]

The Origin of Species was published in 1859 three years after the birth of Rider Haggard, so that the latter grew up in an intellectual climate which took its character from the fierce debate the evolutionary doctrine excited. The remarkable effect this had on his fiction has been examined in this chapter and its influence on Haggard's rendering of the imperial idea shown to be seminal — though not in the crude form that might have been expected from a conjunction of Darwinian principles with Victorian imperial sentiment. This being so, it is astonishing to find Professor Morton Cohen in the only recent full-scale study of his life and works making no reference to Darwin and perhaps even more extraordinarily claiming that

From a personal and spiritual standpoint [Haggard] was not modern. He yearned for the past and spent much of his time investigating ancient cultures.[36]

Disregarding the first sentence, one might have thought that by so spending his time he made himself very much of his age indeed. One can hardly, after all, tax him with whimsical frivolity in his investigation of ancient cultures when his object was the profoundly sober one of a more honest understanding of his own nature and the nature of his time.

At the beginning of this chapter I drew an analogy between Haggard and Kipling in so far as they shared similar views on cultural relativity. The resemblance, perhaps surprisingly, does not go much beyond this, however, and even here one must make reservations, for the origin of these views is far from the same in the two cases.

Certainly Haggard had some sort of belief in the British imperial mission, though one which was much more vague than Kipling's, with an even greater recognition of its transience and its lack of inalienable virtue. His 'philosophy' or idea of nature was, however, so very different from Kipling's that the cultural form of the imperial idea, through which as a literary symbol that philosophy was projected, was itself bound to reflect the difference. The foregoing pages are an attempt to demonstrate the nature both of the disparity and its source, from which it is clear that far from functioning as a symbol of alienation and isolation as it does elsewhere, the idea of empire is used negatively to underline the subservience of all races, creeds and opinions to process and flux, and so to evoke with compassion the community of all creation in a vast, ungoverned movement the genesis of which is as enigmatic as the end is obscure and

D

troubling. The more organic view of man and nature thus posited
with its sympathies and affinities is one altogether foreign to Kipling.

The fuller implications of this may be more clearly established
if one turns once again to J. A. Symonds, described by his recent
biographer as 'a far more typical nineteenth-century figure than a
narrow aesthete like Pater' and one 'touched by many of the cur-
rents that had swept men into a flood of perplexity, doubt and, at
times, despair'.[37] Though he at least knew Haggard — he was a
visitor to the Savile Club of which the latter was a member and
wrote a rather waspish note to Horatio Brown describing Haggard's reaction to Kipling's sudden advent[38] — there is no record
of any communication between them. Yet the two men's response to
evolutionary concepts show some remarkable similarities, and in
at least one place the expression is so similar that it would be interesting to know if it were more than coincidence.[39]

For Symonds, evolutionary theory procured the reconciliation
of God and the Law — the latter being the laws of natural science
— and hence the de-alienation of man and nature. This had been
ensured by the revelation that the whole scheme of things could be
regarded 'as a single organism, advancing methodically through
stages of its growth in obedience to inevitable laws of self-expan-
sion'. The universe is one homogeneous whole 'in which nothing
can be lost and unaccounted for, through which there runs a con-
tinuity of energising forces, and of which we are indisputably conscious members.' And this consciousness — 'the final outcome of
vital processes which started from an inorganic basis' — pervades
all nature since, for him, thought is of the very essence of 'man
considered as a natural product'; consequently we are compelled
to believe that 'there is thought implicit or explicit in all the products which compose this universe'. For Symonds this clearly
establishes the existence and authority of the Universal Mind with
the Spirit 'immanent and everywhere'. His emancipation inspires
him to an almost Carlylean outburst of enthusiasm:

> How far more lovingly we look on Nature now than when we regarded
> it as alien and cursed. It is certainly natural, when inspired by Science, to
> feel true sympathy with beasts and insects, birds of the air and fishes of
> the sea, trees and flowers, and everything that shares the life divine which
> throbs in us. Next to love comes humility; and I need hardly point out
> how Science edifies that virtue. It teaches us that lower forms of life, such,

for instance as parasites which prey upon our bodies in disease, have their places in the scheme, the same raison d'être, while still uncombated in man.[40]

Thus does he dispose of Darwin's revulsion at the thought of the Ichneumonidæ. Haggard's reactions were a little more cautious and moderate: but even if he could not altogether accept the new postulates as grounds for the definition of a Universal Mind, the source of his compassion and humility in the susceptibility of all things to the hazards of chance and change suggests a very real sympathy with the spirit of Symonds's enquiry. At times his emphasis on the organic relation carries him to remarkable lengths. In *The Ghost Kings*, for example, every one of the Tree People has his or her own tree, and a reciprocal life-cycle. Greater than all the others is the Tree of the Tribe and when that is destroyed the whole people are doomed to perish. That the movement described by Symonds was directed towards a happy end, however, Haggard was far from sure. 'Happy endings don't come off,' he has Morris say in *Stella Fregelius* in another Kiplingesque moment. 'The happiness lies in the struggle, you know.'

In its reflection of Haggard's sympathies, Symonds's rendering of current preoccupations helps to make clear the influence of gradualist Darwinian evolutionary theory on the novelist. Of his relationship with Empire taking most of its character from this source enough has now been said. But the subject cannot be left here for from this analysis there emerges a conclusion of great relevance to any study of the idea of empire in its literary embodiment.

It has been noted that in all the record of Haggard's concern with process, with transition, flux and change, he gives no centrality whatsoever to favourite Victorian themes like the value of competition, the providential necessity of war which ensures progress, or that 'beneficent private war which makes one man strive to climb on the shoulders of another and remain there through the law of the survival of the fittest'.[41] Far from celebrating these virtues Haggard, as earlier quotations have demonstrated, treated them with contempt. That he was sorrowfully aware of the struggle for existence is obvious — even that he seemed at times inclined to share Darwin's dark suspicion that it is in some regrettable way a necessary part of human society — but that it should be extolled as a way of life or an attitude of mind is quite foreign to his nature. His refusal to affirm any fundamentally creative role for a doctrine like the survival of the fittest was a refusal to participate in the distortions of Darwinian thinking so common to his age: after all, the survival of the fittest did not ultimately depend on the struggle for existence but on the original accidental variation. As Jacques Barzun notes, 'natural selection can cause nothing but the elimination of the unfit, not the production of the fit'.[42] The primary cause of evolution is not struggle but a random variant *after which* the process of natural selection working through immense stretches of time confirms the form. So that Haggard was getting down to bedrock in querying not whether God had ordained struggle but whether he had ordained anything at all. Darwin's significant contribution had been his emphasis on *chance* variations as a cause: Haggard reveals the authenticity of his *rapport* in instinctively placing his emphasis on the question of design in nature rather than on qualitative comparison of what was designed — so escaping any association with a degenerate political Darwinism.

Something, already alluded to, which adds to this authenticity is the importance to Haggard of an almost infinite extension of time. It is not just that Ayesha is prepared to wait two thousand years for Kallikrates, enduring a variety of incarnations in the process, or that Allan Quatermain should drop hints of a trans-cultural past of quite formidable dimensions: it is that such intelligibility as the world has, actual or possible, depends for him on the vastness of past and future time. And time in such an extension was of the essence of Darwinian thinking: if the relation between the forms of one species and that of another was a temporal one, as Darwin held in opposition to the Aristotelian evolutionary theory, then a gradualism developing imperceptibly through immense spans of time was the inevitable concomitant. And indeed maximum stress is placed on the infinitely slow duration of the process in *The Origin of Species*, where we are reminded, for example, that natural selection 'acts solely by accumulating slight successive, favourable variations, it can produce no great or sudden modification; it can act only by very short and slow steps'; that the human mind 'cannot grasp the full meaning of the term of a hundred million years; it cannot add up and perceive the full effects of many slight variations, accumulated during an almost infinite number of generations'; that the whole history of the world, 'although of a length quite incomprehensible by us, will hereafter be recognised as a mere fragment of time, compared with the ages which have elapsed since the first creature, the progenitor of innumerable extinct and living descendants, was created.'[43]

That Haggard has a very real affinity for the basic characteristics of Darwin's concept of evolution is thus beyond question. And where Empire plays a part in his fiction it is clear that it does so negatively in terms which reflect his 'philosophy' of nature, and these terms, to the extent to which they are consonant with the basic substance of Darwinism do not enjoin conflict, extol dominion nor predicate aggrandisement as the essentially creative factors of evolution or the *sine qua non* of change. Intrinsically they do not immediately suggest a structural analogy with the idea of empire: the latter is, as I suggest in the next chapter, much more closely identified with quite another idea of nature, indeed with quite another concept of evolution.

NOTES

1. *She* (1887), p. 82.
2. Jacques Barzun, *Darwin, Marx and Wagner* (1942), pp. 13–14.
3. *The Witch's Head* (n.d.), p. 246.
4. *Nada the Lily* (1949), p. 216.
5. *Ayesha* (1957), p. 301.
6. *The Way of the Spirit* (1906), p. 286.
7. *Jess* (1888), p. 93.
8. *The Way of the Spirit*, p. 24.
9. J. A. Symonds, *Essays Speculative and Suggestive* (1890), vol. i, p. 7.
10. *Stella Fregelius* (1906), p. 289.
11. *Child of Storm* (1952), p. 72.
12. Ibid., p. 72.
13. Ibid., p. 213.
14. Dedication to *Child of Storm*, p. vi.
15. *Allan Quatermain* (1949), p. 300.
16. Quoted by Morton Cohen, *Rider Haggard. His Life and Work* (1960), p. 262.

17. *Jess*, pp. 185–6.

18. *Allan Quatermain*, p. 171.

19. Ibid., p. 230.

20. *The Witch's Head*, pp. 154–5.

21. *Child of Storm*, p. 15.

22. Ibid., p. 74.

23. Preface to *Nada the Lily*, pp. ix–x.

24. *She*, p. 71.

25. *A Tale of Three Lions* (1951), p. 186.

26. *Jess*, p. 95.

27. *Long Odds* (1951), p. 227.

28. There was no lack of authorities whose writings could have been used to sanction such an interpretation. Darwin's distinguished fellow-anthropologist, A. R. Wallace, put the matter very bluntly: 'It is the same great law of "*the preservation of favoured races in the struggle for life*", which leads to the inevitable extinction of all those low and mentally undeveloped populations with which Europeans come in contact. . . . The intellectual and moral, as well as the physical qualities of the European are superior; the same power and capacities which have made him rise in a few centuries from the condition of the wandering savage with a scanty and stationary population to his present state of culture and advancement, with a greater average longevity, a greater average strength, and a capacity of more rapid increase, — enable him when in contact with the savage man, to conquer in the struggle for existence, and to increase at his expense, just as the more favourable increase at the expense of the less favourable varieties in the animal and vegetable kingdoms, just as the weeds of Europe overrun North America and Australia, extinguishing native productions by the inherent vigour of their organization, and by their greater capacity for existence and multiplication.' [Quoted by J. C. Greene, *The Death of Adam* (New York, 1961), p. 313.]

29. *Ayesha*, p. 278.

30. *Nada the Lily*, p. 39.

31. *Stella Fregelius*, p. 300. It is interesting to set beside this some of Darwin's reflections where he finds it difficult to conceive of 'this immense and wonderful universe, including man with his capacity of looking far backwards and far into futurity, as the result of blind chance or necessity'. Yet he has the physicists' view that the sun with all its planets will in time grow too cold for life and so has to face the 'intolerable thought that [man] and all other sentient beings are doomed to complete annihilation after such long-continued slow progress'. [Francis Darwin, *Life & Letters of Charles Darwin* (1887), vol. 1, p. 312.] 'To think of the progress of millions of years, with every continent swarming with good

and enlightened man, all ending in this, and with probably no fresh start until this our planetary system has been again converted into red-hot gas. *Sic transit gloria mundi*, with a vengeance....' [*More Letters*, ed. Francis Darwin and A. C. Seward (1903), vol. 1, pp. 260–1.]

32. *Jess*, p. 47.

33. *The Witch's Head*, p. 247.

34. Francis Darwin, *The Life and Letters of Charles Darwin*, vol. 2, pp. 311–12.

35. Francis Darwin, op. cit., p. 313.

36. Morton Cohen, *Rider Haggard. His Life and Work*, p. 103.

37. Phyllis Grosskurth, *John Addington Symonds* (1964), p. 326.

38. Morton Cohen (ed.), *Rudyard Kipling to Rider Haggard. The Record of a Friendship* (1965), p. 17.

39. Cf. end of ch. 12, *The Witch's Head* and 'The Philosophy of Evolution'.

40. J. A. Symonds, *Essays Speculative and Suggestive*, pp. 7, 15, 23, 25.

41. Sir Henry Maine, *Popular Government* (1884). Quoted by Jacques Barzun, op. cit., p. 101.

42. Jacques Barzun, op. cit., p. 69.

43. Charles Darwin, *On the Origin of Species* (1902), pp. 424, 433, 439.

CHAPTER THREE

Darwin, Hegel and Marx:
A Changing Dialectic

PROFESSOR F. S. C. NORTHROP, in an illuminating essay, 'Evolution in its Relation to the Philosophy of Nature and the Philosophy of Culture'[1] proposes that the philosophy at the basis of the Darwinian conception of evolution by gradual, minute steps has its source in the philosophy of science 'established for nature generally' of Descartes, Newton and Locke. Galileo and Newton had disposed of the basic premises of earlier Aristotelian evolutionary theory by their repudiation of irreducible or formal causes. Instead it could now be shown that once the 'positions and momenta of the masses of a given system were known, the final state of the system was determined necessarily according to the principle of mechanical causation'.

Darwin was driven to a similar conclusion with the realisation that far from time referring only to the actualisation of the form in matter, as the Aristotelians maintained, the origin of the form as form was itself a temporal event. This entailed, as Professor Northrop points out, that

> The forms or properties defining a given species and the adaptation of that form to its environment is effect rather than cause. The question then arose concerning the mechanism by which this effect is produced.

With the result we are all familiar:

> Upon the basis of biological data of the natural history type alone, Darwin is led to the same rejection of irreducible formal and final causes and to the same conception of natural design and adaptation having its basis in purely mechanical causes to which the physicists Galileo and Newton were guided in their studies of the inorganic world.[2]

And, as described earlier, dominating Darwin's conclusions was the

48

notion of gradualism, of the slow extension of process and change through 'the accumulation of innumerable slight variations'.[3]

So much for the Darwinian evolutionary tradition rooted, largely, in British empirical philosophy. Let us turn now to the examination of another which, it is suggested, has the capacity for a more organic relation to the idea of empire. Moreover it is, significantly, the one which seems to inform the view of reality held by those other writers more intimately connected with the idea of empire who make up the rest of this study. Since the complex material involved will have an important place both as analogy and source, some space will have to be given to delineating its characteristics.

Prior to Kant, Rationalist philosophers such as Descartes, Spinoza and Leibniz saw no discontinuity between the 'science' of metaphysics and those other sciences of mathematics and physics with which they held themselves closely associated; accounting for the facts of science in terms of God's goodness, they saw man's place in the universe as explicable in a moral as well as a scientific light. Kant, however, with his radical distinction between pure or theoretical reason and practical reason promulgated a quite different philosophical basis for the interpretation of the natural order from that of the normative; the truth about the natural order can, for him, be reached only through pure reason and the phenomenal world, while the truth about moral convictions and moral responsibility can only be approached through the practical reason and the noumenal world. The result, of course, was the establishment of a breach between science and ethics.

Confronted with this dichotomy Fichte, Kant's first important follower, resolved the conflict by making even nature itself a logical product of the morally free ego.

He started his enquiry from the basis of the intelligence-in-itself, or, as he called it, the ego. But to identify this ego we have to go behind the objectifiable self, that is self as an object of introspection, to the consciousness that thought the self. Fichte, always careful to demonstrate his proposition fully, illustrated this by commanding the audience listening to his lecture on 'The Vocation of Man' to 'think the wall'. 'Have you thought the wall?' he asked. 'Well then, gentlemen, think him who thought the wall.'[4] Since there will always be an ego which transcends objectification, it is this which Fichte describes as the pure ego. This pure ego is not to be seen, however, as the individual finite ego but as a transcendental infinite activity manifesting itself in a finite consciousness. From this, Fichte establishes what for him was the fundamental proposition of philosophy, namely that the ego posits its own being.

But the ego's original activity is not in itself conscious, and for consciousness to develop a non-ego must emerge in opposition to the ego.

It is certainly true . . . that the Ego is not, and can never become, conscious of itself except under its empirical determinations; and that these empirical determinations necessarily imply something external to the Ego.[5]

So we arrive at Fichte's second basic proposition of philosophy, that the non-ego is opposed to the ego. But if the infinite ego-in-activity *is* infinite and unlimited so is the non-ego of the second basic proposition since it refers to external things in general and not to a particular object. If the affirmation were left at this, then obviously the ego and the non-ego would neutralise each other. So Fichte makes his third basic proposition that within itself the *absolute* ego posits a finite ego and a finite non-ego reciprocally limiting and determining one another.

If the absolute ego then is to be seen as an unlimited activity striving towards consciousness of its own freedom through moral self-realisation, the positing of the non-ego, which Fichte identifies with the world of nature, is a necessary means to the achievement of this end. Self-consciousness then demands the non-ego from which, as one commentator describes it, 'the otherwise unlimited activity of the ego, comparable to a straight line stretching out indefinitely, can recoil, as it were, onto itself'.[6]

Fundamentally, it is, in Fichte's words,

the necessary faith in our own freedom and power, in our own real activity, and in the definite laws of human action, which lies at the root of all our consciousness of a reality external to ourselves;

And he adds:

We are compelled to believe that we act, and that we ought to act in a certain manner; we are compelled to assume a sphere for this action; this sphere is the real, actually present world, such as we find it. . . . From this necessity of action proceeds the consciousness of the actual world; . . . we raise ourselves from [the] abyss, and maintain ourselves above it, solely by our moral activity.[7]

For a very succinct summing up of the argument one might turn again to the commentator already cited:

The absolute ego is to be conceived as activity. And this activity is fundamentally an infinite striving. But striving according to Fichte implies overcoming, and overcoming requires an obstacle to overcome. Hence the ego must posit the non-ego, Nature, as an obstacle to be overcome, as a check to be transcended. In other words Nature is a necessary means or instrument to the moral self-realisation of the ego. It is a field for action.[8]

Nature is thus, in this view, the negation of man, the moral ego, so that the demands of the latter, or of the moral life through the latter, can be seen to prescribe not only moral philosophy but natural philosophy as well: science and scientific knowledge are thus to be seen not as distinct from the moral noumenal order but as a direct consequence of it.

From this examination it also becomes apparent that the structure of reality for Fichte was dictated by the logic of dialectic, the triad being composed of ego as thesis, non-ego as antithesis and the Absolute ego as synthesis resolving the opposition in its own ultimate unity of consciousness incorporating both ego and non-ego. Professor Northrop pursues the significance of this even further:

Since this dialectic governs the coming of Absolute consciousness to self-consciousness, and since according to the philosophy of Kant and his successors all the content of human knowledge whether in nature or culture has to conform to the forms which the knowing consciousness brings to the empirical data of consciousness it follows that everything known, whether in culture or nature, must evolve according to the dialectical law of thesis, antithesis and synthesis, the latter synthesis in turn becoming a new thesis which gives rise to its antithesis thereby leading to a higher synthesis.

Consequently he sees Hegel as simply working out this dialectical theory of evolution 'governed, not by gradualism and slight variations, but by sharp negations and antitheses'.[9]

Thus we have now two points of potential importance to this study. The first is that the novelist Rider Haggard, writing under the powerful influence of Darwinian thinking, did not, when using empire as his *mise en scène*, abstract from that doctrine any such popular theme as the survival of the fittest or the white man's burden. In fact, when he wrote about empire he wrote about transition — the character of whose process in this case was gradualism — about chance and change and about the apparent absence of Providential design. Such themes are inimical to the idea of empire but entirely consonant with the basic propositions of the Darwinian system through which, in consequence, they established their connection with the latter's antecedents in British empirical philosophy and the philosophy of Descartes. Haggard's had been, on the whole, an 'organic' view of man-in-nature: not so fully pantheistic as, say, that of his contemporary Symonds but having much in common with it nevertheless. The consequent want of a man-versus-nature dualism forcefully underlines the fact that strife is not here the essential condition of life nor a method of self-consciousness.

It would appear, therefore, that the system of nature subsumed in Haggard's work, with its very specific evolutionary character, shows no spontaneous affinity with the idea of empire: the tensions of Empire, in other words, have nothing to do with the tensions of Haggard's major concern. The function he allows it is very largely the negative one of providing him with a means for disparaging one of its major premises, cultural absolutism, so that he may assert in its stead his own doctrine of the relativity of all cultures and morality. Interestingly, however, the other 'imperial' writers dealt with here do not follow in this tradition. Their system of nature is much more integral to the basic structure of the idea of empire than Haggard's could ever have been: indeed they identified the one with the other, finding in this idea a logic of evolution identical to that governing their own moral universe. In fact, theirs is the dialectical evolutionary mode largely as it has been described here in its development by Fichte though, of course, elaborated and enlarged in scope by Hegel and Marx. Of its general potential we all know something in this age, but the following comparison of the two traditions together is informative and may be left to sum up. It comes from Lenin's book *Marx–Engels–Marxism*.

In our times, the idea of development, of evolution, has almost fully penetrated social consciousness, but it has done so in other ways, not through Hegel's philosophy. But the same idea, as formulated by Marx and Engels on the basis of Hegel's philosophy, is much more comprehensive, much more abundant in content than the current [Darwinian] theory of evolution. A development . . . in spirals, not in a straight line; a spasmodic; catastrophic, revolutionary development; . . . ; inner impulses for development, imparted by the contradiction, the conflict of different forces and tendencies reacting on a given body or inside a given phenomenon or within a given society; . . . such are some of the features of dialectics as a doctrine of evolution more full of meaning than the current one.[10]

One further connection remains to be established. Two evolutionary modes have been defined and the suggestion has also been made that the one informing the work of those writers most intimately involved with the idea of empire is the Hegelian–Marxist. The link still to be made is between this mode and literary aesthetics; for these authors, writing in the way they did about empire, giving it the symbolic function that they did, describe an interesting development of the Romantic tradition.

To explain the relationship it is necessary to return, briefly, to Kant. The dualism which he postulated between the phenomenal and noumenal worlds is paralleled by a dualism which he found in man's own nature. He was *Homo noumenon* and at the same time *Homo phenomenon*, a dual personality partly rational, partly the creature of desires and inclinations and so of the phenomenal world still. He is conscious of this duality, and having identified his 'real self' with the rationally perfect *Homo noumenon*, it then becomes obligatory for him as phenomenal self to strive towards this idealised picture of himself: what the rational man would do man ought to do. Professor Robert Tucker in his book *Philosophy and Myth in Karl Marx*, describes the situation in these terms:

There is a war going on inside Kantian man. The moral life is a drama of ceaseless conflict within the dualised personality of the human being who is conscious of himself as half-godly and half-human. His duty, as he sees it, is to actualise the godlike noumenal self. This means that he must bend the phenomenal self to his moral will to be absolutely good. He must mould the phenomenal self into the being of absolute perfection.

He attempts to do this by addressing himself in the stern language of the categorical imperative: Thou shalt be perfect. Morality is the system of commands of this order by which the god-like self in man attempts to compel the merely human self to be perfect.[11]

But Kant recognises that the categorical imperative is an ideal which can never be realised: the degree of progression which results from our attempts towards the state is what can be hoped for.

The object of a will that is capable of being determined by the moral law is the production in the world of the highest good. Now the supreme condition of the highest good is the perfect harmony of the disposition with the moral law . . . — a perfection of which no rational being existing in the world of sense is capable at any moment of his life. . . . Since, nevertheless, such a harmony is morally required of us, . . . the pure practical reason forces us to assume a practical progress towards it, in infinitum, as the real object of our will. . . . A finite rational being is capable only of an infinite progress from lower to higher stages of moral perfection.

This, then, was Kant's conception of the moral ideal: an endless struggle towards a goal that would never be achieved. Perhaps some of the characteristics of the Romantic inclination are already suggested. A further move towards the aesthetic rendering of the original Kantian position was provided by Fichte, who, as A. O. Lovejoy noted in 'Schiller and the Genesis of German Romanticism', converted the Kantian conception of the moral ideal as an endless pursuit of a forever unattainable goal into a metaphysical principle. The very nature of all existence now became

an infinite and insatiable striving of the Absolute Ego whereby it first sets up the external world as an obstacle to its own activity, and then gradually but endlessly triumphs over this obstacle. The notion of infinity thus took precedence in philosophy over that of the finite and determinate, the category of Becoming over that of Being, the ideal of activity over that of achieved completion, the mood of endless longing over that of quietude and collectedness of mind.[12]

It is not difficult to argue from the second half of this particularly an emergent antithesis between a Classical mode of thought and a Romantic. And Lovejoy, in tracing Kantian influences upon Friedrich Schlegel whom he sees as originally developing the conception of 'Romantic' poetry shows that the latter's ultimate aesthetic rendering of Kantian ethics made the connection explicit, namely 'that art should be characterised by a constant enlargement of its boundaries and an endless progression towards an unattainably remote ideal rather than by any definitive perfection of form attainable by adhering to immutable laws and narrow limitations of aim'.[13]

Kant accepted the gulf between *Homo noumenon* and *Homo phenomenon* and the tyranny of the former's demands. Hegel, however, was incapable of resting in this dualism; for him the greater awareness was not of an impossibly remote ideal and the contented putting up with it, but of the insatiable appetite of the noumenal world-self. All his energy was directed towards the resolution of the dualism inherited from Kant. Conceiving its basis in the demand of the world-self for a complete fulfilment — complete self-consciousness — he found in the expanding consciousness of 'phenomenal man' the instrument of reconciliation.

A preliminary step for Hegel was the rejection of God as a being external to man; a being whom man might entreat and placate but who remained alien; a being whose objective creation had been the consequence of man's humiliation and demoralisation by men.

The despotism of the Roman Princes had hounded the spirit of man from the face of the earth: deprived of freedom, he was forced to let that which was eternal in him, his absolute, flee into the deity; and the spread of misery forced him to seek and expect blessedness in heaven. The objectification of the deity went hand in hand with the corruption and slavery of man, and it is actually only a revelation and a manifestation of this spirit of the times.[14]

God then was located *in* man. Hegel refused to accept the Kantian assertion of the noumenal self as god-like — it is the God-in-man and in so far as man strives to become God he strives towards self-realisation. The 'sorrow of finitude' *could* be surmounted: he had at once released himself from all constriction and given a divine sanction to the rapacity of his selfhood. The process, with its objective of absolute knowledge, is described by Professor Tucker in these terms:

By Hegel's definition, God is not fully God until he *knows* himself to be God; self-knowledge or self-consciousness in this specific sense belongs to the nature, essence, or 'concept' of God. At the outset of creation, moreover, he lacks the requisite self-consciousness: God is God, but is not yet conscious of himself as such. Hence, the historical process of God's self-realization is essentially a knowing process. Hegel calls it the 'process of becoming in terms of knowledge'.

Further, the organ of God's slowly growing consciousness of himself as God is the mind of man. God passes from primal unconsciousness in the form of nature to ultimate self-consciousness in the person of historical man. The 'phenomenology of mind', or progress of human knowledge in the course of history, is God's passage to self-knowledge. The self-cognitive journey has its final destination in 'absolute knowledge', which is God's completed consciousness of himself and therefore actualization of himself in the mind of the philosopher.[15]

God and the world are one: in other words the world is a divine personality or world-self which Hegel calls *Weltgeist* or *Geist*, meaning 'spirit'. The process by which spirit — altogether synonymous with God — reaches self-consciousness involves its externalisation in some concrete form so that it may apprehend this substantial form as itself. In a sentence which we find many times echoed in Carlyle's work Hegel himself wrote: 'What powers it inherently possesses, we learn from the variety of products and formations which it originates.'[16] And in another which recalls significantly not only Carlyle but a major preoccupation of all of the writers dealt with subsequently in this study: 'The very essence of spirit is activity; it realises its potentiality — makes itself its own deed, its own work — and thus it becomes an object to itself; contemplates itself as an objective existence.'[17]

Man's place in this development is quite clear. He is 'spirit in the act of becoming conscious of itself as spirit'.

As a builder of civilizations, a creator of culture-worlds, he is spirit in the historical continuation of its creative, self-externalizing phase. But in his capacity of knower, he is spirit on the path of self-discovery. His mind, and particularly his religious and philosophical mind, is the organ of the world's emergent consciousness of itself as a subjective being. But inasmuch as this long remains an incomplete, limited consciousness, Hegel defines man as 'finite self-conscious spirit'.

In the process of becoming in terms of knowledge, finite self-conscious spirit overcomes its finitude and rises to the plane of absolute self-conscious spirit, or fully actualized God.[18]

And this urge towards self-knowledge — 'the impulse of spiritual life in itself to break through the hull of nature, of sensuousness, of its own self alienation, and to attain the light of consciousness, namely its own self'[19] — is, as Professor Tucker observes, 'no mere idle curiosity or Platonic wonder but a monstrous and insatiable lust of knowledge. It is a craving in man to pierce the seeming objectivity of the world that confronts him, and grasp it as subjective in nature.' In Hegel's words:

The aim of knowledge is to divest the objective world that stands opposed to us of its strangeness, and, as the phrase is, to find ourselves at home in it: which means no more than to trace the objective world back to the notion — to our innermost self.[20]

The process then is one of reappropriation. Having externalised itself in some 'objective' form in furtherance of its own self-consciousness, spirit must then reintegrate this world and so overcome the divisive effect of this stage in its development. 'Thus Spirit,' says Hegel, 'is at war with itself. It must overcome itself as its own enemy and formidable obstacle.'[21] And it is through the cognitive activity going on in the mind of man that spirit is able to repossess itself in consciousness.

Knowing is spirit's means of reintegration or 'return to itself' out of the state of self-division that obtains when spirit as conscious subject (man) is confronted with spirit as external object (the world). Hegel calls this state 'self-alienation' or 'self-estrangement' (*Selbstentfremdung*). The subject-object relation *per se* is one of spirit's self-alienation. In the subject-object relation spirit apprehends itself as 'otherness' (*Anderssein*). According to Hegel, this means that the object is experienced as an alien and hostile being, as something that stands opposed to the conscious subject. Knowing activity, by which the objective world is divested of its strangeness, is the overcoming of alienation.[22]

The same capacity for protection in a Romantic aesthetic as had been offered in Fichte's rendering of Kant is obvious in all this. Under the influence of these two last, Schlegel had finally convinced himself that those links which had been earlier assumed to bind man to nature were no longer there, and Hegel's redactions gave particular force to the discovery. For in them the alien phenomenal self finally emerges as an alien world. In Professor Tucker's heavily emphasised words, 'the image of man against himself has now

E

turned into an image of man against the world'.[23] In fact, although he underlined other elements in the Romantic response (mostly available already, as Schlegel had realised, via Fichte), what received greatest stress from Hegel and was in turn to be taken up and given a new dimension by Marx was precisely the notion of alienation.

Awareness of the rupture between subject and object and a yearning for reunion is, of course, one of the chief characteristics of Romantic writing.

> What is called Romanticism in England and on the Continent is . . . the concern for the reconciliation of subject and object, man and nature, consciousness and unconsciousness . . .[24]

But though the crisis in which the 'imperial' writers about to be discussed here find themselves is basically Romantic, centred as it is in an intense awareness of this dissociation, they no longer really believe in the possibility of reconciliation. Theirs is a papiermaché grail: it is without intrinsic worth and with a purpose that is purely and confessedly psychological. No longer was there any possible prospect of that matter-spirit continuum which according to Albert Guerard is the proper object of the Romantic experience.[25] (Buchan may be thought something of an exception. His earlier notion of empire as the visible expression of a synthetic philosophy which would satisfy all man's aspirations of reason and soul was very Hegelian. But his 'middle period' is one where he becomes increasingly aware of the illusions on which his world-order depends.) In a sense what they sought now was less reconciliation than 'victory': and the basis of this reaction is certainly to be found in Hegel, for it is he who has projected an alienated world and proclaimed a state of hostility between the world-self or spirit and a world experienced as alien and menacing in its objectivity. If there is in these writers still an occasional glimpse of nostalgia for the object, what is much more obvious is their fear of it, and the aggressiveness of Hegelian spirit is now seen to derive from a defensiveness which admits not just a lack of confidence in the outcome of the engagement but a despairing realisation that the battle is all.

Thus the nature of the dialectic for these writers becomes clear: from the inevitable and necessary opposition of self and anti-self comes the synthesis of consciousness. To them, it is by this process alone that order is introduced into nature — a phenomenology which recalls the fourth possible interpretation of reality just hinted at, but never taken up, in Haggard's work, that what order man finds in nature he himself puts there. It is a reading inherent in the Hegelian dialectic but it again refers us back to Kant who had already made it quite explicit:

> ... the order and regularity in the appearances, which we entitle *nature*, we ourselves introduce. We could never find them in appearances, had not we ourselves, or the nature of our mind, originally set them there.[26]

Through the dialectical struggle, then, for these authors a world essentially illusory is deliberately created whose construction is the means to self-survival. And activity, that same ceaseless, voracious activity which had been for Hegel the essence of spirit, becomes the chief instrument of illusion. Such a world is Kipling's India: for him the imperial idea functioned both as a symbol of consciousness and, in the specific conflict of India with the European, a symbol of the antithesis. For Conrad, empire has more the latter purpose, though at least on one occasion through the rather ambiguous medium of Marlow it is found fulfilling the former.

How closely — and how justly — the imperial idea in its literary expression comes to reflect this developing Romantic form can be seen if we look a little more closely at the central dialectic of these three writers — Kipling, Conrad and Buchan — and its relation to the Hegelian tradition.

Their interpretation of the subject/object relationship results, broadly, in their acceptance of an alien nature and the fact that the end of self-consciousness can only be secured if the alien is appropriated and subdued. Compared with Hegel's objective, it is, of course, a scaled-down self-consciousness and its mechanics are those of a psychological expedient rather than a philosophical system. They look no further ahead than what Hegel called 'finite self-conscious spirit' but the modification is historically just; for after Hegel had come Marx whose great discovery in the work of the former had been the notion that man is God — whereupon for him human self-consciousness became the supreme divinity.

As for the method of self-consciousness, that, too, in these writers strongly recalls the Hegelian system. It is not only in the sequence of externalisation and re-appropriation that the tradition is reflected: much of the machinery of the second stage, too, is the same — that is, assimilation is by means of a process of cognition.

I shall dwell on this at some length in the next chapter when I attempt to describe how Anglo-India and the fabric of Empire served Kipling as a paradigm for the structure of his own moral universe. There is, for example, his explicit appreciation of the Indian Empire's great knowability providing a means of containing the chaos of the objective world. Indeed, we can take as an instance his generalised 'knowingness' which has been so long derided apparently without any realisation that it is an integral, if frequently exasperating, part of the mechanics of his central concern: self-consciousness for him is secure only to the extent to which we are able to familiarise and thereby tame the destructive 'otherness'. The very dramatisation of a principle of cognition is to be found in *Kim*, where the hero joins forces with the Secret Service to repel the subversive enemy: but Kim's own intermittent loss of self-consciousness makes it quite clear that the enemy — and the antidote — is moral rather than political.

A more naïve expression of the same thing is particularly evident in Buchan's earlier fiction where his heroes casually betray themselves as amazingly well-informed about practically everything. Destructive forces are rooted out with unerring prescience from quiet little inns on the Achensee and innocent-looking fur-shops in the Galician quarter of Buda. And in both Buchan and Kipling it is noteworthy that the abrogation of otherness by a cognitive process is preceded, classically, by what could be seen as the externalisation of this alienated world: Kim or, in one of his many impenetrable *alter egos*, Sandy Arbuthnot, in the end turn out to have been one of us all the time. Their 'otherness' is only apparent, not real: but it is a necessary step in the suppression and domestication of what is wild and strange.

In Conrad the same process is to be found, though the greater balance and freer speculation in his work offer it a fuller perspective. Kipling and Buchan, in their explicit and obsessive use of knowing as an instrument of the will to power, had intensified the antithesis between the symbol of consciousness and the destructive element to a point where the work deteriorates into a simple reflection of the classic Freudian neurosis of the conscious mind struggling to suppress the threat which it discerns in the subconscious. Conrad is, in this sense, less neurotic. Characters like Lord Jim, Kurtz or Heyst in becoming more fully aware of themselves do so through coming face to face with the destructive power of their universe. Here knowing is being used as a means of moderating the antithesis, and as such is reflected in Stein's advice to Lord Jim: 'The only way is to the destructive element submit yourself.' What makes for some ambiguity in Conrad, however, is that there are two levels of knowing activity in his work, basically antagonistic in their tendencies. There is the one just referred to, where the end is the moderation of the antithesis. But, of course, the antithesis can only be moderated so far: it cannot be *transcended* unless one finds a transcendental guarantor of self-consciousness and this Conrad — for all his fretful appeal to Immensities, Infinities, Imponderables — failed to achieve. All he can do is to assert, rather lamely, the notion of fidelity to an ideal of self hood — which, as *Nostromo* shows, is far from proof against scepticism. And this ideal of his can only be defined and defended, paradoxically, via a sharpening of the antithesis: by the 'taming' of the destructive element. The method of this conquest is once again very largely cognitive, therefore it is without much surprise that we discover Conrad giving great emphasis to the seaman's 'mystery', celebrating virtues that are highly Kiplingesque: solidarity, a sacrosanct ideal of conduct, discipline and a knowing competence in a practical world where, as for Kipling's John of Burgos, a man's trade is the outside of things, and where the illusion of a universe susceptible to human manipulation can consequently be sustained. God fails to walk upon the waters, so Conrad finds it an irresistible temptation to bow down before the log-book.

For these writers then, the development of the Romantic antinomy leads to a moral imperialism, by which is meant literally the expansion and aggrandisement of self, where, in the classic Hegelian manner, the subject wages a continuous war of conquest against the alien object. And the principal weapon is the thoroughly Hegelian one of cognition. What more natural, then, that they should find the ideal milieu for the dramatisation of their conflict in the sphere of political imperialism? As was beginning to become apparent, the theory of knowledge and the theory of politics have a good deal in common. Hans Kelsen in *The Foundations of Democracy* put it like this:

> ... It is a truism that political theory and that part of philosophy which is called 'ethics' have been in close connection. But there exists also a certain affinity, less generally recognised, between theory of politics and other parts of philosophy, such as epistemology, that is, the theory of cognition. ... The main problem of political theory is the relationship between the subject and the object of domination; the main problem of epistemology is the relation between the subject and the object of cognition. The process of domination is not so different from that of cognition by which the subject tries to be master of his object, by bringing some order into the chaos of sensual perceptions.[27]

And imperialism, of course, intensifies the 'process of domination'.

Thus it is clear that these writers' discovery of a projection for their concern in the field of empire is something other than an exhibition of serendipity on their part. In fact, it is one of the most organic correlatives imaginable — and given their development of what was essentially the Romantic response, one of the most inevitable. For them as writers, political imperialism serves expressly as the translation of the Hegelian system's 'boundless expansionism on the plane of thought'. The need to secure their own identity dictated an incessant war against an alien and chaotic nature with the elusive end in the subjugation of the latter. This crisis, where the principal is at once aggressive and embattled in a foreign and menacing world which he nevertheless seeks to appropriate, is essentially the crisis of empire. The embarkation of the self on its rapacious cognitive conquest to overcome the world's 'otherness' thus finds an equivalent physical expression in the imperial idea. The writers discussed in the following chapters provide plentiful evidence to show that in describing the tensions of political empire they are in fact describing almost literally the precise relations which govern their own moral universe with all its antagonisms and predatory aggression: the harsh moral imperialism, in other words, which is the condition of their self-consciousness.

NOTES

1. See Stow Persons (ed.), *Evolutionary Thought in America* (New Haven, Conn., 1960).

2. F. S. C. Northrop, op. cit., p. 58.

3. Charles Darwin, op. cit., p. 413.

4. Introduction to *Fichte's Popular Works*, trans. and ed. Smith (1889), vol. i, p. 85.

5. J. G. Fichte, 'The Vocation of Man', *Fichte's Popular Works*, trans. and ed. Smith, vol. i, p. 151.

6. Frederick Copleston, *A History of Philosophy*, (1946–), vol. vii, p. 47.

7. J. G. Fichte, 'The Vocation of Man', op. cit., p. 421.

8. Frederick Copleston, op. cit., p. 54.

9. F. S. C. Northrop, op. cit., pp. 66, 67.

10. V. I. Lenin, *Marx–Engels–Marxism* (London, n.d.), p. 11.

11. Robert Tucker, *Philosophy and Myth in Karl Marx* (Cambridge, 1961), pp. 34–35.

12. A. O. Lovejoy, *Essays in the History of Ideas* (Baltimore, 1948), p. 211. His foregoing quotation from Kant's *Critique of Pure Reason* is made up from bk. ii, ch. ii, sect. iv [in Abbot's translation (1883), p. 218].

13. Ibid., p. 216.

14. Hegel, *Early Theological Writings* (quoted by Robert Tucker, op. cit., p. 40).

15. Ibid., p. 46.

16. *Philosophy of History* (1857), p. 77.

17. Ibid., p. 77.

18. Robert Tucker, op. cit., p. 49.

19. G. W. F. Hegel, *Reason in History* (New York, 1953), p. 71.

20. Hegel, *The Logic of Hegel*, p. 74 (quoted by Tucker, p. 49).

21. Hegel, *Reason in History*, p. 69.

22. Robert Tucker, op. cit., p. 49.

23. Ibid., p. 51.

24. René Wellek, 'Romanticism Re-examined', in *Romanticism Reconsidered*, ed. Northrop Frye (1963), p. 130.

25. Albert Guerard, 'The Logic of Romanticism', *Essays and Criticism* (1957), vol. vii.

26. Immanuel Kant, *Critique of Pure Reason*, trans. Kemp Smith (1929), p. 147.

27. Hans Kelsen, 'The Foundations of Democracy', *Ethics*, vol. lxvi (Oct. 1955), no. 1, pt. ii, p. 15.

CHAPTER FOUR

Rudyard Kipling:
The Imperial Simulacrum

Tout commence en mystique et finit en politique.

CHARLES PÉGUY

*Man must wrap himself in a vision, make a house of apparent
form and stability, fixity. In his terror of chaos he begins by putting
up an umbrella between himself and the everlasting whirl. Then he
paints the underside of his umbrella like a firmament. Then he
parades around, lives and dies under his umbrella.*

D. H. LAWRENCE

I

'Y OU'RE one o' the right sort, you are,' says Beerbohm's John
Bull to a lantern-jawed Kipling:

And them little tit-bits o' information what you gives me about my
Hempire — why Alf 'Armsworth 'imself couldn't do it neater, I do
believe. Got your banjo with you tonight? Then empty that there mug
and give us a toon.[1]

This cartoon, along with the more familiar one of Kipling capering
over Hampstead Heath on the arm of 'Britannia 'is gurl', and
strongly reinforced by Robert Buchanan's abusive article 'The
Voice of the Hooligan',[2] set a remarkably durable fashion in
Kipling criticism. His purpose and achievement, they suggest, is
simply to talk of, and to tell people how to think about, the illustrious British Empire: to effect in his countrymen the realisation that they, ahead of all others, have been collectively placed by the
will of the Almighty behind the greatest of his ploughs. The imperial idea, in other words, is to be seen as the causal inspiration of
most, if not all, of his writings.

Since then the position has been modified in some respects, but
whenever the Indian stories come under discussion the Beerbohm–

Buchanan premise comes to the fore in one shape or another.[3] Yet these earlier Indian stories tell much more than an uplifting imperial tale, and can, in fact, bring us nearer than any other category of his fiction to an understanding of his artistic inspiration. Professor W. Y. Tindall has claimed that Kipling's idea of empire 'may be deduced from "Recessional", "The White Man's Burden", and "Loot"':[4] I would suggest, on the contrary, that a much more profound insight into the real nature and function of the imperial idea in Kipling's works can be obtained from 'The Children of the Zodiac', 'The Bridge-Builders', 'At the End of the Passage', 'On the City Wall', and 'Without Benefit of Clergy', where we also see more clearly the relation of that idea to his more fundamental concerns, his deeper artistic vision.

Of course no one would deny that Kipling vigorously beat the imperial drum: nor will anyone seek to contest the fact that a great number of his stories work within an implicit or explicit framework statement reiterating what might be described as the British Imperial Aptitude. Clearly Kipling's artistic inspiration emerges '*en politique*'. But to say this as if it were all there is to be said: to see Kipling as 'the laureate of Joseph Chamberlain's designs', as Professor Tindall does,[5] is to see the surface pattern merely — and sometimes not even that. To go further and suggest that Kipling's relationship to the imperial idea is thus explained is nonsense. It is, after all, the 'mystique' from which his expression emerges that must be explained if we would reach a real understanding of the precise nature of that expression: for the two are linked by the closest sequence of cause and effect. Kipling, much more so than one would at first suspect, in talking about political society is talking about self and individual consciousness. Thus even at his most 'imperial', for instance in 'The Head of the District', he is never being simply political; if we ignore this fact we are closing the door firmly on any hope of understanding what Noël Annan has called 'the riddle of Kipling'. Not only is Péguy's dictum amply illustrated in Kipling's work, it also represents precisely the essential dualism in which his concern centres and in which his dramatic tension has its roots. To comprehend this is, if not to excuse, certainly to explain his faults and to recognise where his virtues actually lie.

2

In the Introduction I referred to the political view of action in imperial fiction as being a source of misconceptions about the imperial writer. That such is the nature of action in Kipling's work has long been axiomatic for many of his most intelligent readers. Professor Tindall's remarks depend upon this interpretation, and its accurate reflection of 'the Spirit of Kipling' is still taken for granted in, for example, highly cultured journalism:

Has the policy of 'being strong east of Suez' . . . any real meaning today, or any future tomorrow? Does the spirit of Kipling still exert its magic in Downing Street, and if so can it be exorcised without betraying our honourable commitments?[6]

Of course in beating the imperial drum Kipling wrote stories of a directly propagandist sort: but even then the number which had this as their *raison d'être* is very small. Of these one of the clearest examples is *The Enlightenments of Pagett, M.P.*, where the Anglo-Indian case is carefully argued and, implicitly, the British presence justified.

But the quotations to be used to establish the character of this type of story reveal something more. They make it clear, for instance, that the story's political statement is not such a reactionary or unthinking dogma as dismissive commentators would have us believe. Perhaps Kipling never fully realised the part played by democracy and capitalism in the foundation of the Empire — in fact he is not in the least interested in first causes — but he was by no means ignorant of capitalism's effects.

. . . it is an elementary consideration in governing a country like India which must be administered for the benefit of the people at large, that the counsels of those who resort to it for the purpose of making money should be judiciously weighed and not allowed to overpower the rest. They are welcome guests here, as a matter of course, but it has been found best to restrain their influence. Thus the rights of plantation labourers, factory operatives, and the like have been protected and the capitalist, eager to get on, has not always regarded Government action with favour. It is quite conceivable that under an elective system the commercial communities of the great towns might find means to secure majorities on labour questions and on financial matters.

They would act at least with intelligence and consideration.

Intelligence, yes: but as to consideration, who at the present moment most bitterly resents the tender solicitude of Lancashire for the welfare and protection of the Indian factory operative? English and native capitalists running cotton mills and factories . . . I merely indicate an example of how a powerful commercial interest might hamper a Government intent in the first place on the larger interests of humanity.[7]

Such benevolent despotism as the story indicates would have been regarded by his Victorian contemporaries as far from immoral: Britain's power to do good was obvious and Kipling was thoroughly Victorian in his insistence that power used in this context was sensible and virtuous, and certainly not to be despised merely because it might be translated into physical force.[8]

The common-sense basis of Orde's argument seemed self-justifying to him. Orde, who, we are carefully told, is a radical in politics, addresses the visiting Pagett, incidentally revealing the impractical abstraction a 'moral' imperialism was:

You and I were brought up together: taught by the same tutors, read the same books, lived the same life, and thought, as you may remember, in parallel lines. I come out here, learn new languages and work among new races: while you, more fortunate, remain at home. Why should I change my mind — our mind — because I change my sky. Why should I and the few hundred Englishmen in my service become unreasonable, prejudiced fossils, while you and your newer friends alone remain bright and openminded? You surely don't fancy Civilians are members of a Primrose league.[9]

The main plank in the defender's platform is that a programme of gradual liberalisation has been embarked upon and the administrator, knowing through years of arduous experience how long such a programme will take to be properly fulfilled, sees it threatened by precipitate action on the part of a few. To him their interference threatens an entire people with a course of action which is disastrously opposed to their real long-term material interests.

Edwards, Burke, Bishen Singh, Rasul Ali Khan, old Jelloo, though propagandist are not entirely unauthentic in their attitude to the emergent Congress Party. With these, however, who are *not* called the case is rather different and one feels both that Congress could have had a better spokesman and that the Anglo-Indian antipathy towards Babus has been extended to Dina Nath. The interesting thing, however, is that the latter refuses to be dismissed: almost in spite of the author, a genuine and, in a wider view, sympathetic character shows itself in his enthusiastic rush of words and his buoyant disregard for 'the mere exceptions to the universal rule'. But always for the administrator, the 'external' man of common sense devoted to things as they are, there looms the crushing practical difficulty:

If there were any political analogy between India and England, if the thousand races of this Empire were one; if there were any chance even of their learning to speak one language . . . this kind of talk might be worth listening to.

It is, of course, not all materialist argument — 'if there were any political analogy' is a pertinent observation and one that troubles Kipling repeatedly. He knows too well that Britain won't hold India in fee for ever, but what will happen? More clearly than many, he saw that there might well be too little common ground for English liberal traditions ever to seed themselves in those imperial, alien territories.

But the material objections are important ones, particularly those involving race and caste problems:

'Pride of race', says Orde, 'which also means race hatred is the plague and curse of India and it spreads far . . . and the race-hatred is only part of it. What's really the matter with Bishen Singh is class-hatred, which unfortunately is even more intense and more widely spread. That's one of the little drawbacks of caste which some of your recent English writers find an impeccable system.'[10]

Here, as elsewhere, there emerges in the tone a half-angry, half-discouraged recognition of the size of the forces which the representatives of progress have to contend with.

That all this amounts to more than simply political statement we can appreciate if we stand back a little from the process of the argument. What we see then is a man who has deliberately chosen as his field of action and of values the material world; a man who has no time for politics based on abstract theories when millions of people are dying through lack of a planned agriculture, lack of medical treatment, and through what Dr. Lathrop describes as 'an all-round entanglement of physical, social and moral evils and corruptions'. In her words the famine- and cholera-ridden people of

India 'require many things more urgently than votes'. And always before the Administrator's eyes there is the reminder of the shortness of the present moment and its value:

Our death rate's five times higher than yours . . . and we work on the refuse of worked out cities and exhausted civilisations among the bones of the dead.[11]

Nineveh and Tyre, we are reminded, were also empires: 'work' and 'worked out' form an inevitable and terrible sequence and one can transcend discouragement only through the knowledge that a selfless expenditure of effort can make the reality of the moment more endurable and enjoyable for a multitude of fellow-humans. Kipling has little time for those visionaries who so easily overlooked present hells in order to build future utopias. Out of the bodies of millions of animalculae nature may have made the rocks, but, as Rider Haggard remarked in a passage quoted earlier, 'the process must have been unpleasant to the living creatures by whose humble means the great strata were reared up'. The Rock of God's far-off purpose didn't concern Kipling; there is no clear evidence that he found it anything other than a myth. But the process of the living moment did — all the more so. There is little enough time to alleviate the sufferings of the world's brief lives and none at all to waste experimenting on emaciated bodies with new forms of government, particularly when these forms are based more on metaphysical speculation than on experience which alone could apprehend the happiness and unhappiness of individuals — the only criterion of government.

Naturally a man (in Town) grows to think that there is no one higher than himself, and that the Metropolitan Board of Works made everything. But, in India, where you really see humanity — raw, brown, naked humanity — with nothing between it and the blazing sky, and only the used-up, overhandled earth underfoot, the notion somehow dies away, and most folk come back to simpler theories. Life, in India, is not long enough to waste in proving that there is no one in particular at the head of affairs. For this reason. The Deputy is above the Assistant, the Commissioner above the Deputy, the Lieutenant-Governor above the Commissioner, and the Viceroy above all four, under the orders of the Secretary of State, who is responsible to the Empress. If the Empress be not responsible to her Maker — if there is no Maker for her to be responsible to — the entire system of Our administration must be wrong. Which is manifestly impossible.[12]

The sting is in the tail: Kipling is not in the least concerned with moral absolutes, and here he is ironically proving not the system against the principle, but the principle against the system. Whether or not there is a Maker, whether or not there is a morality based on responsibility to Him, there is an Administration with its clear justification in the succouring of India's mass of 'raw, brown, naked humanity'. In the light of their crying need, First Causes are luxury commodities which could well be done without. Kipling was thoroughly utilitarian and pragmatic: the standard by which the morality of an idea was to be judged was the practical result which the idea would have when applied in action. Indeed, William James's own definition of pragmatism represents accurately Kipling's attitude: 'For the pragmatist . . . all discarnate truth is static, impotent, and relatively spectral, full truth being the truth that energises and does battle.'[13]

If this leads him, as Hilton Brown complains, to be unduly severe with the 'University-trained hybrids', dismissing them as if they were 'unreal' so that he may concentrate on the cultivator and the ryot, we should remember this outlook and context of thinking. Kipling's eyes, the eyes of Leo in *The Children of the Zodiac*, were always on the ground, the only place where they could do any good, and there he saw millions of people starving from famine and dying from cholera, people who demanded service in order to have their sufferings alleviated, who in mass and in need *were* the real Indian. What good could the abstract theorists from the universities do, unfitted by their training to help in any way, able only to reveal what was better concealed — the agonies of the human dilemma?

Politics, for Kipling, are people: abstract theorising for him is altogether suspect.

'Strict supervision, and play them off one against the other,' said the Mussuck, shovelling down his ice by tureenfuls , . . 'That, Mrs. Hauksbee, is the secret of our Government.'[14]

But it is certainly not, as Mrs. Hauksbee clearly demonstrates — it is a thorough knowledge of the people involved which pays off in the end: and the end of politics, as Tod reminds the Administrator in another story, is also people. Conversely people are politics; they are not metaphysics, or at any rate are not to be reminded that they are — hence the conversion of Aurelian McGoggin, and the many elaborate evasions of 'higher things', which leads on occasion to a deliberate and showy philistinism:

> The bundle [of MS.] needed much expurgation, and was full of Greek nonsense at the head of the chapters, which has all been cut out.[15]

Thus even where the action postulated is of a very traditional and imperial sort, confidently directed to highly edifying ends, Kipling is never being *merely* political. There is in it a sombre commitment to the human community that is far from being a casual by-product of devotion to the imperial idea.

And stories which are propagandist to the extent of *The Enlightenments of Pagett, M.P.* are very few. Even *One View of the Question* does not quite come into the category for there is a strong element of nostalgic fantasy surrounding the story as a result of the author's careful dissociation. Here the narrator is not the sober, responsible Orde but Kipling's ideal Pathan warrior: an expression of frustration at life's refusal to be simple and straightforward, rather than a political statement.

Characterisation throughout the Indian stories has also been made to suffer in the assumption of a purely political link between Kipling and the idea. One need go no further for an example than the case of his notorious Subalterns. Even Professor Bonamy Dobrée in his sensitive study of Kipling in *The Lamp and the Lute* finds them 'perfectly insufferable and not altogether real'.

Yet far from being the hopelessly idealised *élite* of an Imperial *herrenvolk*, these men are, in fact, drawn from actuality by a peculiarly stoic mind. Unreal though they may be to us, they certainly were not so in the nineteenth-century Anglo-Indian scene. For one thing, they were men living and acting within a self-created code of behaviour of quite enormous strength, which by itself made them a little larger than life. Documentary evidence tends, if anything, to exceed even Kipling's picture of their courage, fortitude and enterprise. For this was particularly 'the day of subalterns, boys in age, men in character, blessed with the adventurous ardour and audacity of youth'. 'Few things,' wrote Sir Francis Younghusband,

> are more remarkable in our history than the splendid work done by

young British officers; few things more amazing than the utter ignorance of people in England about the deeds they have done.[16]

It was the day, too, of Sir Henry Lawrence and his 'young men' through whom he created the basis of sound administrative government in northern India. As well as the celebrated John Nicholson these included Lt. Eldred Pottinger, 'The Hero of Herat', Lt. Proby Cantly, who, totally without experience, designed and built the Ganges canal 'on a scale of magnitude hardly conceivable outside India', of Lt. Herbert Edwardes who pacified the wild Bannu tribesmen single-handed. 'How you will laugh', the latter wrote to a friend at home on the day of his appointment as 'a responsible Political Officer' to the notorious Maharajah of Jammu, 'a Lieutenant of Foot advising the King of the Mountains! Such is India.'[17]

As for their dash and spirit and insatiable lust for combat, before dismissing it as mere fiction as Hilton Brown, for example, did, it is worth recalling another of Lt. Edwardes's letters:

... if he takes any pride in the discipline of his corps, he must not grudge the labour by which it is brought about, and which has enabled the regiment to serve with such great distinction all through the late war, and will enable it, I hope, to gain fresh laurels in the one now springing up in the part of the country where I am going. This is a cheerful prospect for us subs. and I am, at all events, lucky in being posted to a regiment which is always called upon when fighting is to be done . . .[18]

One has, in fact, only to dip into the mass of autobiographies, memorials and other works descriptive of the era like *A Year on the Punjab Frontier* (1885), Sir Winston Churchill's *The Story of the Malakand Field Force* (1899), or *A Soldier's Memories* (1917) to realise how far from unreality Kipling's subalterns really were.[19] Filtered through his own uncompromising vision, their code, their endurance and their objectives became more Roman: for so transmitted, these qualities were the essential ones in Kipling's world if man were to achieve any dignity at all and to survive with some degree of integrity during his battle with life.

The story *Only a Subaltern* starts with a quotation from the Bengal Army Regulations,

... not only to enforce by command, but to encourage by example the

energetic discharge of duty and the steady endurance of the difficulties
and privations inseparable from military service.[20]

Duty . . . endurance . . . difficulties . . . privations: attention to
the job in hand and fortitude in the face of all which that will bring
is what constitutes a man and makes his soul. And to aid and fortify
him he has the assistance of his community — in this case the
military community — drawing its spiritual sustenance from the
same ideals:

. . . every one of those legends told him of battles fought at long odds,
without fear as without support; of hospitality catholic as an Arab's;
of friendships deep as the sea and steady as the fighting line; of honour
won by hard roads for honour's sake; and of instant and unquestioning
devotion to the Regiment — the Regiment that claims the lives of all
and lives forever.[21]

What is implicit in this is the machinery, not of militarism or anything like it, but of self-consciousness, identity and moral integrity.
Its components are, very largely, the 'few simple notions' that we
find recommended in Conrad's *Lord Jim*.[22]

Over the years Kipling's Other Ranks have fared better. Even
here, however, accusations of unreality are still frequent. This is
inevitable if, like Mr. Robert Graves, we look upon them simply as
adulterous scallywags on whose imperial doings the sun, with very
good reason, is reluctant to set. According to Mr. Graves they provide clear evidence that Kipling

condoned drinking bouts at hygienic intervals, . . . took something like
the French view of adultery, . . . encouraged fighting with fists and belts
as being an old English habit and better than running amok with rifle
and bayonet, . . . delighted in oaths and ribaldry, and discountenanced
piety while at the same time insisting on certain soldierly virtues such as
loyalty, initiative, comradeship, steadiness under fire, and above all,
personal cleanliness and care of arms.[23]

This is, of course, to ignore the dedication of Barrack-Room Ballads
to Tommy Atkins 'both for your pleasures and your pain'. Kipling
is not identifying his own with the soldier's morality: he is simply
putting before us with all honesty the soldier in action, the soldier
in camp, the soldier in India.

Again, it is really a case of actuality refined through a peculiarly

F

bleak and penetrating vision. These men are all that Mulvaney suggests in the summary of his own life in *The Solid Muldoon*:

> But I've had my day, I've had my day an' nothin' can take away the taste av that! Oh my time past, whin I put me fut through ivry livin' wan av the Tin Commandmints betune Revelly and Lights out, blew the froth off a pewter, wiped my mustache wid the back av me hand, an' slept on ut all as quiet as a little child. . . . Was there any wan in the Ould Rig'mint to touch Corp'ril Terence Mulvaney whin that same was turned out for sedukshin? I niver met him. Ivry woman that was not a witch was worth the runnin' afther in those days, an ivry man was my dearest frind or . . . I had stripped to him an' we knew which was the better av the tu.[24]

— but no Kipling character ever wears his heart upon his sleeve though now and then we may be vouchsafed a glimpse of it. In fact, as though he were anxious lest we had failed to appreciate the depths of their consciousness and sensitivity from these brief insights, Kipling reinforces them on a special occasion for each of the soldiers three in turn: in *The Courting of Dinah Shadd* for Mulvaney, in *On Greenhow Hill* for Learoyd and in *The Madness of Private Ortheris* for the third member of the group.

Of the three, *The Courting of Dinah Shadd* makes clearest the soldiers' appreciation of the public image and the private truth:

> Good cause the Rig'mint has to know me for the best soldier in ut. Better cause have I to know myself for the worst man.[25]

— and the awareness which this brings of the loneliness at the core of their individuality:

> When I woke I saw Mulvaney, the night dew gemming his moustache, leaning on his rifle at picket, lonely as Prometheus on his rock, with I know not what vultures tearing at his liver.[26]

With very great clarity Kipling brings home the intensity of the pressures which these men endured. Forced to serve in the middle of an alien and hostile country in stations like Fort Amara, the petty frustrations of military regimentation swell to intolerable proportions, enormously aggravated by unpleasant and dangerous diseases:

> Since August when it started, it's been stickin' to our tail,
> Though they've 'ad us out by marches an' they've 'ad us back by rail;
> But it runs as fast as troop trains, and we cannot get away,
> An' the sick-list to the colonel makes ten more today.[27]

How thin the barrier is between them and the limit of mental and physical endurance is shown with great insight in for example, *With the Main Guard, Black Jack*, 'Danny Deever' — even in 'Boots'.

Kipling penetrates far enough into the personality and individuality of these characters to show that Tommy, derided at home when times were peaceful, was not only human but was, too, an individual with a capacity for spiritual affliction and self-appraisal, and the possessor of an unsuspected sensitivity which Kipling's predecessors had denied him. Long before the advent of Norman Mailer or Nicholas Monsarrat, Kipling with, perhaps, Stephen Crane, set a new style in military story-telling.[28]

Occasionally Kipling uses these soldiers to indulge his taste for the cut-and-thrust of fierce hand-to-hand fighting. Sometimes these intimate accounts of vivisection merely suggest masochism: certainly something too immediate to his senses to be helpful to his art or meaningful to us:

> The Gurkhas' stall at the bazaar was the noisiest, for the men were engaged — to a nasty noise as of beef being cut on the block — with the kukri, which they preferred to the bayonet; well-knowing how the Afghan hates the half-moon blade.[29]

Elsewhere they are better integrated:

> This jam thing that I'm talkin' about lasted for five minut's good, an' thin we got our arrums clear an' wint in. I misremimber exactly fwhat I did, but I didn't want Dinah to be a widdy at the depot. Thin after some promishkuous hackin' we shtuck agin, an' the Tyrone behin' was callin' us dogs and cowards an' all manner av names; we barrin' their way.
>
> 'Fwhat ails the Tyrone?' thinks I; 'they've the makin's of a most convanient fight here.' A man behind me sez beseechful an' in a whisper: 'Let me get at thim! For the love av Mary, give me room beside ye, ye tall man.' 'An' who are you, that's so anxious to be kilt?' sez I widout turnin' my head, fir the long knives was dancin' in front like the sun on Donegal Bay whin ut's rough.
>
> 'We've seen our dead,' he says, squeezin' into me; 'our dead that was men two days gone! An' me that was his cousin by blood cud not bring Tim Coulan off! Let me get on' he sez, 'let me get to thim or I'll run ye through the back!' ... I gave room to the man an' he ran forward wid the Haymakers' Lift on his bay'nit an' swung a Paythan clear off his feet by the belly-band av the brute, an' the iron bruk at the lockin'-ring. 'Tim

Coulan'll slape aisy tonight', sez he wid a grin; an' the next minut his head was in two halves and he wint down grinnin' by sections.'[30]

Behind this there is more than a narrow self-indulgence; there is a view of life which sees action as in its essence virtuous. Kipling was intensely aware that man in his battle with life purchased victory at the price of ultimate defeat: the Lords of Life and Death merely played with him, offering life, which in spite of himself he grasped, withdrawing it and dealing him death with the same laconic hand. There is a mood, he suggests in extracts like this, which rebels against this frustration and humiliation, and which, in the permitted, fatal moment of defiant activity, seeks to settle a few old scores, and to regain a moiety of self-respect.

We have been told that Kipling had a capacity for savouring pain: it is also clear from a story like *At the End of the Passage* that he was capable of embracing it deliberately if the alternative was to suffer agonies of mental torment. Battle offered the prospect of this and implied the absence of the latter; but it had to be subalterns' action, swiftly and cleanly consummated in the physical presence of the enemy, otherwise it defeated its own purpose, and the horrors of life, to which it had all along been a hopeless and defiant gesture, would be redoubled:

'Don't,' Strangwick squealed, 'I can't stand it! There's nothing on earth creaks like they do! And — when it thaws we — we've got to slap 'em back with a spade! Remember those Frenchman's little boots under the duckboards?'[31]

It is significant that in his later stories when war can no longer be reconciled with heroic personal combat and Homeric ideals, glorification of fighting is heard no more: in fact it never survives translation from its Indian context. Neither the South African war nor, later, the European, allowed him to write as he had done before, they only revealed that an ideal of action conceived in India had no place in *A Sahib's War*. And instead of young men like those in *A Conference of the Powers* came those of *Sea Constables*; and the rich, passive seclusion of a Freemasons' temple is substituted for gay cantonments, vast, burning, challenging deserts and life with action as its mainspring.

Though Kipling may use his soldiers to indulge himself or to project his Homeric ideal, he was, as has been suggested, far too interested in them as individuals to create them simply for this purpose. Although for the most part they are found punctiliously observing the rules, living life in full fealty to the God of Things as They Are, we are left in no doubt as to their awareness of the depths beneath. The Other Ranks, of course, observe the rules in a manner historically different from that of the Subalterns: while the latter conceal their awareness behind reticence and a gentlemanly nonchalance, the common soldier adopts the front of Barrack Room balladry, of garrulousness and belligerence, of scepticism in everything but the chain of command.

When it comes to the Administrator — of whom more will be said in the next section — he is still seen to have an upper lip so stiff as to preclude utterly any explanation of his conduct. Here again to dismiss him as one more example of Kipling's imperial statement is to miss the real significance of his characterisation. What he represents is something which has, in a fundamental sense, less to do with the politics of the imperial idea than with the basic credo of Kipling the artist.

With very little interest and no particular faith in the long term future Kipling most admired the man who had learned to live nobly and usefully in the full consciousness of his ultimate destruction. The whole theme of *The Children of the Zodiac* is in the progression of Leo and the Girl to this particular awareness.

Unremitting work and sacrifice in the present actuality such as the Administrator participated in, was the only meaningful activity. By sharing in it, one not only contributed to the happiness of fellow-humans but also discovered the only means of achieving a personal integrity. The harder and more exhausting the task, undiluted by anything which might make it easier or more congenial, the more fully were all one's powers and energies engaged in the struggle; in such conflict with one's environment alone was there the chance to attain even a passing reality.

Thus if in his notorious story *The Head of the District* Kipling can be seen, on one level, as launching perhaps his most savage and bitter attack on the 'educated native' who presumed to do a Sahib's job, the second level must, at the same time, be kept in mind. For what Grish Chunder Dé threatened was to introduce an entirely different code, and one that would utterly profane the stoic ideal in which Kipling's vision emerged. And if one took away from man his conflict, his fight against overwhelming odds which clearly was to end in defeat, one does nothing less than deprive him of his salvation. Take away man's stoicism and that 'Bulkhead 'twixt Despair and the edge of Nothing' will at once disintegrate.

Earlier in this section I said that to see Kipling's work in political terms imbued with political action, was to see the surface pattern merely and sometimes not even that. This did not deny the occasional political relationship between Kipling and the imperial idea in stories like *The Enlightenments of Pagett, M.P.*, *A Deal in Cotton* and *The Head of the District*: nor did it deny that a political concern could stimulate him to write — as indeed it did in *The Army of a Dream*, written to express Kipling's alarm at the state of Britain's defences *vis-à-vis* the Powers of Europe, and in poems like *Stellenbosch* and *The Islanders*.

But I have also claimed that Kipling is eminently more than a commentator upon a changing political reality. Even where he is dealing with a highly political action or character we are continually being offered insights more characteristic of the artist's eye than that of the political propagandist.

It is on this other area, this deeper layer, so far merely suggested, that I would now like to concentrate. Here action takes all its force and direction from being filtered through Kipling's most powerful moral focus — the vast threatening entity that is India.

3

For the main character in the Indian stories is not the tired, tough, dedicated Administrator nor the resourceful subaltern: the main character is India itself.

Looking over the menacing jungle landscape of the Congo, Marlow, in Conrad's *Heart of Darkness*, had wondered:

Could we handle that dumb thing or would it handle us? I felt how big, how confoundedly big was the thing that couldn't talk and perhaps was deaf as well.[32]

In Kipling the struggle for mastery is evident in every story which has to deal with the country, and nine times out of ten, 'great, grey, formless India'[33] wins. Inevitably it comes to represent the forces of persecution ranged against the individual in his struggle to sustain his identity. Physically and morally it overwhelms and crushes. One's own truths and moral definitions blur and diffuse themselves into meaninglessness, just as they did for Forster's Mrs. Moore. Mrs. Mallowe has, in fact, occasional flashes of Mrs. Moore's perception, observing very clearly the moral destructiveness of India where 'you can't focus anything':[34] and because it is Kipling and not Forster, we are inside India looking outwards through our bars rather than outside looking in with Mrs. Moore's cool clarity of mind.

Faced by a country which can reduce utterly, these beleaguered Anglo-Indians band together in pitiful, blind opposition, doomed to ludicrous failure, however much they speak of Smith as a Bengal man, Jones as a Punjabi. Herded together in The Club, in The Station, in Simla, they insist upon their 'difference' from the rest of India; but even in the bosom of their own community they can not escape the constant awareness of their vulnerability.

Everybody was there and there was a general closing up of ranks and taking stock of our losses in dead or disabled that had fallen during the past year. It was a very wet night, and I remember that we sang 'Auld Lang Syne' with our feet in the Polo Championship Cup and our heads among the stars, and swore that we were all very dear friends.[35]

This is Forster's famous anthem scene viewed from the inside. It is, however, in the outposts that India's malignant power is to be seen at its most active in its relentless war against the aliens.

The night-light was trimmed; the shadow of the punkah wavered across the room, and the 'flick' of the punkah-towel and the soft whine of the rope through the wall-hole followed it. Then the punkah flagged, almost ceased. The sweat poured from Spurstow's brow. Should he go out and harangue the coolie? It started forward again with a savage jerk, and a pin came out of the towels. When this was replaced, a tom-tom in the coolie lines began to beat with the steady throb of a swollen artery inside some brain-fevered skull.[36]

Bound on his wheel, the imperial servant struggled to reduce the hostile mass of India to governable terms, more often than not ending up as

one of the rank and file who are ground up in the wheels of the Administration; losing heart and soul, and mind and strength in the process.

Driven too far there was, of course, always a more dramatic way of conceding victory, though one not likely to evoke a sentimental response from one's colleagues:

'Why didn't you let it go in as suicide?' said Lowndes . . .'No direct proof. A man hasn't many privileges in this country, but he might at least be allowed to mishandle his own rifle. Besides, some day I may need a man to smother up an accident myself. Live and let live. Die and let die.'[37]

And always in the background there lurks the question: just how much effect has the British raj had — the raj so vaunted for its capacity to bring physical and moral good? Mrs. Mallowe, at any rate, has no illusions:

We are only little bits of dirt on the hillsides — here one day and blown down the *khud* the next . . . we have no cohesion.[38]

And she is echoed in *The Bridge-Builders*. The great new work has, on this occasion, withstood the furious hostility of Mother Gunga, but its time will come, for the gulf is not to be bridged: least of all by this sort of work, which, as the clear vision of India's gods ironically reveals, is destructive rather than creative.

'They have changed the face of the land — which is my land. They have killed and made new towns on my banks', said the Mugger. 'It is but the shifting of a little dirt. Let the dirt dig in the dirt if it pleases the dirt,' answered the Elephant.[39]

The Empire, its ideals and works are, by India, utterly reduced in time and space:

'What should their Gods know? They were born yesterday and those that made them are scarcely yet cold,' said the Mugger. 'Tomorrow their Gods will die.'[40]

It is of no use saying that because the Bridge — and Finlayson — have survived the onslaught of the river theirs is the last word and the final triumph. Compared to the commentators whose statements are made from above and beyond time, their expression could scarcely appear more ephemeral.

Not even the most celebrated institutions of the raj were proof against India's inexorable powers of assimilation. British Justice itself, as we see in *Gemini*, was on occasion eroded to the level of a useful new pawn in a very old game, while the Pax Britannica had already sowed the seeds of its own destruction:

'Thanks to your Government,' said Wali Dad . . . 'all our heads are protected, and with the educational facilities at my hand' — his eyes twinkled wickedly — 'I might be a distinguished member of the local administration. Perhaps in time, I might even be a member of a Legislative Council.'[41]

Meanwhile gross materialism advances and the destruction — with no real substitute — goes on:

'Ye should have slain at the beginning,' says Krishna, 'when the men from across the water had taught our folk nothing. Now my people see their work, and go away thinking. They do not think of the Heavenly Ones altogether. They think of the fire-carriage and the other things that the bridge-builders have done, and when your priests thrust forward hands asking alms, they give unwillingly a little. That is the beginning . . .'[42]

Peroo when he first enters the engine-room prays to the low-pressure cylinder ('Not half a bad thing to pray to either,' says Finlayson); and Rao Sahib remarks in almost the same breath,

Now you shall back her out, Hitchcock. I — I do not understand steam-engines.

. . . They are dam'-bore, these religious ceremonies, Finlinson, eh?[43]

Elsewhere Hurree Babu's reflection of the crisis is brought out in an aside:

It is an awful thing still to dread the magic that you contemptuously investigate — to collect folk-lore for The Royal Society with a lively belief in all Powers of Darkness.[44]

The product of the conflict between India and the intruders can best be seen in the Anglo-Indians' immense consciousness of vulnerability and loneliness. The extent of their self-dependence makes itself felt in the remote places where

there is only the isolation that weighs upon the waking eyelids and drives you perforce headlong into the labours of the day. There is no post, there is no one of your own colour to speak to, there are no roads: there is, indeed, food to keep you alive, but it is not pleasant to eat; and whatever of good and beauty and interest there is in your life, must come from yourself and the grace that may be planted in you.[45]

The loneliness of the four young men in *At the End of the Passage* provides another example. The only solidarity is, as has been said of Conrad's characters, the solidarity of isolated victims. These men are lonely, imperial aliens, whose personal identity and that of their group is in daily peril. In their awareness of their alien nature and of the great darkness beyond the circle of light from the club-room window, the supernatural becomes a sublimation of their fear, heavily on the side of the forces of persecution; an acknowledgement of their alien-ness and of the power of India.

The Administrator then, as Kipling creates him, has at his core a terrible irony: he who would 'administer' and govern this vast mass is himself a victim. Stoically he goes through the motions of his trying occupation, appropriating to himself a world and a life completely alien; and the more alien it becomes the more it engrosses until he has no soul of his own left, and can only plod mechanically on until finally engulfed. Mrs. Mallowe says of her husband:

> Government has eaten him up. All his ideas and powers of conversation — he really used to be a good talker, even to his wife — are taken from him by this — this kitchen sink of a Government.[46]

At the End of the Passage illustrates powerfully, if didactically, what this means. The Imperial Demand is for self-sacrifice of a most complete and senseless character, a willingness on the part of the imperial servants to offer themselves up so that the great maw of India may feed upon the offering. The British work in India was a huge, macabre joke which Kipling and a few — but only a few — of his creations saw. The principal character, inert, but possessed of an awesome authority, is India herself. Seen thus the Briton in India becomes microscopically small and his labours puny and futile.

One of Kipling's best short stories — *Without Benefit of Clergy* — derives its excellence from its sympathetic awareness of the human context of this conflict. The brief little tragedy of Holden and Ameera is played out against a background, not of marching feet and thudding rifle-butts as in *On the City Wall*, but of India's silent, malignant and pervasive power. The title refers, of course, to an illicit union, but 'benefit of Clergy' is also a technical phrase originally alluding to the exemption of ecclesiastics from secular jurisdiction. It is thus made clear that there is to be no exemption here either — even for the lovers, for all the purity of their emotions.

From the beginning, the story evokes a sense of helplessness and doom in the face of immensity; and the vehicle through which India demonstrates its tyranny is Ameera herself, whose love for Holden is no less intense than his for her. At the birth of their child, Ameera rejoices that there is 'a bond and a heel-rope between us now that nothing can break'. But she has reckoned without their foe's might and jealousy: Toto dies of 'the seasonal autumnal fever' and presumptuous humanity is beaten down to size.

Throughout, with an admirable manipulation of time and space, the relationship between these humans and India evolves: from the intimate opening, close-focused and personal, 'But if it be a girl?' we move to the desolate end, through a phased depersonalisation, showing us first the grey squirrel, now sole occupant of the bungalow's verandah, 'as if the house had been untenanted for thirty years instead of three days', and lastly nothing at all:

It shall be pulled down and the municipality shall make a road across as they desire from the burning-ghat to the city wall, so that no man may say where this house stood.[47]

Man has shrunk to a mere pinpoint, and a pinpoint which travels across the triumphant mass of India between the City Wall and the burning-ghat.

The Anglo-Indians' main reaction to this ubiquitous persecution is to assert their own cultural morality more fiercely than ever. The result is that they fail to understand the people they govern.

In the west people say rude things about Lalun's profession, and write lectures about it, and distribute the lectures to young people in order that Morality may be preserved. In the East, where the profession is hereditary . . . nobody writes lectures or takes any notice: and this is a distinct proof of the inability of the East to manage its own affairs.[48]

The same theme is expressed more succinctly in the description of Wali Dad making 'an unsuccessful attempt to enter the Roman Church and the Presbyterian fold at the same time', when the missionaries 'found him out and called him names; but . . . did not understand his trouble'. Wali Dad presents, in fact, the most complete picture of what has happened in the collision to people like him.

India has gossiped for centuries — always standing in the bazars until the soldiers go by. Therefore — you are here to-day instead of starving in your own country, and I am not a Mohammedan — I am a Product — a Demnition Product. *That*, also, I owe to you and yours; that I cannot make an end to my sentence without quoting from your authors.

Exhorted to take up his 'place in the world', he becomes even more ironic:

I might wear an English coat and trousers. I might be a leading Mohammedan pleader. I might even be received at the Commissioner's tennis parties where the English stand on one side, and the natives on the other, in order to promote social intercourse throughout the Empire.[49]

Is this a source for Mr. Forster's Aziz and his famous bridge-party? The remark could certainly have come from Aziz.

There is, however, in this discussion of the role of India, one acknowledgement missing: that is to the fascination which it continued to exert while crushing and annihilating. Mrs. Mallowe saw clearly enough the bars of the cage:

I don't suppose a Russian convict under the knout is able to amuse the rest of his gang; and all our men-folk here are gilded convicts.[50]

And outside Simla, more often than not, there was not even the gilding. Yet the colour and the seething abundance of life with which their enemy veiled its malevolence could still attract, quite apart from the fact that, so much having been absorbed by it, they could no longer have a completely independent existence. Kipling reflects the fascination in many places — one thinks of his well-known description of the Grand Trunk in *Kim* (see note 150).

The British may have built the Great Trunk Road, but it is the teeming life of India that erupts upon it: towns have been built and dusty boulevards of Victorian villas, but it is to the riot of the bazaar that one is irresistibly drawn. Even in Lalun's little house the variety was interminable:

Shiahs of the grimmest and most uncompromising persuasion, Sufis who had lost all belief in the prophet and retained but little in God: wandering Hindu priests passing southwards to the Central India fairs and other affairs; Pundits in black gowns . . . bearded headmen of the wards; Sikhs with all the details of the latest ecclesiastical scandal in the Golden Temple, red-eyed mullahs from beyond the border: M.A.s of the University. . . .[51]

To stand back a little, to add a touch of remoteness, was to colour it with an increase of appeal and to generate memories and impressions to be carried away with the imperial servant, when, with his complex of hate and affection, he surrendered his alien citizenship:

There is a pleasant wind among the mulberry trees, and the streams are bright with snow-water, and the caravans go up and the caravans go down, and a hundred fires sparkle in the gut of the Pass, and tent-peg answers hammer-nose, and pack-horse squeals to pack-horse across the drift of the evening. It is good in the North now. Come back with me.[52]

4

India, then, is a great deal more than a geographical expression in the purple language of Empire. And in one of its principal symbolic functions it is seen to embody a central concern of Kipling's — his intense preoccupation with the inexorable sway of the Lords of Life and Death. Death is the one reality: man's highest achievement to live nobly, usefully and bravely in the full knowledge of this fact.

From the start Kipling treated the subject of death in a manner which conflicted with the orthodox Victorian response. Hence his deliberately irreverent approach in defiance both of William Sankey and *sotto voce* funeralism: an approach which Le Gallienne thought exceedingly vulgar but nevertheless profound. To disparage people's response to death was to suggest a close look at their response to life. Understating the event of dying he stresses the wretchedness, the hardship — and the importance — of the present: denied the dignity of ritual and the buttress of false sentiment, death admits its bleak reality. And the medium is India, where

> . . . threadbare Death commands
> Hardly observance . . .'[53]

There is nothing heinous in Little Tobrah's killing of his sister, here where death is not a Glorious End but a sardonic means: a card, admittedly an ace, to be played in a rather shabby game. Where life is cheap ('she was but a little child', says her brother) death is obviously cheapened, though even then the head groom's wife is constrained to ask of Tobrah: 'But who art thou, weak as a fowl and small as a day-old colt, what art thou.'[54] Neither youth nor age has very much significance in such a context, however: experience is the only initiation rite, and in this these children have as much opportunity to be informed as their elders. At the age of eight Tobrah had discovered that a gift of marigolds to the gods was powerless against the depredations of the money-lender Surjan Dass. It is not surprising to find that life in these terms seems to Kipling to invalidate life as reflected in the light of Western fireside mythologies.

Kipling, then, is deliberately challenging certain cherished Western conceptions by showing a context in which they have little validity: where the universal claims of their beliefs look remarkably hollow. (India had been similarly responsible for teaching Mrs. Moore, in *A Passage to India*, the inadequacies of 'poor little talkative Christianity'.) Dying 'decently of zymotic diseases' could be reconciled to these beliefs but Tobrah's act and Pambé Serang's vengeance,[55] the culmination of which was such a 'sad blow to the kind gentleman', could not. In this last story the utter failure of the 'kind gentleman' to understand Pambé takes us back again to Lalun and the two cultures. Neither he nor his type were capable of understanding Pambé and his — not even at their most superficial levels let alone comprehending their attitudes to life and death.

Seen from this angle, life demanded a different approach. For one thing it brought the present actuality into the forefront, and for another, introspective problems of great moral doctrines seemed to be rather less pressing and infinitely less realistic than those of eating.

Implicit in this theme there is for Christianity, if not outright dismissal, the severest censure. In Kipling's eyes this had largely failed because it did not remove the fear of death and the Western world 'still clung to the dread of death more closely than to the hope of life'.[56] Perhaps in some ways this was a good thing.

'I am afraid to be kicked,' said Grish Chunder, 'but I am not afraid to die, because I know what I know. You are not afraid to be kicked but you are afraid to die. If you were not, by God! you English would be all over the shop in an hour, upsetting the balances of power and making commotions.'[57]

But for a man whose whole life was a search for reassurance it was simply one more theory which, on application, proved negative.

There is, in fact, very little evidence anywhere in Kipling's writing of an adherence to Christianity — *The Gardener* is the only story to have a positive reference to Christ. On the other hand, there is much to show that no formal religion would have satisfied him.

In the early stories he is content to imply that Christianity could well be explained simply as a stage in evolution and no more.[58] And many a time his attitude in a Christian would have been irreverent, to say the very least of it: in *On the Gate*, for instance, when we find St. Peter administratively preoccupied with allotting people to their various categories:

'Good!' St. Peter rubbed his hands. 'That brings her under the higher allowance — G.L.H. scale — Greater love hath no man ——'[59]

Or in Ortheris's reference to the 'hanging' prayer:

The Lord giveth an' the Lord taketh awai, — Heasy with that there drop! — Blessed be the naime o' the Lord.[60]

The priest who appeals to him is one like that of Saint Juvans, who was 'learned in death and life', or like Father Dennis, who, in a particular battle, had managed to make his way to the foremost of his boys:

To him crawled Mulcahy, ashen-grey, demanding absolution.
'Wait till you're shot', said Father Dennis sweetly. 'There's a time for everything.'[61]

The Roman Catholic Church, as a matter of fact, always comes out in a more favourable light — simply because it seemed much nearer the humanity it served.

Between himself and the Roman Catholic chaplain of the Irish contingent lay, as Bennett believed, an unbridgeable gulf, but it was noticeable that whenever the Church of England dealt with the human problem she was very likely to call in the Church of Rome.[62]

Or again, by implication:

Bennett looked at him [the lama] with the triple-ringed uninterest of the creed that lumps nine-tenths of the world under the title of 'heathen'.[63]

And there is a splendid picture in *The Record of Badalia Herodsfoot* of the rector who lived in dread of pauperising the poor, would fain have held bazaars for fresh altar-cloths, and prayed in secret for a large new brass bird, with eyes of red glass, fondly believed to be carbuncles.[64]

His distaste was not always with the negative failings of Christianity, and he returns several times to

... the more than inherited (since it is also carefully taught) brutality of the Christian peoples, beside which the mere heathendom of the West Coast nigger is clean and restrained. ...[65]

An example of this Christian brutality can be found in *Lispeth*, and substantiation of Kipling's convictions in a letter quoted by Professor Carrington:

It is my fortune to have been born and to a large extent brought up among those whom white men call 'heathen'; and while I recognise the paramount duty of every white man to follow the teaching of his creed and conscience as 'a debtor to the whole law', it seems to me cruel that white men, whose governments are armed with the most murderous weapons known to science, should amaze and confound their fellow creatures with a doctrine of salvation imperfectly understood by themselves and a code of ethics foreign to the climate and instincts of those races whose most cherished customs they outrage and whose gods they insult.[66]

However, the fact that we possess no satisfying theory on mortality gives us at least something in common with the rest of humanity, something which ought to break down the barriers within and between societies.

'Sing if you never sang before', said the Bull.
'To a mud-spattered villager?' said Leo.
'He is under the same doom as ourselves. Are you a coward?' said the Bull.[67]

There are two stories in particular where man's attitude to death actually becomes the subject. One of these is *On Greenhow Hill* where Private Learoyd gets a chance to reveal something of himself. The superscription from 'Rivals' gives an indication of the story's intended range: it, too, is going to contrast the rival pull of life and death, but with a cynicism which begs evaluation of the manipulators' action.

It is a story of closely packed parallels and contrasts operating at several levels: a forerunner, in fact, of highly complex stories like *Mrs. Bathurst.* There is the contrast in the title, for example: the men are *not* on Greenhow Hill physically or, superficially at least, morally. Greenhow Hill had been the scene of Learoyd's early manhood where he had fallen in love with Liza Roantree, the daughter of a Primitive Methodist stalwart. The sentimentally tragic love-story is developed against the constantly invoked background of the business in hand: the three soldiers, on whom 'the desire of slaughter lay heavy' have set out to shoot a deserter. It is a deliberate devaluation of life, with the hunted man reduced to little more than an animal, doomed to Ortheris's rifle — and Ortheris worried only lest the noise of neighbouring gunfire might scare away his prey. Against this Learoyd tells of his love for Liza, of her consumption, of the death-bed parting. Then comes the crack of Ortheris's rifle, coarsely eloquent in ridicule.

But not even the world of Learoyd's love-story is without its brutal reverse. In the middle of his narrative we are offered a glimpse of Learoyd at the height of the rivalry between him and Barraclough over Liza, in the course of which he is brought to the brink of murder. At which point in his telling of the story,

The thick lips curled back over the yellow teeth, and that flushed face was not pretty to look upon. Mulvaney nodded sympathy, and Ortheris, moved by his comrade's passion, brought up the rifle to his shoulder, and searched the hillside for his quarry, muttering ribaldry about a sparrow, a spout, and a thunderstorm.[68]

The right hand of love is the left hand of death: we are returned to the self-appointed task of the three.

The detail is worked out further in the hypocrisy of the unco' guid Methodists, the would-be godly, and the cynical comparison with the three soldiers at their afternoon's bloodsport: one lot obstructing happiness in the name of God, the other questioning its prescriptive existence by the affirmation of a totally relative morality. For Ortheris at least (but none objects to the shooting) the only absolute is death:

'Wot's the use o'worritin' 'bout these things? . . . you're bound to find all out quicker nor you want to any'ow.' He jerked the cartridge out of the breech-block into the palm of his hand. ''Ere's my chaplain,' he said, and made the venomous black-headed bullet bow like a marionette.

G

''E's goin' to teach a man all about which is which, an' wot's true, after all, before sundown.'[69]

In this world of savage cynicism we hear much of the scentless un-reality of the white violets blooming long past their season 'in the twilight' of the pines. Their repeated appearance in a story of this nature is quite deliberate: they are 'the innocent violets' which Learoyd seizes at the point where he describes his murderous pas-sion. And at the end, unable to obey the sergeant's injunction to forget her ('I've been forgettin' her ever since'), his passion spent but his sense of loss in no way diminished, he throws away 'the wilted clump of white violets'.

Kipling, however, is not usually as cynical and negative as this on the subject. A less bitter — indeed, most positive — story on the same theme is *The Children of the Zodiac*. His experientialism here is something other than the bluff rejection of philosophic hum-bug that it is often taken to be.

Like the last story its comprehension presents some difficulties. How divine, for instance, are the Children of the Zodiac? Certainly, to start with we are told that 'they knew they were immortal gods' but even then there was a greater power — they feared the Houses. As the story progresses, however, their divinity is lessened and Leo ceases to refer to the children of men as 'they' and speaks of 'us' instead: 'What have we done that you should trouble us?' he asks Cancer, one of the Houses. They themselves 'knew' that they were gods, and men 'treated them as Gods' but for most of the story they are of the earth though with traces of their loftier status still in them.[70] At any rate, their full realisation only comes when they learn that they are, in the significantly apt words from another source, 'neither children nor Gods, but men in a world of men'.[71] During the time when they persisted in seeing themselves as gods they understood nothing of human affairs. When stories of death and dying and requests for his help were brought to the Bull, he would only 'lower his huge head and answer, "What is that to me?"' Nor could they ever understand laughter: and laughter like love is community.

The first sign of their growing understanding appears when Leo kisses the Girl; there is a comparison to be made here between this act and that which introduced Adam and Eve to the mortal world of men. 'Leo kissed the Girl and all Earth felt that kiss, and the Girl sat down on a hill and the water ran out of her eyes';[72] this immediately suggests,

> Earth felt the wound, and Nature from her Seat
> Sighing through all her works gave signs of woe
> That all was lost.[73]

In one sense all was lost here too, in another all was won. Through the kiss — the human kiss — they have opened the door on the human world and closed it on the supernatural.[74] Immediately afterwards the Girl claims understanding and almost as soon we see the first intimations of mortality:

> 'We have come to the end of things,' said the man quietly.
> 'This that was my wife ——'
> 'As I am Leo's wife,' said the Girl quickly, her eyes staring.[75]

It is the Girl, too, who understands why the old man, after complaining of having to live, tries to escape death. There is the growing realisation that they are not immortal.

> 'Leo we must learn more about this for their sakes.'
> 'For *their* sakes,' said Leo very loudly.
> 'Because *we* are never going to die,' said the Girl and Leo together, still more loudly.[76]

Their fears are confirmed when Leo asks Scorpio why he should trouble the children of men, and receives their answer in his question, 'Are you so sure that I trouble the children of men alone?' The Bull, the Ram and the Twins all admit their ultimate mortality and their need to keep working — though all explicitly find life like this unpleasant. Then Leo finds his own fate in the House of the Crab, though by this time he has realised his identity with the sons of men. There follows the final rejection of their status as gods and of their mythical immortality:

> Next morning they returned to their proper home, and saw the flowers and the sacrifices that had been laid before their doors by the villagers of the hills. Leo stamped down the fire with his heel, and the Girl flung the flower-wreaths out of sight, shuddering as she did so.[77]

And when the villagers visited them they found not gods but simply 'a man and a woman with frightened white faces sitting hand in hand on the altar-steps.'

They will not, however, give in to despair but take heart from the fact that while they know the worst in store they do not know the best that love and life — the present life — can bring. They discover laughter, defiant laughter, in the very teeth of Death's decree.

But Leo, and it is impossible to dissociate Kipling from him here, found it hard to accept the reality of death; and after an evening of pleasant, happy company, redolent of a Stalky-like health, life and vigour, he woke up with the poignant realisation:

'Every one of those people we met just now will die ——'
'So shall we', said the Girl sleepily. 'Lie down again, dear.'
Leo could not see that her face was wet with tears.[78]

But Leo's fears could not be stilled and he went in search of the Bull so tired after his walk that (happily) all his contemplation was taken up by the beautiful straight furrows he had made that day.

'Well', said the Bull, 'what will you do? . . . you cannot pull a plough . . . I can and that prevents me from thinking of the Scorpion.'[79]

Leo, however, finds that he can sing and though he would have liked 'to lie down and brood over the words of the Crab', he is persuaded to continue singing. First he sang the song of the fearless but soon discovered another much more powerful.

This was a thing he could never have done had he not met the Crab face to face. He remembered facts concerning cultivators, and bullocks, and rice fields that he had not particularly noticed before the interview, and he strung them all together, growing more interested as he sang, and he told the cultivator much more about himself and his work than the cultivator knew. The Bull grunted approval as he toiled down the furrows for the last time that day, and the song ended, leaving the cultivator with a very good opinion of himself in his aching bones.[80]

So Leo becomes the Singer, the Poet, the Writer or simply the Artist, whose job it is to secure just such an effect as this. Boldly he has confronted his destiny and now through his efforts, man will be helped towards dignity, integrity and self-respect, as well as to the modicum of happiness which he is permitted.

It was after this that Leo made the Song of the Bull who had been a God and forgotten the fact, and he sang it in such a manner that half the young men in the world conceived that they too might be Gods without knowing it. A half of that half grew impossibly conceited and died early. A half of the remainder strove to be Gods and failed, but the other half accomplished four times more work than they would have done under any other delusion.[81]

A delusion it remains, but without it existence would not be possible.

And now the last vestiges of divinity have disappeared from the Children of the Zodiac.

The Star of Aldebaran was crusted with caked dirt on the Bull's forehead, the Ram's fleece was dusty and torn, and the Twins were only babies fighting over the cat on the doorstep.[82]

Gradually all god-like attributes have left them and Man is now as they portray him.

With the Girl's death Leo knew — in terms again highly suggestive of the Fall — 'all the sorrow that a man could know including the full knowledge of his own fall who had once been a god'. But he continued to sing the same song, teaching fortitude and denying any facile, mystic optimism.

One of his listeners interrupted him as he was singing.

'Leo,' said he, 'I have heard you telling us not to be afraid for the past forty years. Can you not sing something new now?'

'No,' said Leo, 'it is the only song that I am allowed to sing. You must not be afraid of the Houses, even when they kill you.'

The man turned to go, wearily, but there came a whistling through the air and the arrow of the Archer was seen skimming low above the earth, pointing to the man's heart. He drew himself up, and stood still waiting till the arrow struck home.

'I die,' he said quietly, 'it is well for me, Leo, that you sang for forty years.'

'Are you afraid?' said Leo . . .

'I am a man, not a god,' said the man. 'I should have run away but for your songs. My work is done, and I die without making a great show of my fear.'

'I am very well paid,' said Leo to himself. 'Now that I see what my songs are doing, I will sing better ones.' [83]

But the Artist in the middle of his work is struck down by the Crab. And at the end it is emphasised that he makes the same remark as all human beings, 'Why have you come for me now?'

Then he too draws himself up, and, recalling the godhead he

once thought he possessed, he reaffirms his fearlessness, and Kipling with a careful touch completes his story's development:

'What is that to me?' said the Crab.

These were the words used by the Bull at the beginning about the lives of men whom he failed to understand, now they are applied to Leo by the only real God: Death. But the noble spirit of man can be made a worthy adversary, and he who said 'I am a man, not a god', placed himself far higher than he knew.

Having faced the painful fact of his own ultimate extinction clearly and honestly the artist must dedicate himself to the world of actuality, for it is the only world, and by his work increase in some small way the limited sum of happiness which humans, under their inescapable sentence of death, can enjoy: it is his duty to 'draw the Thing as he sees It for the God of Things as They are'.[84] Wreaths of marigolds presented to gods which are not gods will do nothing to ameliorate the lot of the children of men; but if the poet, the artist, can show them how to live with the maximum of fortitude and pleasure while doing nothing to minimise the stark certainty or finality of death, his contribution is infinite. Above all he must be in the world of men — there is his 'proper home'. And lest the prospect would appear to be unsupportable, we are to remember that we know the worst of life — death — before we know the best; and the combination of such awareness and at least a mildly hopeful anticipation of what the present life may bring justifies existence, though it compels us to recognise freshly and fully the pleasures and importance of the present, of the moment. Of course it stresses self-sufficiency and the prime importance of giving one's attention to actuality and the stoic virtue of brave endurance in the face of crushing forces, but in Kipling's view what else is there to do except sit and weep? It has been said of Conrad that under his stoicism there flowed a bleak and terrible disbelief — the same could be said of Kipling, particularly as he is shown here; the bleakness, however, is at least illumined by the clarity of the vision.

In his later work a different note makes itself heard on the subject. Not that references to it are less frequent — to the contrary — but where earlier there was usually a nobility about it as part of defiant action against overwhelming forces, there is easily discernible now a note of defeat. Portson, Maddingham, Winchmore of Sea Constables replace The Infant, Bobby Wick and Tallantire with a terrible middle-aged disillusionment — even the names connote dyspeptic lawyers and moribund city brokers. The cruelly-bereaved Burgess says 'There's not much left for middle-aged people, just at present',[85] and the poignancy of the sham optimism supplies all the endorsement needed.

This, then, is his pronouncement on the omnipresent questionings of life and death: it is at the same time, as I have tried to show, so much more, since in it is included a writer's manifesto. Edmund Wilson has said that Kipling lacked faith in the artistic vocation:[86] at this point in his development, at any rate, nothing could be further from the truth. The artist, by sharing fully in their existence has identified himself completely with the world of men. Tried and tested in the fires of human experience, he has at last attained the knowledge and position which enables him to tell the cultivator 'much more about himself and his work than the cultivator knew' and, at the end of his song, to leave him, 'with a very good opinion of himself in his aching bones'. Surely in the light of his poems and stories this can be construed as a record of Kipling's own intention; it is certainly within this definition that most of his achievement lies. Far from revealing a lack of faith, *The Children of the Zodiac* gives to the artist with the utmost confidence and clarity of purpose, a stirring call to arms. 'This', Kipling is saying with great decisiveness, 'is the role of the Artist, and here is the America in which it must be effected.' But there is no need to invent a coda:

> Yet they who use the Word assigned,
> To hearten and make whole,
> Not less than Gods have served mankind
> Though vultures rend their soul. [87]

5

From all that has been said it would appear that the basis of action in these stories has shown itself as far from 'imperial' or political. The enquiry can now be advanced further by putting together the facts that have emerged about the actors.

What sort of being is the Kipling character fundamentally? A man with a burning cause, perhaps, to make the deserts blossom as the rose? A man with the conviction that the world is best ruled by an aristocracy of blood — bluest and best of which is to be found in British veins? Something of these elements are there, but their acknowledgement leaves the surface hardly scratched.

He is, first of all, a man whose vision, far from delighting him with rich and glorious prospects, is bleak and austere. Of his own individuality he is immensely aware and hence of his loneliness.

'I am Kim — Kim — Kim — alone — one person — in the middle of it all.'[88]

The burden of sustaining moral integrity is recognised as his alone, and involvement seems to offer the only solution:

All that while he felt . . . that his soul was out of gear with its surroundings — a cog-wheel unconnected with any machinery . . . but of a sudden easy, stupid tears trickled down his nose, and with an almost audible click he felt the wheels of his being lock up anew on the world without. Things that rode meaningless on the eyeball an instant before slid into proper proportion. Roads were meant to be walked upon, houses to be lived in, cattle to be driven, fields to be tilled, and men and women to be talked to. [89]

This is, in fact, the major theme of *Kim*. The point is not, as Edmund Wilson claims, that Kim sells out his Indian 'half' in order to demonstrate that white will out and that a Son of the Blood will always in the last event return to the Blood. Such an interpretation misconstrues and underrates the meaning of Kim's search and the seriousness of the problem which faces him.

Once again the problem is one of identity. 'I too am a Seeker,' says Kim to the Hindu bairagi, 'though Allah alone knoweth what I seek.'[90] The knowledge of what prompts his doubts and his search is not, however, confined to Allah: they arise, we learn, when one lets the mind 'go free upon speculation as to what is called personal identity'.[91]

'Who is Kim — Kim — Kim?'

He squatted in a corner of the clanging waiting-room rapt from all other thoughts; hands folded in lap, and pupils contracted to pin-points. In a minute — in another half second — he felt he would arrive at the solution of the tremendous puzzle; but here, as always happens, his mind dropped away from these heights with the rush of a wounded bird . . .[92]

All through Kipling's work — though most noticeably in his imperial stories — we find him insisting on the virtue of confining one's attention and effort to dealing with actuality. This is, of course, far from denying or deriding the reality of the non-actual. To the contrary it is a deliberate acknowledgement of it: only, according to Kipling, one can't live in such a realm. The logical alternative is therefore quite clear:

> When you have to attend to . . . the mere incidents of the surface, the reality — the reality, I tell you, fades. The inner truth is hidden — luckily, luckily.[93]

— which was exactly the point made by the Bull in *The Children of the Zodiac*. If one does attempt to live in these regions what, Kipling asks, holds things together?

> 'I am Kim. I am Kim. And what is Kim?'[94]

So Kim chooses involvement, and significantly it is with the Secret Service — the force for law, order and control, the force above all others which can bring against the insidious powers of disruption and disintegration an equally insidious weapon cast from stealth, dissimulation and all-knowingness. Idiomatically, the power that India exerts over Kim and, indeed, over most of the character-victims already discussed, differs little from that which it exerted over Fielding in Forster's *Passage to India*: it is the power which destroys values, reduces sustaining categories to meaninglessness and sends Fielding back to the world of definitions, and distinctions, back to the other Peninsula 'smaller and more exquisitely shaped', back to form and to beauty — just as it sends Kim back to the Secret Service.

A few like the Lama may be able to survive in the realm of abstraction by resort to an other-worldly, but by no means untroubled, mysticism. But this can only mean a withdrawal from the human community which is, ultimately, wholly selfish. It is to the Lama that the Jat farmer comes in his distress but it is to Kim's practical medicines that he owes his child's recovery. Yet the Lama's characterisation remains one of the most finely sympathetic in all Kipling's work, and because it is so, one of the most generously conceived. For Kipling's acute awareness of the vulnerability of individual integrity and identity led him to give little quarter to those who worshipped any God other than that of Things as they Are: the illusion of actuality as reality could not be sustained half-heartedly. Consequently we find him deriding Grish Chunder Dé and, at the end of *The Children of the Zodiac* for instance, denouncing those who weaken or refuse to shoulder the burden entailed in accepting the hegemony of his God.

But the strength of the non-actual, which this acknowledges, remains, and in *Kim*, despite the terror which it holds for the author, one form of it achieves honest, courageous and sympathetic expression. Allied to its more purely aesthetic quality and to its humanity in other spheres, it is this consideration which seems to me to justify the book's claim to be Kipling's greatest single work. 'This is no longer the Kipling of *Without Benefit of Clergy*,' writes Edmund Wilson:[95] but isn't it?

I have said that the strength of the non-actual is to be found acknowledged in one way or another throughout Kipling's work. In the later as well as the earlier stories we find him repeatedly coming back to supernatural themes or to dealing with men in some way obsessed — men who are literally taken possession of by something larger and more powerful than themselves. Contrary to the view held by Noël Annan I would suggest that Kipling's 'Ghost' stories are always symptomatic of something deeper than a mere momentary fancy for 'the trivial fashionable ideas of the nineties which people express by saying "Wouldn't it be fun if. . .?"'[96] Whether we take *The Lost Legion*, *At the End of the Passage*, *The Mark of the Beast*, *In the Same Boat* or *The Woman in his Life* what we have presented to us is self-possession versus possession — or the threat of possession — by the non-self. This last nameless quantity is, as I have tried to show, an ever-present menace for Kipling.

> A stone's throw out on either hand
> From that well-ordered road we tread
> And all the world is wild and strange;[97]

What is wild and strange is destructive. Nameless and shapeless, this malignant force haunts his work in capitalised abstractions: it is a 'Thing' or an 'It': it is 'the Horror passing speech';[98] it is — very frequently — a Face that is faceless, depersonalised, dehumanised. Such, for instance, are the Faces, mildewed and half-eaten, which

Miss Henschil sees in her nightmares,[99] or the Face in *A Matter of Fact* whose 'horror . . . lay in the eyes, for those were sightless — white, in sockets as white as scraped bone, and blind' [100] or the one we encounter in 'La Nuit Blanche':

> Then a Face came, blind and weeping,
> And It couldn't wipe Its eyes,
> And It muttered I was keeping
> Back the moonlight from the skies[101]

Mrs. Bathurst is the story of a man who is killed not by the woman he loves but by his obsession with his love for her. Whatever Vickery says to the Captain it involves an act which is, we learn, tantamount to throwing the gunsights overboard. He has, in fact, opted out of this world of focus and order so that he may indulge his obsession to the full: he has sold out his identity completely.

'You!' he said. 'What have you got to complain of? — you've only 'ad to watch. I'm *it*.'[102]

And again in this story the travesty of a face is made to symbolise the man's moral disintegration:

. . . it reminded me of those things in bottles in those herbalist shops at Plymouth — preserved in spirits of wine. White an' crumply things — previous to birth as you might say.[103]

One makes, or possesses, one's own self in the world of actuality: if one allows, as all these characters have done, anything else to intrude or take over, selfhood and identity got with such careful and laborious delimitation of a world, crumble into chaos:

for Truth is a naked lady, and if by accident she is drawn up from the bottom of the sea, it behoves a gentleman either to give her a print petticoat or to turn his face to the wall and vow that he did not see.[104]

All this reinforces the conclusions to be drawn from the previous section. The real crux of the Anglo-Indian/India relationship — and of the relationship between Kipling and Imperial India — is here and it is not in the least political. To regard its agonies — so well brought out in *At the End of The Passage* — as a simple description of the triumph of British fortitude under extreme conditions, is to misread completely Kipling's artistic vision. For the conflict is spiritual and tragically inescapable. These Anglo-Indians may writhe and suffer under their relentless persecution, be, like Otis Yeere, 'ground up in the wheels of the Administration; losing heart and soul, and mind and strength, in the process',[105] yet, paradoxically, their existence depends on just this conflict. For these men are less the victims of empire than of the wider necessity which decrees that man shall live for ever at the edge of the pit, snatching his identity from the limbo of non-existence lying at his feet. The conflict between their personal lives and the empire they serve is only a reflection of that more fundamental dialectic between self and destructive non-self. And from this permanent state of war there can be no opting out on any terms whatsoever, since only by the closest engagement can even a momentary existence and identity be secured. Only by immersing oneself fully in the world of actuality can one achieve integrity. This had been Stein's advice in *Lord Jim* and the whole point of *The Children of the Zodiac*.

The Kipling character in dedicating himself so completely to his duty was really only paying lip-service to the Queen-Empress: what was served, fundamentally, was his own moral integrity. Self-sacrifice of the sort Kipling recommends is self-assertion; through devotion to the actualities of duty one preserves identity and individuality and keeps chaos at bay.

Kipling's feeling for humanity as well as his sensitive portrayal of the Anglo-Indian stems from this recognition of the immeasurable preciousness of the individual self in 'man', and of the unceasing battle with the Lords of Life to which man is ineluctably joined in defence of this core.

Such a realisation, such a concern, can only stem from the most lucid clearsightedness. For Kipling as for Conrad there is a crisis of realisation — such as Leo experiences — when man faces his destiny clearly and without illusions. But whereas Conrad projected this in explicit artistic statement through characters like McWhirr and Mitchell on the one hand and Lord Jim on the other, Kipling leaves it largely unprojected. The crisis is part of his own experience and though it obviously informs his work it very rarely becomes the subject. (Perhaps what he lacks, artistically, is the services of a reliable Marlow.) And the fact that this is so, that it informs but is scarcely ever realised in artistic terms, has an unfortunate effect upon his characterisation. So much of it obviously springs from this crisis, but in the presentation of the individual character all traces are frequently concealed with the result that the real dynamic of his tension is largely denied him in the moment of his advent; he arrives post-crisis with a well-bred resolve to say nothing about it. Consequently his inevitable courage, fortitude and endurance have too often the dead unreality of a *fait accompli*. Kipling seems to shrink nervously from bringing the crisis into the public world of his characterisation, but his awareness of it cannot be suppressed.[106] Adherence to a code, insistence on discipline and the stiff upper lip are in the Kipling hero indications not of shallow-mindedness but of a deep sensitivity which has allowed him to see far into 'the wheel and the drift of Things'.

In *At the End of the Passage*, however, one is permitted to see something of the crisis; the tone, even allowing for the didacticism — the story is designed to emphasise the hazards of the Anglo-Indians' lot — is one of defeatism rather than idealism, of pessimism rather than hope. Hummil is utterly broken by the loneliness, monotony and physical hardship of his existence. Mottram of the Indian Survey spends his time trying to get a sub-surveyor to understand 'that an error of five degrees in an angle isn't quite so small as it looks'. Spurstow, the doctor, is involved in a cholera outbreak where the course of events is 'Chlorodyne, opium pill, chlorodyne, collapse, nitre, bricks to the feet, and then — the burning-ghat', and Lowndes, of the Civil Service with 'the miserable intrigues of an impoverished native state', where even his life was potentially forfeit to their petty scheming. And all to what end? Their work is of no innate value; it is of use only in so far as it sustains the sense of their own integrity, though when carried to certain extremes it is no good even for this. Typically, it is in the author's comment in the epigraph that we come nearest to an explicit recognition of this:

> And the soul of man is turned from his meat,
> Turned from the trifles for which he has striven
> Sick in his body and heavy hearted. . . .

The essential context of the crisis is, however, suggestively present in a great number of his stories. It is there, for instance, in the Lama's frequent references to the illusions of actuality in *Kim* —

references which do not always confidently posit an optimistic alternative.

'Be content,' said he. 'There is great work forward. When this madness is over there is a recompense.' 'Ay, there is a recompense when the madness is over, surely?' the lama muttered half to himself.[107]

Hope — or even oblivion — seems often far away:

'I have no less than three [sons] — Rissaldar-majors all — in the regiments.' 'And they likewise, bound upon the Wheel, go forth from life to life — from despair to despair,' said the lama below his breath, 'hot, uneasy, snatching.'[108]

It is there, too, in the constant reminders of mortal futility:

[The hare] limped from her form and ran across to a disused Mahomedan burial-ground, where the jawless skulls and rough-butted shank bones, heartlessly exposed by the July rains, glimmered like mother o'pearl on the rain-channelled soil.[109]

To weather the crisis a certain 'drill' is demanded: loyalty to a fixed standard of conduct, for instance —

It was gently but firmly borne in upon him that the regiment was his father and his mother and his indissolubly wedded wife, and that there was no crime under the canopy of heaven blacker than that of bringing shame on the regiment which was the best-shooting, best drilled, best-set-up, bravest, most illustrious and in all respects most desirable Regiment within the compass of the Seven Seas.[110]

And again:

All ritual is fortifying. Ritual's a natural necessity for mankind. The more things are upset, the more they fly to it.[111]

And a further necessity is, as we have seen, an activist attention to the job in hand, which means, of course, commitments. One might demonstrate something of the consistency of this theme by taking one last, very explicit statement from a much later, non-Indian story:

. . . he found that the reaction following prolonged research loses much of its grey terror if one knows one can at will bathe the soul in the society of plumbers (all the water pipes had chronic appendicitis), village idiots (Jimmy had taken Midmore under his weak wing and camped daily at the drive gates), and a giant with red eyelids whose every action was an outrage.[112]

Commitment, of course, means community, and for Kipling, clearly, it is community with a purpose — the reassurance of integrity. Society is of value not because of the particular morality on which it is based but — as for the administrative hierarchy referred to earlier — for the effect it secures.

6

Man is alone: this realisation is the core of Kipling's artistic vision:

... that primal instinct of independence which ante-dates the social one and makes the young at times a little difficult ... comes from the dumb and dreadful epoch when all that man knew was that he was himself, and not another, and therefore the loneliest of created beings.[113]

Consciousness of individuality meant simultaneous consciousness of estrangement — of the

horror of desolation, abandonment, and realised worthlessness which is one of the most real of the hells in which we are compelled to walk.[114]

And inevitably this led to the antidote being sought in society.

One of the few advantages that India has over England is a great Knowability. After five years' service a man is directly or indirectly acquainted with the two or three hundred Civilians in his province, all the Messes of ten or twelve Regiments and Batteries, and some fifteen hundred other people of the non-official caste. In ten years his knowledge should be doubled, and at the end of twenty he knows, or knows something about, every Englishman in the Empire, and may travel anywhere and everywhere without paying hotel-bills.[115]

But such reinforcement was not to be had free of charge: it demanded, in fact, an important sacrifice.

Not till [man] abandoned his family tree and associated with his fellows on the flat, for predatory or homicidal purposes, did he sacrifice his personal independence of action or cut into his large leisure of brooding abstraction necessary for the discovery of his relations to his world. This is the period in our Reverend Ancestor's progress through Time that strikes me as immensely the most interesting and important.[116]

That this should be the period of greatest importance for Kipling is of the utmost significance, for it is that fundamental moment of truth when the great conflict between self and society comes into being. The self in isolation is wholly vulnerable to the forces of disintegration as Decoud in Conrad's *Nostromo*, Hummil in *At the End of the Passage* and Dawse in *The Disturber of Traffic* discovered. So reassurance of integrity is sought in society and commitment:

> A veil 'twixt us and thee, dread Lord
> A veil 'twixt us and thee
> Lest we should hear too clear, too clear,
> And unto madness see.[117]

But as we have heard, this involves sacrifice: for the creation of society inevitably means, for the individual, a partial surrender of integrity. And here we have the real source of the essential tension in and behind Kipling's writing. Half-way between Marx and Sartre he reveals the great human paradox that man can only exist in society which he alone can create out of his own precious store of selfhood: thus every contribution to society is an erosion of the self which it is designed to identify and protect. When society demands too great a contribution it must be resisted for it would mean erosion to the point of complete assimilation: Mulvaney, while admiring the Roman Catholic Church, found that it was not one for a weak man 'bekaze she takes the body and the sowl av him', and, in a later non-Indian story, *The Mother Hive*, the doctrine 'we and The Hive are one' is completely rejected. If, on the other hand, too little is given to society, then the latter loses coherence and the core of the self is once more left unprotected and wholly vulnerable. So everyone must concede something. Even the powerful tiger and the wolf must submit to having their freedom restricted and must not change their hunting grounds without due warning:

> He will frighten every head of game within ten miles, and I — I have to kill for two these days.[118]

Real freedom — which means freedom to preserve responsibility and integrity — can only be achieved through a certain degree of organisation and law:

> Lead us again, O Akela. Lead us again, O man-cub, for we be sick of this lawlessness, and we would be the Free People once more.[119]

There is one statement in his work which above all others goes furthest towards explaining 'the riddle of Kipling'; at the same time it seems to me to justify, in the most succinct terms, the interpretation which has been suggested in the foregoing pages:

For the eternal question still is whether the profit of any concession that a man makes to his Tribe, against the light that is in him, outweighs or justifies his disregard for that light.[120]

In a way, Imperial Anglo-India came nearest offering Kipling the ideal nourishment for his ethic of crisis. There the present actuality took all one's time, attention and energy; and the friendship and support of a tightly-knit 'knowable' community, though never becoming too intimate nor seeking to break down the barriers of that guarded inner privacy, yet linked individuals in a fortifying alliance against the powers of darkness and disintegration. Not surprisingly after this, Kipling's characters appear to need rather than to love each other:

The players were not conscious of any special regard for each other. They squabbled whenever they met; but they ardently desired to meet, as men without water desire to drink. They were lonely folk who understood the dread meaning of loneliness.[121]

On all but a very few occasions Kipling was too jealous and uncertain of his own soul ever to be magnanimous.

In the examination of what is involved in Kipling's expression of the imperial idea we have discovered that the real core of his inspiration is his concern for moral integrity. This seems to me of importance not only in that it allows us a new light in which to see his creative expression and affords us an explanation of his personal and political attitudes but also because it does, I think, demonstrate that Kipling's response to life can be wholly understood in literary terms. This has hitherto never been admitted and its possibility has even been explicitly denied by Noël Annan in his study of Kipling's place in the history of ideas.[122]

For Mr. Annan the question Kipling asks is 'what holds society ... together?'[123] But from what has been said in this chapter it would not seem to be 'the' question, which was much more nearly 'what holds the individual together?' One sociological bias leads to another: 'when (Kipling) asked what forces kept the groups in

H

this bewildering society together, he found the answer as Durkheim had, in the forces of social control'.[124] Again, as far as Kipling is concerned, this is to put the cart before the horse. When he alludes to the forces of social control he does so not as a sociologist intent on demonstrating 'how society works',[125] but as a creative artist profoundly concerned with the individual's struggle to sustain identity, seeing in these forces a means whereby this might be achieved. Society for Kipling was something which the individual deliberately and necessarily creates in order to establish, identify and protect the self. It is the product of the conflict between the individual's consciousness of his essential estrangement and the need to preserve his own moral integrity: the conflict so clearly delineated in the statement quoted on page 105: the conflict out of which Kipling's writing evolves.[126]

But Kipling rarely leaves it as a conflict; frequently — too frequently — he imposes a settlement, and it is for this reason, I would suggest, rather than for that advanced by Mr. Annan that 'his views and morality have received such harsh treatment'.[127] 'Il n'y a pas de signe dans le monde,' Sartre announces,[128] but Kipling though he more than suspects this truth firmly resolves that signs there will be, and all the paraphernalia of self reassurance comes into being — religion, law, customs, morality and the rest.

The general application of the sociological analogue to this distorts rather than clarifies, and leads to a confusion of ends and means: it certainly fails — almost inevitably — to identify the real source of Kipling's creativity. And given the basis of this distortion — the view that 'Kipling is . . . seldom interested in individuals as such',[129] the pattern of Mr. Annan's complaint is foreseeable. He is bound to find Kipling guilty of ignoring the effect of social morality on the individual — how it amplifies, corrupts or ennobles his character. He is bound to find that Kipling's 'in-group theories' are 'too simple-minded',[130] that, when dealing with 'those alleviations of social pressures upon men, such as laughter, mirth, vitality or love', he conceives of them 'as social forces existing apart from the individuals who experience them',[131] and that his characters are one thing and his social theory another.

In fact, Kipling does not show us the effect of the social process simply because the conflict lies between the individual and the concept, not the fact, of society, and the reason why Mr. Annan fails to find consciousness of isolation in his work is because he is looking for it in the wrong place. Once Kipling imposes his settlement and affirms man's place in society, the crisis is past, or at any rate papered over. But the isolation of man who has discovered his own essential loneliness remains his preoccupation and emerges in varying guises and strength in, for instance, Hummil, Dawse and Wali Dad: in *Beyond the Pale*, *Little Tobrah*, *The Children of the Zodiac* and *The Bridge-Builders*.

'The centre of Kipling's world is society,' Mr. Annan claims,[132] but this is true, paradoxically only in so far as it means the individual, for Kipling's world remains entirely solipsist. He is not in the least bit interested in society, or its particular morality as absolutes in themselves, but only in so far as they are essential to the self's existence. From this comes his cynicism and his acceptance of so many of the moral definitions of his caste in despite of his own awareness:

... one cannot visit a loafer in the Serai by day. Friends buying horses would not understand it ... .[133]

Or:

He was going to marry Miss Castries, and the business was his own business ... with a man in this condition mere words only fix him in his purpose. Of course he cannot see that marriage in India does not concern the individual but the Government he serves.[134]

Even his appreciation of human nature is not ultimately as disinterested as one might expect. A really magnanimous, unhampered, outgoing warmth of feeling for humanity is present only sporadically in his work, although his awareness of the human dilemma was, as I have tried to indicate, acute. In *Without Benefit of Clergy* and in *Kim*, for instance, we do, of course, find such warmth, but all too often it is reined and snaffled by his own selfishness. *The Children of the Zodiac* might be taken for an expression of profound feeling and sympathy for struggling humanity, and so it is — until the last few lines when Kipling rounds hysterically on those who weaken and let the jungle in:

After [Leo's] death there sprang up a breed of little mean men, whimpering and flinching and howling because the Houses killed them and theirs, who wished to live forever without pain. They did not increase their lives, but they increased their own torments miserably. ... .[135]

And in *Beyond the Pale* his sympathy is likewise flawed by his cynical insistences on the observance of the man-made boundaries to human love in the interests of self-security.

The source of Kipling's pessimism and conservatism, then, was not a Burke-like distrust of human nature; but neither was he a conservative without a cause as Mr. Annan suggests.[136] The attainment of selfhood and, for this end, the preservation of illusions in the face of nada, provided him with an all-absorbing concern. From this there came, on the one hand, his acute awareness of man's dilemma, his sympathy for struggling humanity and his conception of the role of the artist: and on the other, his fundamentally selfish view of society with all that that implied for those who failed to recognise where their responsibilities lay. What these early Indian stories reveal, in fact, is a man desperately working to establish an economy of the self which will preserve a balance between the psychotic perils of total alienation and the demands and inroads made on the integrity of the self in a 'healthy' commitment to society.

If this is the nature of his conservatism it seems to me useless to talk of his 'Toryism' and to make disparaging comparisons with Johnson, Burke and Scott — as Lionel Trilling does in his essay in *The Liberal Imagination*:

he is not generous, and although he makes much to-do about manliness, he is not manly; and he has none of the *mind* of the few great tories. His toryism often had in it a lower-middle-class snarl of defeated gentility, and it is this rather than his love of authority and force that might suggest an affinity with fascism. His imperialism is reprehensible not because it *is* imperialism but because it is a puny and mindless imperialism. In short Kipling is unloved and unlovable not by reason of his beliefs but by reason of the temperament that gave them literary expression.[137]

As for the *snarl* in his 'Toryism' it is less the snarl of defeated gentility than of the dog in the manger: and his Imperialism is frequently offensive not because it *is* imperialism but because it isn't. For Kipling could never be disinterested enough to commit himself to a cause of any self-transcendent objectivity whatsoever. Empire in general and the Indian Empire in particular was simply a Place des Signes, where the signs could be more securely guarded and where he himself could find refuge and reassurance in his frontiersmen's ideals. Elsewhere Professor Trilling has written that 'ideas, if they are large enough and of a certain kind are not only not hostile to the creative process, as some think, but are virtually inevitable to it'.[138] This indicates precisely the inhibiting factor in Kipling: his essential, creative idea is ultimately not large or generous enough, and, inevitably, it shrinks the other ideas brought in as vehicles. The imperial idea itself is heavily circumscribed by his unrelenting egotism, frequently lacking even the largeness it is found possessed of in the works of Buchan. All this makes Kipling conservative, but, in relation to his art, mean-white rather than true-blue.

7

The basis of action in the Kipling story is not fundamentally political in character: nor is the empire there as a symbol of the author's confidence either in a dynamic progress or in the viability of the British way of life. Indeed the very possibility of creative achievement is spurned:

It is but the shifting of a little dirt. Let the dirt dig in the dirt if it pleases the dirt . . .

His is a pessimistic vision: and though on occasion he may pay lip-service to an idea of progress it is never more than this and is always fitful and without intrinsic value.

To him as to Conrad the end of action was to be found in the preservation of the individual's identity and self-consciousness. In his activity man realises his own potential for selfhood and is objectified. To fortify himself he conspires with others to erect certain codes and institutions in a large-scale repeat of the exercise, so that he is able to reappropriate to himself their substantial existence and through them come to have a definite place in the world and *be* something.

This 'concept' of action is what firmly allies Kipling to the anti-positivist school of social thinkers. Man's conduct was not determined by a universal law but by a non-rational, highly subjective, psychological need: and for Kipling, as for others, that need was emphatically the reassurance of his own moral integrity.[139]

It is quite clear from this why the criterion of moral action for Kipling should be whether or not it is structural: he would, one feels, have readily subscribed to Fichte's interpretation of man's relationship to society:

> The social impulse . . . belongs to the fundamental impulse of man. It is man's vocation to live in Society — he *must* live in Society; — he is no complete man, but contradicts his own being, if he live in a state of isolation . . .[140]

So Kipling found himself totally committed to a principle of order and stability through a massive opposition to the entropic or disintegrative forces of the universe. To the effects of this on his art I have already alluded in the preceding pages of this chapter. Of the ironic, even cynical, detachment of sympathy which was one of its consequences I might offer just two reminders:

> . . . one cannot visit a loafer in the Serai by day. Friends buying horses would not understand it. . . .

> He was going to marry Miss Castries, and the business was his own business . . . with a man in this condition mere words only fix him in his purpose. Of course he cannot see that marriage in India does not concern the individual but the Government he serves.

Implicit in this sort of action is the 'illusion of a mastered destiny', in Conrad's phrase: the illusion that a human determination of events is possible. But, like Conrad, he never forgets that it *is* an illusion, fostered to conceal the chaos that lies beneath.

Like one of the greatest social thinkers in the anti-positivist tradition, Georges Sorel — whom he resembles far more closely than he does Durkheim — he has something approaching a horror of what this distinguished contemporary described as 'natural nature'. To Sorel 'natural nature' was 'a mysterious even malignant Fate, an arbitrary and meaningless force that constantly threatens to overwhelm the spheres conquered by human reason'.[141] And the particular mode of Sorel's response to the threat strengthens the affinity, for he sought the antidote in 'artificial nature', which was the construction imposed on the chaos of reality by scientists and technicians in order to tame it. This, as I have tried to point out, is precisely the *métier* of the Kipling character: his heroes are all, in this sense, scientists and technicians.

The analogy with Sorel's response to nature illuminates another of Kipling's interests which finds expression in his stories: his fascination with the world of machinery in tales like 'The Ship that

Found Herself' and '.oo7'. The machine was one of the most powerful adjuncts of man's efforts to command through the creation of an 'artificial nature'. Henry James failed to understand this when he complained of Kipling's 'deterioration':

> ... he has come steadily from the less simple in subject to the more simple — from the Anglo-Indians to the natives, from the natives to the Tommies, from the Tommies to the quadrapeds, from the quadrapeds to the fish, and from the fish to engines and screws.[142]

And Edmund Wilson simplifies grossly for the same reason, explaining Kipling's increasing addiction to 'animals, insects and machines' as the expression of a need to find 'characters which will yield themselves unresistingly to being presented as parts of a system'.[143] In fact, to Kipling as to Sorel the machine is a major expression of man's ability to understand and control the forces of nature.[144]

One can go further still in the analogy between Sorel and Kipling: for the role that empire plays in the latter's fiction would identify it in Sorel's terminology as one of the great creative myths. A myth to Sorel was the indispensable incentive to action: 'We do nothing great', he writes 'without the help of warmly-coloured and clearly-defined images, which absorb the whole of our attention.'[145] And he quotes with approval a remark from Newman's *Grammar of Assent*:

> Strictly speaking, it is not imagination that causes action; but hope and fear, likes and dislikes, appetite, passion, affection, the strings of selfishness and self-love. What imagination does for us is to find a means of stimulating those motive powers; and it does so by providing a supply of objects strong enough to stimulate them.[146]

To Sorel the value of the myth did not in the slightest depend on the actual attainment of the professed ends but on the movement itself.

Both Sorel and Kipling were very well aware that man 'would probably never abandon his inertia if he had a perfectly clear view of the future':[147] action, courage in the face of destructiveness, could only be sustained by the help of these evocative illusions. And for Kipling, the challenge of Empire had just such a function. For it offered, to adapt another of Conrad's remarks, the barbed hook of action baited not only with the illusion of progress but also with a multiplicity of self-gratifying images such as, 'la mission civilisatrice', the White Man's Burden, the Man of Destiny and so on. Certainly it provided man with an image 'towards which he could work in the fulfilment of his own possibilities'.[148]

So well does this fit the theory of myths that when Sorel is found mourning the extinction of 'the heroic myths which had such great popularity at the beginning of the nineteenth century'[149] we might question whether Victorian England with the powerful assistance of Rudyard Kipling had not found themselves another in the idea of empire.

8

It was unfortunate, though in the circumstances inevitable, that Kipling chose to enunciate his 'eternal question', and to impose his frequent settlements in the physical context of a political idea — particularly of this political idea. For in crystallising into a dogma imperialism demonstrated its own unreality in the trend of political thinking, at which moment Kipling was found to be giving it his wholehearted support. His guilt was obvious to all — so obvious that it concealed the fact that, fundamentally, he was *not* writing in order to express the idea of empire. A 'surface' pattern of a political character there might be, but beneath what he was to make known as the commonplaces of imperial routine Kipling described a world of chaos — and a self-system to go with it. Given the idea, he reacted to it in the way any artist would — by finding in it a means through which to express his own artistic vision. Awareness of man's essential estrangement, illumined with such clarity in the imperial alien's relationship to his hostile environment, and of his compulsive need to armour himself against the effects of this, is the far from contemptible dynamic which motivates Kipling's work.

I said at the beginning that if we understood the peculiar relevance of Péguy's dictum to an interpretation of Kipling we would be able to explain his faults and to see where his virtues really lay. The flaw which the subsequent analysis suggested is a major one, but it would never be so if it did not spring from a context of major virtue. If his artistic vision is continually being cramped and confined, emerging finally — in the widest sense — 'en politique': if his basic awareness tends repeatedly to disappear in the imposition of solutions, and his sympathy for humanity in the fear that the dykes will not hold: we cannot, nevertheless, deny this awareness or its fundamental role as the inspiration of his creativity. It is of the first importance to get the sequence right: 'politique', whether in the wider sense or in the narrower one of a shallow and ephemeral political idea, is neither the measure nor the source of his artistic vision. That was based on something much more vital, much more enduring — an acute awareness of man's essential isolation and an agonised consciousness of the razor's edge on which he must balance to sustain his moment of existence.

NOTES

1. 'De arte poetica', *Cartoons*: 'The Second Childhood of John Bull', 1911.

2. In *The Contemporary Review*, lxxvi (Dec. 1899).

3. A notable exception is the criticism of Professor Bonamy Dobrée, whose essay in *The Lamp and the Lute* (Oxford, 1929), and British Council pamphlet on Kipling are far more suggestive than most full-scale studies.

4. W. Y. Tindall, *Forces in Modern British Literature* (New York, 1947), p. 65.

5. Ibid.

6. *New Statesman*, Jan. 1965.

7. *The Enlightenments of Pagett, M.P.*, pp. 136–7. All references are to the Sussex Edition. An additional index of the stories as they occur in individual volumes, together with their date of first publication, is to be found at the end.

8. See James Fitzjames Stephen, *Liberty, Equality, Fraternity* (1874), e.g. p. 237:
'Strength in all its forms is life and manhood. To be less strong is to be less of a man, whatever else you may be.'
Or, p. 243:
'Society rests ultimately upon force in these days just as much as it did in the wildest and most stormy periods of history.'

9. *The Enlightenments of Pagett, M.P.*, p. 109.

10. Ibid., pp. 116–17. This would indicate that, contrary to some opinions, Kipling did not find the caste system congenial.

11. *The Enlightenments of Pagett, M.P.*, p. 143.

12. *The Conversion of Aurelian McGoggin*, p. 154.

13. William James, *The Meaning of Truth* (New York, 1909), p. 204.

14. *The Education of Otis Yeere*, p. 7.

15. *To be Filed for Reference*, p. 433.

16. Quoted by Maud Diver in 'The British Subaltern in India', *Blackwood's Magazine*, cclvii (June 1945), p. 385.

17. E. Edwardes, *Memorials of the Life and Letters of Sir Herbert Edwardes* (1917), vol. 1, p. 65.

18. Ibid., vol. 1, pp. 17–18.

19. Kipling's idealisation of the sympathies between British officer and Pathan warrior has, too, some basis in fact — cf. Sir George Young-husband's *A Soldier's Memories*, pp. 50–51.

20. *Only a Subaltern*, p. 111.

21. Ibid., p. 114.

22. As my next chapter shows, there are many similarities between Kipling and Conrad: the passage just quoted, however, markedly invites a stylistic comparison — particularly with *An Outcast of the Islands*, pp. 54–55 (quoted on p. 141).

23. *The Common Asphodel* (1949), p. 216.

24. *The Solid Muldoon*, p. 52.

25. *The Courting of Dinah Shadd*, pp. 50–51.

26. Ibid., p. 72.

27. 'Cholera Camp'.

28. The extent of his innovation was recognised by some at the time: 'Here be no inanities of the Officers' Mess, no apotheosis of the gilded and tawny-mustachio'd dragoon, no languid and lisping lancer, no child-sweethearts, none, in fact, of the sentimental paraphernalia familiar to readers of modern military fiction.' (Review of *Soldiers Three* in *The Spectator*, 23 March 1889, p. 403.)

29. *Drums of the Fore and Aft*, p. 414.

30. *With the Main Guard*, p. 74.

31. *A Madonna of the Trenches*, p. 201. Kipling was not the only one to recognise the peculiar quality of frontier warfare where 'the uncertainty and importance of the present reduce the past and future to comparative insignificance and clear the mind of minor worries'. [W. S. Churchill, *The Story of the Malakand Field Force* (1899), p. 253.]

32. Joseph Conrad, *Heart of Darkness*. All quotations are from the Medallion Edition of Conrad's works (1925–8). (The Uniform Edition has the same pagination.)

33. *Kim*, ch. v, p. 128.

34. *The Education of Otis Yeere*, p. 10.

35. *The Mark of the Beast*, p. 250.

36. *At the End of the Passage*, p. 206.

37. Ibid., p. 199.

38. *The Education of Otis Yeere*, p. 10.

39. *The Bridge-Builders*, p. 32.

40. Ibid., p. 32.

41. *On the City Wall*, p. 352.

42. Ibid., p. 40. Cf. Mr. Wilson's comment that in Kipling 'there is always the implication that the British are bringing to India modern improvements and sounder standards of behaviour'. ['The Kipling that Nobody Read', in *The Wound and the Bow*, (1961), p. 104.]

43. *The Bridge-Builders*, p. 47.

44. *Kim*, ch. x, p. 244.

45. *The Judgment of Dungara*, p. 256.

46. *The Education of Otis Yeere*, p. 9.

47. *Without Benefit of Clergy*, p. 188.

48. *On the City Wall*, p. 343.

49. Ibid., pp. 350, 359.

50. *The Education of Otis Yeere*, p. 9.

51. *On the City Wall*, p. 349.

52. *Dray Wara Yow Dee*, p. 242.

53. *Rebirth*.

54. *Little Tobrah*, p. 384.

55. *The Limitations of Pambé Serang*.

56. Quoted by Professor Dobrée. ('Rudyard Kipling' in *The Lamp and the Lute*.)

57. *The Finest Story in the World*, pp. 213–14.

58. See *Weland's Sword*, pp. 17–19.

59. *On the Gate*, p. 257.

60. *Black Jack*, p. 109.

61. *The Mutiny of the Mavericks*, p. 240.

62. *Kim*, ch. v, p. 114.

63. Ibid., ch. v, p. 118.

64. *The Record of Badalia Herodsfoot*, pp. 397–8.

65. 'They', p. 323.

66. Charles Carrington, *Rudyard Kipling* (1955), p. 361.

67. *The Children of the Zodiac*, p. 477.

68. *On Greenhow Hill*, p. 94.

69. Ibid., p. 87.

70. The confusion arises, I think, from the fact that there are elements of three different myths interwoven. The first is, of course, the familiar

Zodiacal one, the second, less obvious, is the parallel with Adam and Eve and the third is derived from Indian mythology — Krishna, for instance, being a god but spending his life on earth. From these elements he is really constructing a myth of his own.

71. 'England's Answer'.

72. *The Children of the Zodiac*, p. 466.

73. *Paradise Lost*, bk. ix, l. 782.

74. Cf. also *The Finest Story in the World*, where the same sequence occurs. Human love and marriage is constantly, and almost bitterly, seen by Kipling to mean the closing of the doors of finer perception and the final pronouncement of man's condemnation to an existence of mundane experience.

75. *The Children of the Zodiac*, p. 467.

76. Ibid., p. 468.

77. Ibid., p. 474.

78. Ibid., p. 475.

79. Ibid., p. 476. This is, of course, a large part of the feeling behind Kipling's insistence on the sovereign good of work. Generally speaking, it is a very Victorian insistence; Carlyle, Froude and Kingsley all supported this aspect of the doctrine, while Tennyson recommended 'the persevering performance of daily duty as the best medicine for paralysing doubts and the safest shelter under the storm either of practical or of speculative life'.

80. Ibid., p. 477. This paragraph is the clearest manifesto for the artist in all Kipling's work.

81. Ibid., pp. 482–3.

82. Ibid., pp. 479–80.

83. Ibid., p. 484.

84. 'When Earth's last Picture is Painted.' Cf. ' "My trade's the outside of things," said John quietly. "I have my patterns . . . in my craft a thing done is done with. We go on to new shapes after that" ' (*The Eye of Allah*, p. 312). Or again: ' "There's less risk for a craftsman who deals with the outside shapes of things" ' (ibid., p. 291). Yet all this cannot hide — indeed, it frequently emphasises — Kipling's searching behind the mere fact.

85. '*In the Interests of the Brethren*', p. 56.

86. 'The Kipling that Nobody Read', in *The Wound and The Bow*, p. 134.

87. 'A Recantation' (1917).

88. *Kim*, ch. xii, p. 304.

89. Ibid., ch. xv, pp. 382–3.

90. Ibid., ch. xi, p. 251.

91. Ibid., ch. xi, p. 250.

92. Ibid., ch. xi, p. 251.

93. Joseph Conrad, *Heart of Darkness*, p. 93.

94. *Kim*, ch. xv, p. 383.

95. Edmund Wilson, op. cit., p. 112.

96. N. G. Annan, 'Kipling's Place in the History of Ideas', in *Victorian Studies* (June 1960), p. 345. It should be noted that Annan does not make this a sweeping judgement. He excepts certain stories where the supernatural elements do seem to him to be 'images of deeper spiritual crisis'.

97. Superscription to *In the House of Suddhoo*.

98. 'Helen All Alone'.

99. *In the Same Boat*, p. 81.

100. *A Matter of Fact*, p. 265.

101. 'La Nuit Blanche'.

102. *Mrs Bathurst*, p. 366.

103. Ibid., p. 360.

104. *A Matter of Fact*, p. 274.

105. *The Education of Otis Yeere*, p. 21.

106. Even his maligned 'journalism' with all its poses, knowingness and carefully cultivated sardonic onlooking is, principally, an aspect of this reaction.

107. *Kim*, ch. iii, p. 71.

108. Ibid., p. 72.

109. *The City of Dreadful Night*, p. 407.

110. *Only a Subaltern*, pp. 113–14.

111. '*In the Interests of the Brethren*', p. 59.

112. '*My Son's Wife*', pp. 346–7.

113. 'Independence' in *A Book of Words*, pp. 221–2.

114. 'Values in Life', ibid., p. 19.

115. *The Phantom 'Rickshaw*, p. 135.

116. 'Independence', op. cit., pp. 218–19.

117. Epigraph to *The Disturber of Traffic*.

118. *Mowgli's Brothers*, p. 7.

119. '*Tiger! Tiger!*', p. 120.

120. 'Independence' in *A Book of Words*, p. 232.

121. *At the End of the Passage*, p. 193.

122. *Victorian Studies* (June 1960), p. 325.

123. Ibid., p. 346.

124. Ibid., p. 327.

125. Ibid., p. 325.

126. Mr. Edmund Wilson's claim (op. cit., p. 113) that 'the fiction of

Kipling . . . does not dramatise any fundamental conflict because Kipling would never face any' does not seem to me tenable. His expression of the imperial idea involves a profound conflict as, in their different ways, *Without Benefit of Clergy, Beyond the Pale, Lispeth, On the City Wall, At the End of the Passage, Kim, The Children of the Zodiac* — to name only a few stories — exist to prove.

127. Cf. op. cit., p. 346.

128. *L'Existentialisme* (Paris, 1951), p. 47.

129. N. G. Annan, op. cit., p. 347.

130. Ibid., p. 348.

131. Ibid., p. 346.

132. Ibid., p. 325.

133. *To Be Filed for Reference*, p. 426.

134. *Kidnapped*, p. 186.

135. *The Children of the Zodiac*, p. 486.

136. Op. cit., p. 346.

137. Lionel Trilling, 'Kipling', in *The Liberal Imagination* (1961), p. 125.

138. Trilling, 'The Meaning of a Literary Idea', ibid., pp. 293–4.

139. Further reference to the anti-positivists will be made in the last chapter. Briefly, the description is applied to those social thinkers who, in the later nineteenth century, found Social Darwinism to have so corrupted the eighteenth century Rationalist tradition by its insistence on environment and heredity as governing factors, that little independence of action was left to the human intellect. To this extent their protest was in defence of the 'freely speculating mind'; but their object was far from a purist return to 'orthodox' Augustan principles.

Certainly they shared with the Rationalists faith in the freedom and power of man's intellect, but they deprecated their firm attachment of it to the ball-and-chain of a Newtonian universe. It is, in fact, because of their rejection of the eighteenth century's mechanistic direction of thought with its readiness to elucidate the nature of man and society neatly in terms of natural science that they are to be found categorised as the 'anti-positivists'.

Interestingly, Kipling himself is quite explicit in his dislike for the positivists as he makes clear in his references to Herbert Spencer in *Kim*, pp. 319, 341, and in his opening diatribe against both Comte and Spencer in *The Conversion of Aurelian McGoggin*.

140. J. G. Fichte, 'The Vocation of Man in Society', in J. G. Fichte, *Popular Works*, vol. 1, p. 163.

141. Richard Humphrey, *Georges Sorel. Prophet Without Honour* (New Haven, Conn., 1951), p. 136.

142. *The Letters of Henry James*, ed. Lubbock (1920), vol. 1, p. 278.

143. Edmund Wilson, op. cit., pp. 136–7.

144. 'If there is something that is most specifically social in human activity, it is the machine. It is more social than language itself.' [Georges Sorel, *L'Ancienne et la Nouvelle Métaphysique*, (*D'Aristo te à Marx*) (Paris, 1935), p. 201.]

145. Georges Sorel, *Reflections on Violence*, trans. T. E. Hulme and J. Roth (Illinois, 1950), p. 168.

146. Ibid., p. 57.

147. Georges Sorel, 'Les Aspects juridiques du socialisme', *Revue socialiste* (Oct. 1900), p. 397 (quoted by Richard Humphrey, op. cit., p. 171).

148. Richard Humphrey, op. cit., p. 220.

149. Georges Sorel, *Reflections on Violence*, p. 56.

150. 'The Grand Trunk at this point was built on an embankment to guard against winter floods from the foothills, so that one walked, as it were, a little above the country, along a stately corridor, seeing all India spread out to left and right. It was beautiful to behold the many-yoked grain and cotton waggons crawl over the country roads: one could hear their axles, complaining a mile away, coming nearer, till with shouts and yells and bad words they climbed up the steep incline and plunged on to the hard main road, carter reviling carter. It was equally beautiful to watch the people, little clumps of red and blue and pink and white and saffron, turning aside to go to their own villages, dispersing and growing small by twos and threes across the level plain. . . .

'By this time the sun was driving broad golden spokes through the lower branches of the mango-trees; the parakeets and doves were coming home in their hundreds; the chattering, grey-backed Seven Sisters, talking over the day's adventures, walked back and forth in twos and threes almost under the feet of the travellers; and shufflings and scufflings in the branches showed that the bats were ready to go out on the night-picket. Swiftly the light gathered itself together, painted for an instant the faces and the cart-wheels and the bullocks' horns as red as blood. Then the night fell, changing the touch of the air, drawing a low, even haze, like a gossamer veil of blue, across the face of the country, and bringing out, keen and distinct, the smell of wood-smoke and cattle and the good scent of wheaten cakes cooked on ashes. The evening patrol hurried out of the police-station with important coughings and reiterated orders; and a live charcoal ball in the cup of a wayside carter's hookah glowed red while Kim's eye mechanically watched the last flicker of the sun on the brass tweezers.'

CHAPTER FIVE

Joseph Conrad:
A Window on to Chaos

*Isolation is the sum-total of wretchedness to man. To be cut off,
to be left solitary: to have a world alien, not your world; all a
hostile camp for you; not a home at all, of hearts and faces who
are yours, whose you are! It is the frightfulest enchantment: too
truly a work of the Evil One. To have neither superior, nor in-
ferior, nor equal, united manlike to you. Without father, without
child, without brother. Man knows no sadder destiny. 'How is
each of us', exclaims Jean Paul, 'so lonely in the wide bosom of
the All!' Encased each as in his transparent 'ice-palace'; our
brother visible in his, making signals and gesticulations to us; —
visible, but forever unattainable: on his bosom we shall never rest,
nor he on ours. It was not a God that did this; no!*

THOMAS CARLYLE

Mes sœurs, n'aimez pas les marins:
La solitude est leur royaume.

JEAN COCTEAU

C ONRAD was as intensely aware as Kipling of man's moral
isolation and fragile consciousness. The impression he made
upon Bertrand Russell was of a man who

> thought of civilised and morally tolerable human life as a dangerous
> walk on a thin crust of barely cooled lava which at any moment might
> break and let the unwary sink into fiery depths.[1]

Yet in a way this is a better description of Kipling than of Conrad
for the latter in no way sought to avoid a confrontation with the
destructive element: indeed it was an essential part of experience
and understanding.

Once again the imperial idea offers, in its innate tensions, a moral
correlative for the exploration of the antithesis between conscious-

ness and the hostile principle by which it is menaced. Conrad, however, is the only one of the writers discussed here who explicitly relates the expansionist behaviour of self to that of the State, comparing the political imperialism of the latter with what I have called the moral imperialism of the individual consciousness intent on establishing itself in space. Action as a method of self-consciousness and a mode of expansionism for self and state alike receives full acknowledgement in this passage from 'Autocracy and War':

> The intellectual stage of mankind being as yet in its infancy, and States, like most individuals, having but a feeble and imperfect consciousness of the worth and force of the inner life, the need of making their existence manifest to themselves is determined in the direction of physical activity. The idea of ceasing to grow in territory, in strength, in wealth, in influence — in anything but wisdom and self-knowledge is odious to them as the omen of the end. Action, in which is to be found the illusion of a mastered destiny, can alone satisfy our uneasy vanity and lay to rest the haunting fear of the future.[2]

Perhaps one can ascribe to this scale of thinking the poignancy with which the tragedy of individuals in the Malaysian stories is at the same time felt to be the tragedy of their nation. Certainly alienation while it is clearly an individual moral problem is shown to have much wider ramifications. In fact, Conrad uses the ethnic conflict endemic in imperialism to explore the process of alienation much more fully than Kipling.

In general, however, the relationship between man and empire follows a pattern by now recognisable. Whether as administrator, trader or adventurer the imperial intruder in his embattled consciousness provides the most dramatic evidence of the moral struggle which his physical presence symbolises. Transposed to an altogether alien milieu — to the field of empire from which, by definition, organic unity and social cohesion are debarred — he is made brutally aware of his vulnerability when confronted with the malevolence of the unfamiliar.

Not only is he deprived of all the mechanical aids to self-consciousness which man's social organisation exists to provide, he finds that these are now replaced by a primitive and malignant environment which calls in question the very foundations of his moral integrity.

I

... dull as they were to the subtle influences of surroundings, they felt themselves very much alone, when suddenly left unassisted to face the wilderness; a wilderness rendered more strange, more incomprehensible by the mysterious glimpses of the vigorous life it contained. They were two perfectly insignificant and incapable individuals, whose existence is only rendered possible through the high organisation of civilised crowds. Few men realise that their life, the very essence of their character, their capabilities, and their audacities, are only the expression of their belief in the safety of their surroundings. The courage, the composure, the confidence; the emotions and principles; every great and every insignificant thought belongs not to the individual but to the crowd: to the crowd that believes blindly in the irresistible force of its institutions and of its morals, in the power of its police and its opinion. But the contact with pure unmitigated savagery, with primitive nature and primitive man, brings sudden and profound trouble into the heart. To the sentiment of being alone of one's kind, to the clear perception of the loneliness of one's thoughts, of one's sensations — to the negation of the habitual, which is safe, there is added the affirmation of the unusual, which is dangerous; a suggestion of things vague, uncontrollable, and repulsive, whose discomposing intrusion excites the imagination and tries the civilised nerves of the foolish and the wise alike.[3]

This, of course, is the real burden of Kipling's story *Beyond the Pale*.

The antagonism of the environment is subtly amplified in the invaders' confrontation with the native race. Together they question the Europeans' belief in their own action, compelling them to the demoralising realisation that their code is not, after all, universal; that in certain situations their comforting reflection will not be returned, for to some neither their ideas nor their actions are meaningful or comprehensible. Simultaneously, while thus exposed to the threat of moral annihilation, they succeed in demolishing the integrity of native life by their inevitable failure to appreciate its forces and values.

It is, in fact, this reciprocal destructiveness which produces the main creative antithesis of early stories like *Almayer's Folly* and *An Outcast of the Islands* — though as we shall see it represents an idea of nature subsumed throughout the entirety of Conrad's writing.

'Where do you come from?' she said, impulsive and inconsequent, in a passionate whisper. 'What is that land beyond the great sea . . . from which nothing but misfortune ever comes to us — who are not white . . .'[4]

How stupidly blind to their own destruction and to the implications of the situation the 'specimens of the superior race' could be, is shown by those who

looked on native life as a mere play of shadows. A play of shadows, the dominant race could walk through unaffected and disregarded in the pursuit of its incomprehensible aims and needs.[5]

Although he was well aware that, in any case, 'no two human beings understand each other. They can understand but their own voices',[6] Conrad stands back in astonishment at such complete absence of understanding. Not only do the best on either side fail to understand each other, but even those in the same group are encased in their individual ice-palaces: Lingard, for instance, never comes near to understanding Willems.

The strife which stems from this elementary cause is almost limitless.

'If I ever spoke to Patalolo like an elder brother, it was for your good, for the good of you all,' said Lingard with great earnestness.

'This is white man's talk,' exclaimed Babalatchi with bitter exultation. 'I know you. That is how you all talk while you load your guns and sharpen your swords; and when you are ready, then to those who are weak you say; "Obey me and be happy, or die!" You are strange you white men. You think it is only your wisdom and your virtue and your happiness that are true. You are stronger than the wild beasts, but not so wise. A black tiger knows when he is not hungry — you do not. He knows the difference between himself and those that can speak; you do not understand the difference between yourselves and us — who are men. You are wise and great — and you shall always be fools.'[7]

But Lingard still does not understand:

'Apa! Apa! What is the matter?' he murmured soothingly. 'Whom did I kill here? Where are my guns? What have I done? What have I eaten up?'[8]

Their utter isolation from the ethos of each other's lives is pointed brilliantly:

'Had you come a day sooner, Tuan, you would have seen an enemy die. You would have seen him die poor, blind, unhappy — with no son to

dig his grave and speak of his wisdom and courage. Yes; you would have
seen the man that fought you in Carimata many years ago, die alone —
but for one friend. A great sight to you.'

'Not to me,' answered Lingard. 'I did not even remember him till
you spoke his name just now. You do not understand us. We fight, we
vanquish — and we forget.'

'True, true,' said Babalatchi, with polite irony; 'you whites are so
great that you disdain to remember your enemies.' [9]

Not only are they impenetrable to each other's truths — they
destroy them; the Orang Blanda have made a mockery of the life-
forces of the native community and put nothing which has any
meaning in its place.

You whites have taken all: the land, the sea, and the power to strike,
and there is nothing left for us in the islands but your white man's
justice; your great justice that knows not anger.[10]

And native life, with its incomprehensibility and organisation
unrecognisable as such to the alien, subtly destroys the white man's
faith in his fellow-white man — in fact, in White Men as an exclusive and self-identifying group.

'Oh, damn it,' exclaimed Lingard — then went on in Malay, speaking
earnestly. 'Listen. That man is not like other white men. You know he is
not. He is not a man at all. He is . . . I don't know.'[11]

He is, of course, a man in all but the Stalky and Co. sense in which
Lingard is speaking. He is the reminder that a good man in this
sense — a good chap, a fine fellow — doesn't really exist; that he is
nothing but a myth made corporate, raised in the interest of brotherhood and integrity. Willems calls everyone's bluff: he is again the
ubiquitous betrayer, the Judas of the Conrad system. Against this,
Lingard's proud reiteration 'I am white' sounds particularly desperate and hollow.

All this failure in understanding finds expression in racial antagonism but what is really illuminated is human fragility and loneliness. It is this and its unhappy consequences which form the
substance of these colonial stories. Willems, for example, had
realised that it was not the fear of death that frightened him but the

unreasoning fear of this glimpse into the unknown things, into those
motives, impulses, desires he had ignored, but that had lived in the breasts
of despised men, close by his side, and were revealed to him for a second,

to be hidden again behind the black mists of doubt and deception. It was not death that frightened him: it was the horror of bewildered life where he could understand nothing and nobody around him; where he could guide, control, comprehend nothing, and no one — not even himself.[12]

And his reaction here can be put alongside his behaviour at Omar's death. When, in his 'foreignness' he had violated the sanctity of *their* moral order:

At the first hour of the morning he sat up — he so weak — and said plainly some words that were not meant for human ears. I held his hand tightly, but it was time for the leader of brave men to go amongst the Faithful who are happy. They of my household brought a white sheet, and I began to dig a grave in the hut in which he died. She mourned aloud. The white man came to the doorway and shouted. He was angry. Angry with her because she beat her breast, and tore her hair, and mourned with shrill cries as a woman should. Do you understand what I say, Tuan? That white man came inside the hut with great fury, and took her by the shoulder, and dragged her out. Yes, Tuan. I saw Omar dead, and I saw her at the feet of that white dog who has deceived me. I saw his face grey, like the cold mist of the morning; I saw his pale eyes looking down at Omar's daughter beating her head on the ground at his feet. At the feet of him who is Abdulla's slave.[13]

The whole account of the Aissa/Willems relationship — indeed the whole theme of *An Outcast of the Islands,* is one of complete incomprehension: of that incomprehension which exposes and ultimately destroys a man. The unfolding story is graduated by the slow disintegration of Willems, as his moral being, fragment by fragment, drops back into pre-social chaos. First the exotic attracts, then it puzzles, then repels; and finally, given no relief, destroys. Only too clearly Willems came to recognise this. Aissa never did.

'Aissa! How can I live here? Trust me. Believe in me. Let us go away from here. Go very far away! Very far; you and I!'
He did not stop to ask himself whether he could escape, and how, and where. He was carried away by the flood of hate, disgust and contempt of a white man for that blood which is not his blood, for that race which is not his race; for the brown skins; for the hearts false like the sea, blacker than night. This feeling of repulsion overmastered his reason in a clear conviction of the impossibility for him to live with her people. He urged her passionately to fly with him because out of all that abhorred crowd he wanted this one woman, but wanted her away from them, away

from that race of slaves and cut-throats from which she sprang. He
wanted her for himself — far from everybody, in some safe and dumb
solitude. And as he spoke his anger and contempt rose, his hate became
almost fear. . . .[14]

But Aissa does not understand.

And while she listened she felt a slowing down of her heart-beats as
the meaning of his appeal grew clearer before her indignant eyes, as she
saw with rage and pain the edifice of her love, her own work, crumble
slowly to pieces, destroyed by that man's fears, by that man's falseness.
Her memory recalled the days by the brook when she had listened to
other words — to other thoughts — to promises and to pleadings for
other things, which came from that man's lips at the bidding of her look
or her smile, at the nod of her head, at the whisper of her lips. Was there
then in his heart something else than her image, other desires than the
desires of her love? other fears than the fear of losing her? How could
that be? Had she grown ugly or old in a moment? She was appalled,
surprised and angry with the anger of unexpected humiliation; and her
eyes looked fixedly, sombre and steady, at that man born in the land of
violence and of evil wherefrom nothing but misfortune comes to those
who are not white. Instead of thinking of her caresses, instead of forget-
ting all the world in her embrace, he was thinking yet of his people; of
that people that steals every land, masters every sea, that knows no mercy
and no truth — knows nothing but its own strength. O man of strong
arm and of false heart! Go with him to a far country, be lost in the throng
of cold eyes and false hearts — lose him there! Never! He was mad —
mad with fear; but he should not escape her! She would keep him here
a slave and a master; here where he was alone with her; where he must
live for her — or die. She had a right to his love which was of her making,
to the love that was in him now, while he spoke those words without
sense.[15]

Both think of the other side as false; both are concerned — perhaps
only can be concerned — solely with their own truth. The point,
too, is that such incomprehension is self-destructive: one's own
truths, undermined, disintegrate.

Aissa's answer is to throw a kriss at Willems:

Was this the answer to his pleading, to the hot and living words that
came from his heart? Was this the answer thrown at him like an insult,
that thing made of wood and iron, insignificant and venomous, fragile
and deadly.[16]

The climax of the book is inevitable and wholly consistent with this theme of incomprehension:

Hate filled the world, filled the space between them — the hate of race, the hate of hopeless diversity, the hate of blood; the hate against the man born in the land of lies and of evil from which nothing but misfortune comes to those who are not white. And as she stood, maddened, she heard a whisper near her, the whisper of the dead Omar's voice saying in her ear: Kill![17]

Its conclusion is the bitter hopelessness of Aissa's ultimate realisation:

She added after a pause — 'There has been a time when I could understand him. When I knew what was in his mind better than he knew it himself. When I felt him. When I held him. . . . And now he has escaped.'

'Escaped? What? Gone away?' shouted Lingard.

'Escaped from me,' she said; 'left me alone. Alone. And I am ever near him. Yet alone.'

Her hands slipped slowly off Lingard's shoulders and her arms fell by her side, listless, discouraged, as if to her — to her, the savage, violent, and ignorant creature — had been revealed clearly in that moment the tremendous fact of our isolation, of the loneliness impenetrable and transparent, elusive and everlasting; of the indestructible loneliness that surrounds, envelops, clothes every human soul from the cradle to the grave, and, perhaps, beyond.[18]

As had been the case for Kipling, Conrad reveals that his fear of the wilderness stems from the fact that he knows the enemy to be already within the gates. *Heart of Darkness*, for example, takes most of its strength from the interplay of the internal and external sources of corruption. Kurtz is, of course, the dramatic embodiment of this movement but Marlow as the 'external' observer underlines and enlarges its significance. Confrontation with the primitive, unorganised native discloses a horrible and unsuspected affinity between him and the sophisticated alien which makes clear just how much of an assumption, how much of a carefully erected, entirely superficial thing, individual identity is. One's own moral organisation depends upon the degree of social organisation experienced environmentally. And when this is exposed as brutally as it is by these primitive people the whole basis of integrity is undermined.

The earth seemed unearthly. We are accustomed to look upon the shackled form of a conquered monster, but there — there you could look at a thing monstrous and free. It was unearthly and the men were — No they were not inhuman . . . that was the worst of it — this suspicion of their not being inhuman.[19]

Physical nature may, then, be an emblem of corruption — a projection of that chaotic nature which includes in its totality of 'otherness' the destructive element. And it is an inescapable condition of the colonist's imperial presence just as it is of man's self-consciousness.

Very funny this terrible thing is. A man that is born falls into a dream like a man who falls into the sea. If he tries to climb out into the air as inexperienced people tend to do, he drowns — nicht wahr? No! I tell you the way is to the destructive element submit yourself and with the exertions of your hands and feet in the water make the deep, deep sea keep you up.[20]

Stein's advice to Jim offers a method of consciousness not unlike that recommended by Kipling, for submission to the 'destructive element' is a clear option for involvement in the natural world.

The issue was the same one that had perplexed Kipling — 'whether the profit of any concession that a man makes to his Tribe, against the light that is in him, outweighs or justifies his disregard for that light'. Involvement is, however, an inescapable necessity and if, in one sense, it means self-immolation, in the process the individual will have made his soul. As such it is a change rung upon a theme also heard frequently in Buchan — 'Though thou slay me yet will I trust in Thee.'

What captivated my fancy was that I, Axel Heyst, the most detached of creatures in this earthly captivity, the veriest tramp on this earth, an indifferent stroller going through the world's bustle — that I should have been there to step into the situation of an agent of providence. I, a man of universal scorn and unbelief . . . Funny position wasn't it? . . . I had in a moment of inadvertence, created for myself a tie. How to define it precisely I don't know. One gets attached in a way to people one has done something for. But is that friendship? I am not sure what it was. I only know that he who forms a tie is lost. The germ of corruption has entered his soul.[21]

This, of course, is the reverse of the theme of loneliness and, naturally, is equally pervasive throughout Conrad's fiction. It forms the subject of *Victory* where any chance of defending one's integrity through complete withdrawal from society is shown to be hopeless. Heyst, 'by a system of restless wandering, by the detachment of an impermanent dweller amongst changing scenes'[22] tried to do just this — to obey his father's dying injunction, 'Look on — make no sound', and he failed completely. Both Heyst and Jones are outcasts, one is passively anti-social the other actively and destructively, the difference putting them at opposite ends of any conventional scheme of social morality. Yet both are in a wider sense immoral:

> The gentleman on the bed said he could assure me of one thing; and that was that his presence here was no more morally reprehensible than mine.
> 'We pursue the same ends,' he said, 'only perhaps I pursue them with more openness than you — with more simplicity.'[23]

Both insist on their isolation, both are failures and the cause of their failure is the same — neither has been able to escape the consequences of his anti-social creed. Both are, in fact, destroyed by the forces of involvement. Heyst whose life 'ought to have been a masterpiece of aloofness'[24] had seen clearly that his defeat was implicit in his offer of help to Morrison but the *coup de grâce* for both him and Jones comes through Lena — the symbol of compassion, pity and involvement, as woman so often is in Conrad's work.[25]

Repeatedly Jones (the name itself is significant) and his henchmen are presented as the evil, destructive forces of the world in which man must, nevertheless, immerse himself.

> Here they are, the envoys of the outer world . . . evil intelligence, instinctive savagery, arm in arm. The brute force is at the back.[26]

> I, my dear sir? In one way I am — yes, I am the world itself, come to pay you a visit. In another sense I am an outcast — almost an outlaw. If you prefer a less materialistic view, I am a sort of fate — the retribution that waits its time.[27]

One cannot, then, run away from life and remain whole that way. Association with the human community is a moral necessity: ties must be formed however painful and hazardous it may be to do so. One is forcibly reminded of Kipling's devotion to the God of Things as They Are, although there is an altogether significant difference in the degrees to which the destructive element is allowed a dramatic function.

Georges Sorel had been insistent on the falsity of trying 'to detach the individual from the great universal process in which human experience lies'.[28] Conrad no less vigorously than Kipling endorses this opinion, directing us firmly back to the human community, to duty and sacrifice, and a familiar morality of action. Salvation can be found in abstractions no more for him than for Kipling or Sorel:

> Visionaries work everlasting evil on the earth. Their Utopias inspire in the mass of mediocre minds a disgust of reality and a contempt for the secular logic of human development.[29]

To seek refuge in such a sphere is another instance of 'immoral detachment'.

> 'What do you say? . . . I an aristocrat!'
> 'Oh! I don't mean that you are like the men and women of the time of armours, castles, and great deeds. Oh no! They stood on the naked soil, had traditions to be faithful to, had their feet on this earth of passions and death which is not a hothouse. They would have been too plebeian for you since they had to lead, to suffer with, to understand the commonest humanity. No, you are merely of the topmost layer, disdainful and superior, the mere pure froth and bubble on the inscrutable depths which some day will toss you out of existence. But you are you! You are you! You are the eternal love itself — only, O Divinity, it isn't your body, it is your soul that is made of foam . . .'[30]

In this story (one of Conrad's worst) Miss Moorsom's deliberate intellectualisations are shown up in all their insincerity. 'Here I stand for truth itself,' she says and it is left to Renouard to destroy her meaningless pretensions and to bring her down to earth which in itself alone contains reckonable value.

Describing his daughter, the professor points the message.

> Yes, she's clever, open-minded, popular, and — well — charming. But you don't know what it is to have moved, breathed, existed, and even triumphed in the mere smother and froth of life — the brilliant froth. There thoughts, sentiments, opinions, feelings, actions too, are nothing

but agitation in empty space — to amuse life — a sort of superior debauchery, exciting and fatiguing, meaning nothing, leading nowhere. She is the creature of that circle. And I ask myself if she is obeying the uneasiness of an instinct seeking its satisfaction, or is it a revulsion of feeling, or is she merely deceiving her own heart by this dangerous trifling with romantic images. And everything is possible — except sincerity, such as only stark, struggling humanity can know.[31]

The human community is all and Miss Moorsom's superficial intellectualism is merely 'intellectual debauchery in the froth of existence'. Her abstractions meant nothing in the face of Renouard's great passion: its spontaneity, sincerity and humanity gave it truth and validity to be measured against the reality of human experience. Miss Moorsom, who is the direct opposite of Emilia Gould, talks in her *unemotional* voice of a 'sacred debt' and 'a fine duty' — and cuts herself off.

Such absorbing interest in the community is, of course, self-protective, and consequently anything endangering it gets an extreme personal reaction. Thus the hostility to Donkin in *The Nigger of the Narcissus*; the menace of the amoral soul essentially undermines those who depend upon an obviously ordered system. There is a similar reaction to the insidious threat of destruction from James Wait who creates and manipulates the destructive force of uncertainty.

It is interesting that Conrad's symbolism portraying the dialectical relationship which his idea of nature predicates is dominated by that of the ship (the archetypal image of unity and integrity) threatened by subversive and destructive elements, and that of the White Man (collectively a self-identifying cultural 'quantity') threatened with corruption by an alien environment. Confrontation for both is inevitable and, if either is to survive, the same — and Kiplingesque — demand has to be met: total fidelity to 'what is nearest to hand and heart in the short moment of each human effort'.

I was learning to clap my teeth smartly before my heart flew out, when I shaved by a fluke some infernal sly old snag that would have ripped the life out of the tin-pot steamboat and drowned all the pilgrims; I had to keep a look-out for the signs of dead wood we could cut up in the night for next day's steaming. When you have to attend to things of that sort, to the mere incidents of the surface, the reality — the reality, I tell you fades. The inner truth is hidden — luckily, luckily.[32]

But if one has to get down into the arena and face the destructive element one has at least the invaluable consolation of communion with the rest of humanity — indeed, it could be called the interim object of the exercise since to Conrad, as to Kipling, integration in society and a 'known' environment generally, allows one to demarcate a world and discern a personal identity.

... to us the limits of the universe are strictly defined by those we know. There is nothing for us outside the babble of praise and blame on familiar lips, and beyond our last acquaintance there lies only a vast chaos; a chaos of laughter and tears which concerns us not.[33]

Or again in *Under Western Eyes*:

He raised his voice.
'You are a son, a brother, a nephew, a cousin — I don't know what — to no end of people. I am just a man. Here I stand before you. A man with a mind. Did it ever occur to you how a man who had never heard a word of affection or praise in his life would think on matters on which you would think first with or against your class, your domestic tradition — your fireside prejudices? ... Did you ever consider how a man like that would feel? I have no domestic tradition. I have nothing to think against. My tradition is historical. What have I to look back to but that national past from which you gentlemen want to wrench away your future? ... You come from your province but all this land is mine — or I have nothing ... And what can you people do by scattering a few drops of blood on the snow? On this Immensity. On this unhappy Immensity! I tell you ... that what it needs is not a lot of haunting phantoms that I could walk through — but a man.'[34]

Here, too, we are reminded of Kipling (and, incidentally, of the Carlyle epigraph to this chapter). Perhaps his most explicit comment is in *Lord Jim*:

The spirit of the land, as becomes the ruler of great enterprises, is careless of innumerable lives. Woe to the stragglers! We exist only insofar as we hang together.[35]

The submission Stein required of Lord Jim is clearly not made without reservation — it explicitly demands battle not capitulation for it involves the confrontation of consciousness with, and not its secession to, the destructive element.[36] Compared with Kipling and Buchan, Conrad — as has been already pointed out — was, by exposing this essential tension so fully, moderating the anti-thesis and achieving the greater artistic success. But, also to repeat, this moderation can only be carried so far. There comes a point, except perhaps for the mystic, where a reservation has to be made, a basic irreducible moment of fidelity to one's own self-consciousness: and at that moment the conflict becomes inevitable.

Simple fidelity to oneself is, however, not sufficient to withstand the onslaught as Decoud's fate demonstrated. Even scepticism must have belief to breed on — though it might be, in Marlow's phrase 'a deliberate belief'.[37] In a lack of such lay Kurtz's fatal deficiency: we are told that 'he could get himself to believe anything, any-thing', which spells dissolution rather than cohesion.

What is required, therefore, is adherence to an ideal which in being necessarily beyond the self must carry a measure of protection. Certainly there is nothing but corruption to be expected from deeds enacted on a basis of materialism, as is manifested in the character of Charles Gould whose 'worthiness of life was bound up with success'.[38]

'No!' interrupted the doctor. 'There is no peace and no rest in the development of material interests. They have their law and their justice. But it is founded on injustice and is inhuman; it is without rectitude, without the community and the force that can be found only in a moral principle . . .'
'Is it this we have worked for, then?'
The doctor lowered his head. He could follow her silent thought. Was it for this that her life had been robbed of all the intimate felicities of daily affection which her tenderness needed as the human body needs air to breathe?[39]

Even empire itself, though it can never be justified, may admit an idealism which atones for much:

They [the Romans] were no colonists; their administration was merely a squeeze, and nothing more, I suspect. They were conquerors, and for that you want only brute force — nothing to boast of, when you have it, since your strength is just an accident arising from the weakness of others. They grabbed what they could get for the sake of what was to be got. It was just robbery with violence, aggravated murder on a great scale, and men going at it blind — as is very proper for those who tackle a darkness. The conquest of the earth, which mostly means the taking it away from those who have a different complexion or slightly flatter noses than ourselves, is not a pretty thing when you look into it too much. What redeems it is the idea only. An idea at the back of it; not a sentimental pretence but an idea; and an unselfish belief in the idea — something you can set up, and bow down before, and offer a sacrifice to . . .[40]

Those without any tincture of idealism, 'the buying and selling gang which bosses this rotten show', the 'pilgrims' in *Heart of Darkness*, for example, are repeatedly exposed by Conrad. In *An Outpost of Progress* it is done with splendid irony:

They also found some old copies of a home paper. That print discussed what it was pleased to call 'Our Colonial Expansion' in high-flown language. It spoke much of the rights and duties of civilisation, of the sacredness of the civilising work, and extolled the merits of those who went about bringing light and faith and commerce to the dark places of the earth. Carlier and Kayerts read, wondered, and began to think better of themselves. Carlier said one evening waving his hand about, 'In a hundred years, there will be perhaps a town here. Quays and ware-houses and barracks, and — and — billiard-rooms. Civilisation, my boy, and virtue — and all. And then chaps will read that two good fellows, Kayerts and Carlier, were the first civilised men to live in this very spot!' Kayerts nodded, 'Yes, it is a consolation to think of that.'[41]

Ben Jonson's laconic observation that a certain degree of soul is necessary to every man if only to save us the expense of salt is enlarged by Carlyle: 'For all human things do require to have an Ideal in them; to have some Soul in them . . . were it only to keep the Body unputrefied.'[42] Conrad's Marlow goes to the extent of finding even in the sartorial discrimination of the Company's Chief Accountant in the midst of the demoralising jungle some sort of homage to this divinity:

Moreover I respected the fellow. Yes; I respected his collars, his vast cuffs, his brushed hair. His appearance was certainly that of a hairdresser's dummy; but in the great demoralisation of the land he kept up his appearance. That's backbone. His starched collars and got-up shirt-fronts were achievements of character.[43]

A similar fastidiousness had once reflected the integrity of Willems, that other 'confidential clerk' in *An Outcast of the Islands*. When the discipline of his code which had its centre in his exaggerated regard for his own reputation had broken down, the corruption is revealed in the incoherence and dilapidation of his appearance.

He stood at last before Almayer — a masquerading spectre of the once so very confidential clerk of the richest merchant on the islands. His jacket was soiled and torn; below the waist he was clothed in a worn-out and faded sarong.[44]

Fidelity to one's selfhood is, of course, fidelity to an ideal and the link between this and an apparently impersonal, extraneous ideal, say of service, is obviously a close one. 'Man must serve always something greater than himself' we are reminded in *Under Western Eyes*: if he does not the core is left hollow and ready for invasion.

Even for those armoured in such an ideal there are still moments of terrible doubt when the machinery which sustains the conception is brought to a standstill. The worst of these involve

the doubt of the sovereign power enthroned in a fixed standard of conduct. It is the hardest thing to stumble against; it is the thing that breeds yelling panics and good little quiet villainies; it's the true shadow of calamity.[45]

And these moments can be, as they were for Brierly, fatal. Jim's action in deserting his ship destroyed Brierly because the latter had identified his own integrity with the sanctity of the Merchant Naval officer's code. There was nothing left for him to live by once he had seen his 'sovereign power' brutally desecrated on the altar of Jim's irresponsible selfishness. Jim had, in fact, executed the threat *vis-à-vis* Brierly that we find implicit in Kipling's Grish Chunder Dé.

Fidelity has, of course, to be a tried and tested fidelity. Though he may be found on frequent occasions to be oversimplifying his position —

Those who read me know my conviction that the world, the temporal world, rests on a few very simple ideas; so simple that they must be as old as the hills. It rests notably among others on the idea of fidelity.[46]

— we are never allowed to forget that simple ideas without any real awareness will never secure the highest place in Conrad's estimation. McWhirr, Lingard, Don Pepe, Mitchell, all live within this code but they are not represented as the ideal. Conscious adoption of the idea is necessary, and this can only be gained through an experienced sensibility. When Conrad has Marlow say:

Hang ideas! They are tramps, vagabonds, knocking at the back-door of your mind, each taking a little of your substance, each carrying away some crumb of that belief in a few simple notions you must cling to if you want to live decently and would like to die easy.[47]

he is, in Kiplingesque terms, pronouncing the creed but not the whole creed. You have to be bitten by the dog before the hair can help you and the biting in this case is an ironical but inescapable necessity.

A crisis of realisation with all its desolation and uncertainty was, as Carlyle insisted, the *sine qua non* of true insight into Being. And if the conflict from which it arises cannot be finally resolved at least the newly acquired awareness will remain.

To me nothing seems more natural than that the Son of Man ... should be carried of the spirit into the grim Solitudes, and there fronting the Tempter do grimmest battle with him; defiantly setting him at naught till he yield and fly. Name it as we choose: with or without visible Devil, whether in the natural desert of rocks and sand, or in the populous moral desert of selfishness and baseness — to such Temptation are we called. Unhappy if we are not! Unhappy if we are but half-men, in whom that divine handwriting has never blazed forth ... Yes, to me also was given, if not victory, yet the consciousness of Battle, and the resolve to persevere therein while life or faculty is left ...

A vain interminable controversy ... touching what is at present called Origin of Evil, or some such thing, arises in every soul since the beginning of the world; and in every soul, that would pass from idle suffering into actual Endeavouring, must first be put an end to. The most, in our time, have to go content with a simple, incomplete enough suppression of this controversy; to a few some Solution of it is indispensable. In every new era, too, such Solution comes out in different terms; and ever the Solution of the last era has become obsolete and is found unserviceable. For it is man's nature to change his Dialect from century to century; he cannot help it though he would.[48]

Conrad shared something of Carlyle's disdain for those who never saw behind the veil, but there was for him no final Solution of the sort Carlyle found — nor such suppression of the controversy as we find in Kipling's work. For, undeniably, the latter evaded a direct confrontation with the subject of moral annihilation, and while fully acknowledging the extent to which man lived alone, spent most of his effort elaborating the necessity of a method of integration.[49] The pit was really far too close for him to write about it. It is not surprising, therefore, that we should find Conrad in the course of his exploration making explicit much that is only hinted in Kipling's work. Even then, though it is consequently tempting to talk of Kipling's failure of nerve in this respect one must not forget that if this happened it did so because of a hypersensitivity to the chaos of existence, not because of incomprehension or a lack of insight. Though intensely aware of it, he, unlike Dawse in *The Disturber of Traffic*, refused to look through the crack in the floor, pasting over it, instead, sheet after sheet of paper patterned with heroic deeds and the glowing images of indissoluble friendship and fidelity. But alas, the unbearable heat of summer explosively revealed it again, and when repaired with Duty and Sacrifice the wet season mildewed it and brought out strange, chaotic shapes lurking unsuspectedly behind the gay design.

The process is, very largely, the one described in the quotation from Lawrence used as an epigraph to the previous chapter. In that same essay Lawrence goes on to draw an antithesis which illustrates remarkably well the distinction between Kipling's position and that of Conrad:

Man fixes some wonderful erection of his own between himself and the wild chaos, and gradually goes bleached and stifled under his parasol. Then comes a poet, enemy of convention, and makes a slit in the umbrella; and lo! the glimpse of chaos is a vision, a window to the sun. But after a while, getting used to the vision, and not liking the genuine draught from chaos, commonplace man daubs a simulacrum of the window that opens on to chaos, and patches the umbrella with the painted patch of the simulacrum . . . So that the umbrella at last looks like a glowing open firmament, of many aspects. But alas! it is all simulacrum, in innumerable patches.[50]

Conrad never attempted the same fabrication as Kipling indulged in. What the individual depended on never for a moment had any separate reality: and man himself is ultimately nothing but 'an unforeseen accident which does not stand close investigation'.[51]

All this being so why should we talk grandly about ideals of Service, of Duty, of Sacrifice? Why talk about ideals? Kipling did, although suspecting the true nature of affairs, and to this extent is,

K

compared with Conrad, the lesser spirit. As the latter rightly saw and openly admitted, there was only one ideal — Fidelity. Fidelity to oneself. Selfish? Perhaps, but in preserving oneself one is preserving others. There is, in fact, no such thing as self, only selfhood — an equipose which we either maintain or don't. The pretence that 'isms' can have independent meaning is thus shown up for the pointless sham it is. Imperialism and all other 'isms' must be an attempt of the selfhood to establish itself in space as well as in time. In other words, an attempt to turn selfhood into self. Thus we find identity in our own expression: by our 'isms' shall ye know us. Kipling was quite clear about this: 'It is true', he had once concluded aptly in an address to the Stationers' Company, 'that our existence was forced on us by that providential itch for self-expression.'

All that Conrad could offer, then, was fidelity to simple ideas and a highly pragmatic idealism. Physical labour and the solidarity of the human community were to be his only consolation:

From the hard work of men are born the sympathetic consciousness of a common destiny, the fidelity to right practice which makes great craftsmen, the sense of right conduct which we may call honour, the devotion to our calling and the idealism which is not a misty winged angel without eyes, but a divine figure of terrestrial aspect with a clear glance and with its feet resting firmly on the earth on which it was born.[52]

Clearly Conrad as well as Kipling would have agreed with Carlyle in his conclusion that 'All Works, each in their degree, are a making of Madness sane.' His concern with duty, fidelity and devotion to craft is, once again, a reflection of the notion that man is himself responsible for whatever order there is in nature:

For a moment I had a view of a world that seemed to wear a vast and dismal aspect of disorder, while, in truth, thanks to our unwearied efforts, it is as sunny an arrangement of small conveniences as the mind of man can conceive. But still — it was only a moment: I went back into my shell directly. One *must* — don't you know? . . .[53]

And the task of the writer is seen to be the reassurance of the community's integrity — just as it had been defined in *The Children of the Zodiac*. If the writer succeeds he may

perchance attain to such clearness of sincerity that at last the presented vision . . . shall awaken in the hearts of the beholders that feeling of unavoidable solidarity; of the solidarity in mysterious origin, in toil, in joy, in hope, in uncertain fate, which binds men to each other and all mankind to the visible world.[54]

Conrad's art, however, carries him far beyond the limits of this definition whereas Kipling seeks to fulfil it, narrowly, to the very letter. Yet Conrad's descriptions of merchant-sailing and sailors makes a large part of Kipling's attitude towards the Anglo-Indian fully explicit:

> The successive generations that went out to sea from these Isles went out to toil desperately in adventurous conditions. A man is a worker. If he is not that he is nothing. Just nothing — like a mere adventurer. Those men understood the nature of their work, but more or less dimly, in various degrees of imperfection. The best and greatest of their leaders even had never seen it clearly, because of its magnitude and the remoteness of its end. This is the common fate of mankind, whose most positive achievements are born from dreams and visions followed loyally to an unknown destination. And it doesn't matter. For the great mass of mankind the only saving grace that is needed is steady fidelity to what is nearest to hand and heart in the short moment of each human effort. In other and in greater words, what is needed is a sense of immediate duty, and a feeling of impalpable restraint.[55]

The necessary intensity this reflects of one's surrender to the God of Things as They Are, explains the emphatic insistence in the works of all three writers, Conrad, Kipling and Buchan, on an ideal of competence. Acutely conscious of the chaotic truth, their characters pay an exaggerated deference to what they and their fellow-humans have conspired to accept as reality. Their triumphant achievements in this field postulate a principle of order, comforting them with the illusion of a universe that is not insusceptible to human control and a destiny which it may yet be possible to master. In all three authors we therefore find the same autocratic thirst for power and an admiration of resolute, imperious action.

> He was an adventurer of the sea, an outcast, a ruler, — and my very good friend. I wish him a quick death in a stand up fight, a death in sunshine; for he had known remorse and power, and no man can demand more from life.[56]

The same factor promotes Conrad's pleasure in the Lingard-type which is a reflection of the bland, harmonious face of the world.

It is not the world altogether, but it is pleasant to think of it as such. Fury naturally follows for those who 'blow the bloody gaff' — for Donkin and for Wait and for the Willems-type 'ranging over the islands and disturbing the harmony of the universe by robbery, treachery and violence'.[57] They ignore the formulas which are a necessary part of the illusion and whose function Carlyle defined so succinctly:

> Formulas? There is no mortal extant, out of the depths of Bedlam, but lives all skinned, thatched, covered with Formulas; and is, as it were, held in from delirium and the Inane by his Formulas.[58]

The illusion is, then, of the first importance; all-important in fact. 'What does the price matter if the trick be well done', Conrad asks in one of his stories. And the narrator in *Karain* reflects on the fate of

> all the men that wander amongst illusions; of the illusions as restless as men; of the illusions faithful, faithless; of the illusions that give joy, that give sorrow, that give pain, that give peace; of the invincible illusions that can make life and death appear serene, inspiring, tormented or ignoble.[59]

But though the illusion is precious, is, in the words of Robert Penn Warren's study,[60] the mark of human achievement, it is of vital importance to remember that it *is* an illusion.

This view of the two realities is profoundly pessimistic and hardly to be summed up as Jocelyn Baines does as 'a sense of unreality and fatality'. He himself quotes an extract from a letter where the conclusion, he admits, is implicitly that of contracting out:

> The attitude of cold unconcern is the only reasonable one. Of course reason is hateful, — but why? Because it demonstrates (to those who have the courage) that we, living, are out of life, — utterly out of it. The mysteries of a universe made of drops of fire and clods of mud do not concern us in the least. The fate of a humanity condemned ultimately to perish from cold is not worth troubling about. If you take it to heart it becomes an unendurable tragedy. If you believe in improvement you must weep, for the attained perfection must end in cold, darkness and silence. In a dispassionate view the ardour for reform, improvement, for virtue, for knowledge and even for beauty, is only a vain sticking up for appearances, as though one were anxious about the cut of one's clothes in a community of blind men.[61]

Clearly if there is to be the necessary 'faith' in progress the illusion has to be maintained and, as in Kipling, action supplies the method.

Action — the first thought or perhaps the first impulse, on earth! The barbed hook, baited with the illusion of progress, to bring out of the lightless void the shoals of unnumbered generations.

And, as in Kipling, action can have its own morality irrespective of its particular end.

By heavens! there is something after all in the world allowing one man to steal a horse while another must not look at a halter. Steal a horse straight out. Very well. He has done it. Perhaps he can ride. But there is a way of looking at a halter that would provoke the most charitable of saints into a kick.[62]

Sometimes his remarks on the subject could serve as a definition of Kipling's doctrine:

After three days of waiting for the sight of some human face, Decoud caught himself entertaining a doubt of his own individuality. It had merged into the world of cloud and water, of natural forces and forms of nature. In our activity alone do we find the sustaining illusion of an independent existence as against the whole scheme of things of which we form a helpless part.[63]

And sometimes they are couched in extremely Kiplingesque terms:

The companions of that piratical and son-less Aeneas are dead now, but their ghosts wander over the water and the islands at night — after the manner of ghosts — and haunt the fires by which sit armed men, as is meet for the spirits of fearless warriors who died in battle. There they may hear the stories of their own deeds, of their own courage, suffering and death, on the lips of living men. That story is told in many places. On the cool mats in breezy verandahs of Rajahs' houses it is alluded to disdainfully by impassive statesmen, but amongst armed men that throng the courtyards it is a tale which stills the murmur of voices and the tinkle of anklets; arrests the passage of the siri-vessel, and fixes the eyes in absorbed gaze. They talk of the fight, of the fearless woman, of the wise man; of long suffering on the thirsty sea in leaky canoes; of those who died . . . Many died.[64]

As in Kipling, then, action — 'the enemy of thought and the friend of flattering illusions'[65] — holds a central position among Conrad's tenets. But he never sought to forget that faith in activity was, ultimately, a mere expedient trumped up in order to secure an appallingly specious victory.

I have occasionally alluded to a Conradian idea of nature in these pages while examining its refraction in the idea of empire. It is possible now to look afresh at this idea, to say a little more about its character which will in turn enable us to define more closely Conrad's place in the Romantic tradition and the relationship of that tradition to the idea of empire.

To the question of how a Romantic would respond to a tropical rather than a lakeland nature we have in Conrad one answer — though he was so much of his own time that a tropical nature was an inevitable choice. Reflecting the now accepted alienation of subject from object and the subsequent enmity of a nature that means everything describable as non-self, the nature-symbol no longer provides what F. W. Bateson called 'the synthetic link between the conscious and the sub-conscious mind'.[66] Instead it indicates the perils which menace the conscious mind and heavily underlines its loneliness.

Kipling had once described man as 'at war with his surroundings in a world that does not care', but Conrad, though offering plenty of evidence that he shared the sentiment, has at the same time more of the Romantic yearning to prove it otherwise. In consequence, nature in his writings instead of reflecting simply chaos and anarchy sometimes discovers a spiritual vitality and a mystery: an entrée to which has for Conrad, almost in spite of himself, a baffled enchantment.

He looked into that great dark place odorous with the breath of life, with the mystery of existence, renewed, fecund, indestructible; and he felt afraid of his solitude, of the solitude of his body, of the loneliness of his soul in the presence of this unconscious and ardent struggle, of this lofty indifference, of this merciless and mysterious purpose, perpetuating strife and death through the march of ages. For the second time in his life he felt, in a sudden sense of his insignificance, the need to send a cry for help into the wilderness, and for the second time he realised the hopelessness of its unconcern.[67]

These moments are, however, clearly in the 'if only . . .' category. F. A. Lea once described Romanticism as the rediscovery of religion but emphasised that any theology which emerged had, for the genuine Romantic writer, to be one 'containing nothing that scepticism could impugn'. Because this condition could never be satisfied for him, Conrad's nostalgia for communion remains unindulged. Predominantly the alien natural world is a source of moral danger with its insidious power to corrupt a permanent reminder of the individual's vulnerability. As a result the Romantic concern for unity and harmony has been seen to contract to an appeal for solidarity — with inevitable recourse to all the other Kiplingesque slogans like discipline, loyalty, duty and idealism which could be made so satisfactorily to represent the imperial ethos.

Nature, then, is now a hostile principle but engagement with it is essential to self-consciousness: Stein's advice to Lord Jim had fully acknowledged the necessity — 'to the destructive element submit yourself and with the exertions of your hands and feet in the water make the deep, deep sea keep you up'. This paradox of an essentially destructive nature offering, nevertheless, a method of salvation is one which has much in common with an ambivalence acknowledged among the Romantic poets. It is, in fact, the fusion of two conceptions of nature which Professor Northrop Frye has polarised in Wordsworth and De Sade.

For Wordsworth the reality of Nature is manifested by its reflection of moral values; for De Sade the reality is concealed by that reflection. It is this ambivalent sense (for it is ambivalent, and not simply ambiguous) of appearance as at the same time revealing and concealing reality, as clothes simultaneously reveal and conceal the naked body, that makes *Sartor Resartus* so central a document of the Romantic movement. We spoke of Wordsworth's Nature as a mother-goddess, and her psychological descent from mother-figures is clearly traced in 'The Prelude'. The corngoddess in Keats' 'To Autumn', the parallel figure identified with Ruth in the 'Ode to a Nightingale', the still unravished bride of the Grecian urn, Psyche, even the veiled Melancholy, are all emblems of a revealed Nature. Elusive nymphs or teasing and mocking female figures who refuse to take definite form, like the figure in 'Alastor' or Blake's 'female will' types; terrible and sinister white goddesses like La Belle Dame sans Merci, or females associated with something forbidden or demonic, like the sister-lovers of Byron and Shelley, belong to the concealed aspect.

He adds later that Wordsworth's is a landscape nature and that this landscape is a veil dropped over the naked nature of screaming rabbits and gasping stags, the nature red in tooth and claw which haunted a later generation . . . But the more pessimistic, and perhaps more realistic, conception of nature in which it can be a source of evil or suffering as well as good is the one that gains ascendancy in the later period of Romanticism and its later period extends to our own day.[68]

Carlyle was particularly aware of the ambivalence sometimes voicing it in a manner notably analogous with Conrad's:

Nature, Universe, Destiny, Existence, howsoever we name this grand unnamable Fact in the midst of which we live and struggle, is as a heavenly bride and conquest to the wise and brave, to them who can discern her behests and do them; a destroying fiend to them who cannot. Answer her riddle, it is well with thee. Answer it not, pass on regarding it not, it will answer itself; the solution for thee is a thing of teeth and claws . . .

Even to the discerning and meritorious, nature will turn out to be 'but partially for him; will be wholly against him, if he constrain her not'. And his summary of man's situation is delivered in strikingly Conradian terms:

. . . a waste ocean threatens to devour him; if he front it not bravely, it will keep its word. By incessant wise defiance of it, lusty rebuke and buffet of it, behold how it loyally supports him, bears him as its conqueror along.[69]

The marine imagery is particularly appropriate here, for to Conrad the sea is, as it is for W. H. Auden, 'that state of barbaric vagueness and disorder out of which civilisation has emerged and into which unless saved by the effort of God and man, it is always liable to relapse'.[70] And out upon this sea Conrad puts man's ship freighted with those instruments which alone can ensure his survival. So that just as the exotic land menacing the imperial adventurer had been, the sea with its ship is also his expression of the Romantic ambivalence.

What are you, after all? Oh yes, we know. The greatest source of potential terror, a devouring enigma of space. Yes. But our lives have been nothing if not a continuous defiance of what you can do and what you may hold; a splendid and material defiance carried on in our plucky cockleshells, on and on beyond the successive provocations of your unreadable horizons.

Ah but the charm of the sea! Ah, yes, charm enough. Or rather a sort of unholy fascination as if an elusive nymph whose embrace is death, and a Medusa's head whose stare is terror. That sort of charm is calculated to keep men morally in order.[71]

As it proved to be in the case of Rudyard Kipling, the fundamental character of Conrad's work is found in his great awareness of man's essential estrangement. And for him, too, the tensions of empire serve to symbolise the struggle for consciousness, revealing in the process man's total dependence on the familiarity of his surroundings. But in Conrad the mind transcends the limits set for itself and the full extent of the predicament is ruthlessly exposed and explored — despite all his protestations of being content with a few simple notions and the task of reassuring the community of its integrity.

Repeatedly Kipling's basic awareness disappeared in the strong recommendation in which his appraisal of the human situation was nearly always made to terminate. For Conrad the awareness is the subject and the appraisal an end in itself. He makes no attempt to impose a solution nor to conceal the truth: and the most he offers as a *modus vivendi* is the starkest minimum — a steady, ever-conscious fidelity to one's own selfhood.

In the light of his courageous refusal to seek refuge in any cynical compromise, as well as for other reasons, it would be grossly mistaken to epitomise Conrad as 'the Kipling of the South Seas'. Nevertheless it is clear that the affinity is considerably more seminal than those who first coined the phrase ever imagined.

NOTES

1. Bertrand Russell, *Portraits from Memory* (1956), p. 82.
2. 'Autocracy and War', in *Notes on Life and Letters*, p. 107. All quotations are from the Medallion Edition of Conrad's works, 1925–8 (the Uniform Edition has the same pagination). The date of first publication of works referred to will be found in the bibliography.
3. *An Outpost of Progress*, pp. 88–89.
4. *An Outcast of the Islands*, p. 144.
5. *Victory*, p. 167.
6. *Almayer's Folly*, p. 179.
7. *An Outcast of the Islands*, p. 226.

8. *An Outcast of the Islands*, p. 226.

9. Ibid., p. 227, and see pp. 231–2 for another excellent example.

10. Ibid., p. 229.

11. *An Outcast of the Islands*, p. 230.

12. Ibid., p. 149.

13. Ibid., p. 228.

14. Ibid., p. 152.

15. Ibid., pp. 152, 153.

16. Ibid., p. 155.

17. Ibid., p. 359.

18. Ibid., p. 250.

19. *Heart of Darkness*, p. 96.

20. *Lord Jim*, p. 214.

21. *Victory*, pp. 198–200.

22. Ibid., p. 90.

23. Ibid., pp. 319–20.

24. Ibid., p. 174.

25. Emilia Gould, for example, or the blacksmith's wife in *Under Western Eyes* whose influence is described in these terms: 'He had become a dumb and despairing brute, till the woman's sudden, unexpected cry of profound pity, the insight of her feminine compassion discovering the complex misery of the man under the terrifying aspect of the monster, restored him to the ranks of humanity' (p. 124).

26. *Victory*, p. 329.

27. Ibid., p. 379.

28. R. Humphrey, *Georges Sorel*, p. 88.

29. Quoted by Jocelyn Baines, *Joseph Conrad* (1960), p. 365.

30. *The Planter of Malata*, p. 77.

31. Ibid., pp. 40–41.

32. *Heart of Darkness*, p. 93, and cf. p. 105.

33. *An Outcast of the Islands*, p. 198.

34. *Under Western Eyes*, p. 61.

35. *Lord Jim*, p. 223.

36. Cf. '[I do not] think resignation the last word of wisdom. I am too much the creature of my time for that' (*A Personal Record*, p. xxi).

37. *Heart of Darkness*, p. 94.

38. *Nostromo*, p. 85.

39. Ibid., pp. 511–12.

A study of *Nostromo* does not come within the scope of this book, but it is, of course, a story about moral corruption against a background of economic imperialism. The somewhat obvious leitmotive of the two 'gringo' adventurers who perished in their search for treasure, points the baleful influence of 'material interests', specifically represented in the book by the San Tomé mine. But as the story develops it comes to question the basic capacity of any personal ideal to withstand corruption. Not even the sensitive and aware Emilia Gould goes unscathed: she suppressed the information which Decoud brought her, so allowing the silver to come down from the mine — and ultimately bringing about the death of both Decoud and Nostromo. The latter, whose integrity is based on his conviction of his reputation's inviolability is also betrayed — he who had 'lived his own life on the assumption of unbroken fidelity, rectitude and courage'. However, he at least achieves — somewhat confusingly — a degree of triumph in transplanting an idea of himself to the mind of Linda whose protestation of devotion promises her remembrance.

40. *Heart of Darkness*, pp. 50–51.

41. *An Outpost of Progress*, pp. 136–7.

42. Thomas Carlyle, *Past and Present*, pp. 189–90.

43. *Heart of Darkness*, p. 68.

44. *An Outcast of the Islands*, p. 87.

45. *Lord Jim*, pp. 50–51.

46. *A Personal Record*, p. xxi.

47. *Lord Jim*, p. 43.

48. Thomas Carlyle, *Sartor Resartus*, pp. 147, 151.

49. It should be noted that this is less marked in the later stories.

50. D. H. Lawrence, 'Chaos in Poetry', in *Selected Literary Criticism*, ed. Beal (1955), p. 90.

51. *Victory*, p. 196.

52. 'Tradition', in *Notes on Life and Letters*, p. 194.

53. *Lord Jim*, p. 313.

54. *The Nigger of the Narcissus*, p. x.

55. 'Well Done', in *Notes on Life and Letters*, p. 190, and cf. *The Secret Agent*, p. 53.

56. *Karain*, pp. 8–9.

57. *An Outcast of the Islands*, p. 209.

58. Thomas Carlyle, *Past and Present*, p. 129.

59. *The Return*, p. 176.

60. Robert Penn Warren, 'The Great Mirage', in *Selected Essays* (New York, 1958).

61. Baines, op. cit., p. 449.

62. *Heart of Darkness*, p. 78.

63. *Nostromo*, p. 497.

64. *An Outcast of the Islands*, pp. 54–55.

65. *Nostromo*, p. 66.

66. F. W. Bateson, *English Poetry: A Critical Introduction* (1950), p. 126.

67. *An Outcast of the Islands*, p. 337.

68. Northrop Frye, 'The Drunken Boat', in *Romanticism Reconsidered*, ed. Frye (1963), pp. 20–21.

69. Thomas Carlyle, *Past and Present*, pp. 7, 198, 199.

70. W. H. Auden, *The Enchafèd Flood*.

71. 'Well Done', in *Notes on Life and Letters*, pp. 184–5.

CHAPTER SIX

John Buchan:
The Church of Empire

*The essence of the system was not preaching or propaganda,
though it was prolific of both, but the attempt to crystallise a
moral ideal in the daily life of a visible society, which should be at
once a Church and a State.*

R. H. TAWNEY

I

So far, in these studies, we have discovered the real nature of the
imperial idea to be, for Kipling and Conrad, something remote
from politics: something altogether organic to their total artistic
vision which itself springs from their sensitivity to the unpalatable
fact of man's essential isolation.

The same is true in the case of Buchan. But if, for the other two,
and Kipling especially, the empire had something of the quality of
myth, for the earlier Buchan it was dogma: and where for Kipling
the imperial idea was more a self-system than a social or political
blueprint, for Buchan it was both. Investing empire with an altogether ecclesiastical significance he looked on it as a God-given
means whereby man in his secular condition could be integrated
with his spiritual ideal.

Perhaps it was just because the empire was for him not so much
a symbol as a way of life that he alone of the three writers discussed
here found its earlier significance ultimately inadequate. The vision
which had found a congenial vehicle for the expression of its moral
dialectic in the 'practical ideal' of Empire was a developing one:
and when the vehicle itself revealed its inherent weakness and
instability his reorientation was accelerated.

Buchan's unremitting search for a synthetic philosophy which would satisfy all of man's aspirations and accord him the completest self-fulfilment gives a moral basis even to the slightest of his adventure stories.

We want a key to life, an ideal which will leave out nothing and completely satisfy the hunger in our hearts. When you were a child and invented fairy-lands you brought into them everything you loved — cats and dogs and toys and people — and so with the bigger fairy-land we make when we grow up. Everything shades sooner or later into metaphysics, and the humblest difficulty — if we press it home — brings us within hailing distance of the Infinite.[1]

For a moment it seemed that imperialism offered just such a philosophy. In the end, however, what had actually appeared to be the great cathedral itself was dwarfed to an ante-chapel before his greater and infinitely more humble discovery.

Since the literary significance of the imperial idea is here so markedly part of a developing process the following chapter takes a much more synoptic view of the writer's work than was the case in the preceding studies. In any event, the number of purely 'imperial' novels is very small, though in another sense they are all of this character. Certainly very few avoid all contact with the imperial idiom whether it manifests itself in virile sons of empire like Hannay and Peter Pienaar, called in to supplement the native resources of Sir Archie Roylance and Sandy Arbuthnot, or in the numerous flatly assertive statements of the race's imperial capacity. In the last section of this chapter it is made clear just how much the 'philosophy' of the early Buchan hero reflects the creed of his author's 'Church of Empire': a creed which, as the intervening sections show, turned out to be remarkably sterile.

2

When in *Sick Heart River* Eric Ravelston says of Francis Galliard, 'I thought there was something pathological about his marvellous vitality',[2] we are aware of having, at one time or another, come to a similar conclusion about most of the Arbuthnot–Hannay–Roylance set, as they sweep the earth in their romantic and tireless conquest of space. Only, of course, we are aware that this malaise has its roots not in the body but — as in Galliard's case — in the mind.

Action in Buchan is of a familiar duality. There is Puritan

activism, holding idleness a sin before God and work an ethical duty, and there is what might be called 'existential' activism practised in order to externalise and identify the self or to fortify moral integrity. The second variety may sometimes manifest itself in a Homeric ideal:

> 'Gift this guerdon and grant this grace,
>   That I bid good-e'en,
> The sword in my hand and my foot to the race,
> The wind in my teeth and the rain in my face.'
>   'Be it so', said the Queen.[3]

— or in a simplified version of the Kipling–Conrad doctrine which we find Wratislaw recommending in *The Half-Hearted*:

The great things of the world have all been done by men who didn't stop to reflect on them. If a man comes to a halt and analyses his motives and distrusts the value of the thing he strives for, then the odds are that his halt is final. You strive to strive and not to attain.[4]

Leithen sustains the same argument in rather more Conradian terms in *The Gap in the Curtain*.

The pastoral world was not mine; my world was down below in the valley where men and women were fretting and puzzling. . . . I no longer thought of them as on a raft looking at misty seas, but rather as spectators on a ridge, trying to guess what lay beyond the next hill. Tavanger and Mayot and Goodeve — they were all at it. A futile game, maybe, but inevitable, since what lay beyond the hill was life and death to them. I must recapture the mood for this guessing game, for it was the mainspring of effort and therefore of happiness.[5]

Such convictions will, of course, bring their possessors into conflict with those who base their conduct on a more uncompromising, intellectualist position. Launcelot Wake, for instance, only gets by because in Blenkiron's words 'a nootral can have a share in a scrap as well as a belligerent',[6] and he worthily seizes his opportunity. The 'laboratory of thought' — the pacifist enclave of Biggleswick — full of 'an abundance of young men mostly rather weedy-looking, but with one or two well-grown ones who should have been fighting',[7] comes in for a severe drubbing, particularly with 'our fellows out there . . . sweating blood to keep these fools snug' [8] in mind. It was, of course, their 'babyish innocence' that lay at the bottom of their attitude and thus some leniency could be shown for their waywardness, although it was a lot to ask any man to sojourn for long in their company:

> You have got to sink down deep into the life of the half-baked, the people whom this war hasn't touched or has touched in the wrong way, the people who split hairs all day and are engrossed in what you and I would call selfish little fads. Yes. People like my aunts and Launcelot, only for the most part in a different social grade.[9]

Nevertheless it would be a mistake to assume a lack of awareness in Buchan or an ignorance of what he was rejecting: even more so that he was merely expressing the contemptuous view of a bluff, hearty, athleticism for all 'rootless intellectuals' whose talk was 'the kind of thing you would expect — terribly knowing and disillusioned and conscientiously indecent'.[10] He saw perfectly clearly what the price would be:

> ... you can't bring yourself down to the world of compromises, which is the world of action. You have lost the practical touch. You muddled your fight with Stocks because you couldn't get out of touch with your own little world in practice, however you might manage it in theory. You can't be single-hearted. Twenty impulses are always pulling different ways with you, and the result is that you become an unhappy, self-conscious waverer.[11]

The call to Action and Doing ('You are one of the *doers*, Mr. Brand,' says the intellectual Jimson wistfully, 'and I could find it in my heart to envy you')[12] should for the good of the soul be answered, but the cost will not be light. A large part of one's sensibility must be shut off: and the restless search for absolutes forcibly made to terminate in an enthusiastic welcome for the illusory superlative. The self is being brought firmly under control, horizons are lowered and sacrifice made to Kipling's God of Things as They Are. His world has been determined: the dangerous element has been safely anaesthetised and there now remains only the assumption of the requisite ideals for his redefined world, and the descent into the arena.

> 'What would you call the highest happiness, Lewie?' he asked.
> 'The sense of competence,' was the answer, given without hesitation.
> 'Right. And what do we mean by competence? Not success! God knows it is something very different from success! Any fool may be

successful, if the gods wish to hurt him. Competence means that splendid joy in your own powers and the approval of your own heart, which great men feel always and lesser men now and again at favoured intervals. There are a certain number of things in the world to be done, and we have got to do them. We may fail — it doesn't in the least matter. We may get killed in the attempt — it matters still less. The things may not altogether be worth doing — it is of very little importance. It is ourselves we have got to judge by. If we are playing our part well, and know it, then we can thank God and go on. That is what I call happiness.'[13]

Even then, there are times when the dangerous element seems too near consciousness and things — even within the chosen world — threaten Lewie with defeat.

He had got his chance and the rest lay with himself. It was a chance of high adventure, a great mission, a limitless future. At the thought the old fever began to rise in his blood. . . . And then there came back on him, like a flood, the dumb misery of incompetence which had weighed on heart and brain. The hatred of the whole struggling, sordid crew, all the cant and ugliness and ignorance of a mad world, his weakness in the face of it, his fall from common virtue, his nerveless indolence — all stung him like needle points, till he cried out in agony. Anything to deliver his soul from such a bondage, . . .[14]

The answer is found in vigorous, decisive action, in more and wilder doing, in an increasing self-renunciation which leads to its logical conclusion — the glorious last stand at the mouth of the Pass against impossible odds, and the sacrificial offering of the battered body lying 'wrinkled across the path'.

No man any more should call him a dreamer. It pleased him to think that, half-hearted and sceptical as he had been, a humorist, a laughing philosopher, he was now dying for one of the catchwords of the crowd. He had returned to the homely paths of the commonplace, and young, unformed, untried, he was caught up by kind fate to the place of the wise and the heroic.[15]

'I will not link my fortunes to one who is half-hearted, for in this cause it must be venture all,' says Sabine to Peter in *The Blanket of the Dark*.[16] Total, single-hearted commitment to the job in hand is the resolution arrived at in *The Half-Hearted*, one of Buchan's earliest novels, where Lewie makes his soul in a desperate engagement on the battle-line of empire.

L

The vulgar little fears, which, like foxes, gnaw at the roots of the heart, had gone, even the greater perils of faint hope and a halting energy. The half-hearted had become the stout-hearted. The resistless vigour of the strong and the simple was his.[17]

And from then (1900) until *The Blanket of the Dark* (1931) it is not openly controverted.

So far there is a strong resemblance to Kipling both in the thinking and in the resolution. But Buchan was one of Professor Teufelsdröckh's few for whom a solution was indispensable: a solution of compromises would not do.

Long before 1931 the anaesthetic had begun to weaken, and an occasional restlessness flowed across the stern, refined image. But the image, on the whole so clear, is first cut in this early story. Later it becomes familiar enough to bore: the rigidity of the concept is reflected in the rigidity of the image. Hannay's character is established hopelessly beyond doubt, but in Lewie we see that character being slowly put together and taking shape, with real doubt and uncertainty and a great deliberateness. Even physical features are seen here to be in process of evolution: Lewie's face is 'keen, kindly, humorous, cultured, with strong lines ending weakly, a face over-bred, brave and finical'.[18] But by the end these too have become the prototype for Hannay, Clanroyden and the rest; and the strong lines end as strongly as they began. It is interesting to compare Wratislaw's words to Lewie in *The Half-Hearted* with Bullivant's to Hannay in *Greenmantle*. Both men are presented with difficult and perilous assignments. Wratislaw is speaking in the first, Bullivant in the second:

I am giving you the brave man's choice, Lewie. You will be going out to uncertainty and difficulty and extreme danger. On the other hand, I believe in my soul it will harden you into the man you ought to be. Lord knows I would rather have you stay at home.[19]

I may be sending you to your death, Hannay — Good God, what a damned task-mistress duty is! — If so, I shall be haunted with regrets, but *you* will never regret. Have no fear of that. You have chosen the roughest road, but it goes straight to the hill-tops.[20]

Hannay takes a few seconds to make up his mind, Lewie three days. The image was created by the latter's decision and for the next twenty years at least it represented the idiom of Buchan's fiction —

but, as Bullivant demonstrates, becoming a completely unreal and theatrical mask in the process.

With this careful definition and delimitation of space comes its corollary in his attitude to time. So he looks back to time that has been mastered — to the petrification of time past: often to the ordered, gracious, stable England of one of his favourite authors, Izaak Walton. Feeling himself dwarfed by the inscrutable forces of nature and conscious of little but the 'feeble unit' of the self and the vastness of time, this careful hoarding and reckoning gave a precious rootedness:

> No man can harm us of the old England and the older blood. Kings and nobles and priests may pass but we remain. Ours is the *fallentis semita vitae*, which is beyond the ken of the great.[21]

Hob of Kipling's Puck stories represents exactly the same quality. Buchan, whose search for self-fulfilment constantly threatened to end in self-effacement, lingered over the prospect it offered of a final retreat from the great struggle:

> In that moment I had a kind of revelation. I had a vision of what I had been fighting for, what we all were fighting for. It was peace, deep and holy and ancient, peace older than the oldest wars, peace which would endure when all our swords were hammered into ploughshares. It was more; for in that hour England first took hold of me. Before, my country had been South Africa, and when I thought of home it had been the wide sun-steeped spaces of the veld or some scented glen of the Berg. But now I realized that I had a new home. I understood what a precious thing this little England was, how old and kindly and comforting, how wholly worth striving for . . . in that hour I had a prospect as if from a hilltop which made all the present troubles of the road seem of no account. I saw not only victory after war, but a new and happier world after victory, when I should inherit something of this English peace and wrap myself in it till the end of my days.[22]

In this context it is not surprising to find on one occasion Hannay rather wistfully recognising Peter Pienaar's genius 'for living in the moment' and on another Leithen envying 'the people who live happily in the present'. For Buchan with his greater sensitivity such a way out was impossible: for him the movement of time was distressingly clear and to it those ideals evolved to establish the self were hopelessly, inevitably, vulnerable.

It was about myself that I felt most dismally. Lombard's youth had gone, but so had my own. Lombard was settled like Moab on his lees, but so was I. We all make pictures of ourselves that we try to live up to, and mine had always been of somebody hard and taut who could preserve to the last day of life a decent vigour of spirit. Well, I kept my body in fair training by exercise, but I realized that my soul was in danger of fatty degeneration. I was too comfortable. I had all the blessings a man can have, but I wasn't earning them. I tried to tell myself that I deserved a little peace and quiet, but I got no good from that reflection, for it meant that I had accepted old age ... Then I became angry with myself. 'You are a fool,' I said. 'You are becoming soft and elderly, which is the law of life, and you haven't the grit to grow old cheerfully.' That put a stopper on my complaints, but it left me dejected and only half-convinced.[23]

The same feeling, it might be remembered, is found in Kipling's post-war writings, and largely from the same cause. Instances of it in Buchan's work could be multiplied: there is Leithen, for example, who deliberately tried to recreate his life at Oxford and his early days at the Bar.

It wasn't sentiment but a deliberate attempt to put the clock back, and, by recalling the feelings of twenty-five, to convince myself that I had once been a strong man ...[24]

And there is his frequent recognition of the emphasis which war gives to disruption and change. It might be possible under special circumstances to penetrate the gap in the curtain: it was certainly impossible to forget that it was there. Man, to preserve his moral integrity, immerses himself in the world of actuality which lies in front of the curtain, but he is aware of what lies beyond: 'Civilisation anywhere is a very thin crust.'[25] The actual is in constant conflict with the non-actual, the self with the non-self, in Buchan's fiction:

'This hill-top is bad for me,' he once told her. 'I have no facts to work upon and I begin to make pictures. Wasn't it Napoleon who said that we should never think in pictures, but always look at things as if through a telescope — bring reality close to one, but always reality?'

'Isn't that begging the question?' the girl replied. 'Reality for us is what we make of things. We may make them conform to our pictures. It is what we all do. ...'[26]

Reality, that is, is self-created, with no external validity or justification — an illusion of the mind. Aware of this, though not pushing his awareness any further, Buchan saw, like Conrad, the need for working within the framework of the illusion. And he worked to some purpose, bringing to bear on his world an intelligence which sifted and analysed the facts with a notable discrimination:

Most countries will flatter her [America] and kowtow to her and borrow money of her, but they hate her like hell. Trust them not to help matters by interpreting her case sympathetically. Inside her borders she has half a dozen nations instead of one, and that is where Castor comes in. A situation like that, when she was forced to act and yet didn't want to and didn't know how to, might, if properly manipulated, split her from top to bottom. Look what happened in the Civil War, and she was an integrated nation then compared to what she is now.[27]

It was, too, an imaginative intelligence, which enabled him to predict the pattern of a later 'reality'.

'You may hear people say . . . that submarines have done away with the battleship, and that aircraft have annulled the mastery of the sea. That is what our pessimists say. But do you imagine that the clumsy submarine or the fragile aeroplane is really the last word of science?'

'No doubt they will develop,' I said, 'but by that time the power of the defence will have advanced also.' He shook his head. 'It is not so. Even now the knowledge which makes possible great engines of destruction is far beyond the capacity of any defence.'[28]

His remarkable understanding of the political aspect of this reality led him to his percipient comments later in the same story. The passage is a long one but requires to be quoted in full: Lumley is talking of his knowledge of great extra-social intelligences:

'Let us say that they distrust the machine. They may be idealists and desire to make a new world, or they may simply be artists, loving for its own sake the pursuit of truth. If I were to hazard a guess, I should say that it took both types to bring about the results, for the second find the knowledge and the first the will to use it.'

A recollection came back to me. It was of a hot upland meadow in Tyrol, where among acres of flowers and beside a leaping stream I was breakfasting after a morning spent in climbing the white crags. I had picked up a German on the way, a small man of the Professor class, who did me the honour to share my sandwiches. He conversed fluently but quaintly in English, and he was, I remember, a Nietzschean and a hot rebel against the established order. 'The pity,' he cried, 'is that the reformers do not know, and those who know are too idle to reform. Some day there will come the marriage of knowledge and will, and then the world will march.'

'You draw an awful picture,' I said. 'But if those extra-social brains are so potent, why after all do they effect so little? A dull police-officer, with the machine behind him, can afford to laugh at most experiments in anarchy.'

'True,' he said, 'and civilisation will win until its enemies learn from it the importance of the machine. The compact must endure until there is a counter-compact. Consider the ways of that form of foolishness which today we call nihilism or anarchy. A few illiterate bandits in a Paris slum defy the world, and in a week they are in jail. Half a dozen crazy Russian *intellectuels* in Geneva conspire to upset the Romanovs, and are hunted down by the police of Europe. All the Governments and their not very intelligent police forces join hands, and hey, presto! there is an end of the conspirators. For civilisation knows how to use such powers as it has, while the immense potentiality of the unlicensed is dissipated in vapour. Civilisation wins because it is a world-wide league; its enemies fail because they are parochial. But supposing . . . anarchy learned from civilisation and became international. Oh, I don't mean the bands of advertising donkeys who call themselves International Unions of Workers and such-like rubbish. I mean if the real brain-stuff of the world were internationalised. Suppose that the links in the cordon of civilisation were neutralised by other links in a far more potent chain. The earth is seething with incoherent power and unorganised intelligence. Have you ever reflected on the case of China? There you have millions of quick brains stifled in trumpery crafts. They have no direction, no driving power, so the sum of their efforts is futile, and the world laughs at China. Europe throws her a million or two on loan now and then, and she cynically responds by begging the prayers of Christendom. And yet, I say, supposing . . .'

'It's a horrible idea,' I said, 'and, thank God, I don't believe it possible. Mere destruction is too barren a creed to inspire a new Napoleon, and you can do with nothing short of one.'

'It would scarcely be destruction,' he replied gently. 'Let us call it iconoclasm, the swallowing of formulas, which has always had its full retinue of idealists. And you do not want a Napoleon. All that is needed is direction, which could be given by men of far lower gifts than a Bonaparte. In a word, you want a Powerhouse, and then the age of miracles will begin.'[29]

Lumley's argument is far too cogent for us to classify his creator as either impercipient or unrealistic.

Buchan — quite justifiably — would today have argued that all this has taken place, that the idealist and the artist, the knowledge and the will, have met up in the communist scientist. Only, such organisation is not anti-civilisation but anti-Western 'civilisation'; and when Buchan uses the word he really means society as he knows it. It is, however, interesting to notice that he posits the alternative 'civilisation' himself, almost without noticing it.

> But there is one kind of fanatic whose strength comes from balance, from a lunatic balance. You cannot say that there is any one thing abnormal about him, for he is all abnormal. He is as balanced as you or me, but, so to speak, in a fourth-dimensional world. That kind of man has no logical gaps in his creed. Within his insane postulates he is brilliantly sane. Take Lenin for instance. That's the kind of fanatic I'm afraid of.[30]

The insanity of the fourth-dimensional world only means that the speaker finds it utterly repugnant and inimical to his own fundamentals.

Reality, then, was a man-made thing begetting in turn concepts like 'society' and 'civilisation' whose illusory independent existence all men conspire to maintain:

> 'You forget one thing,' I said — 'the fact that men really are agreed to keep the machine going. That is what I called the "goodwill of civilisation".' He got up from his chair and walked up and down the floor . . .
> 'You have put your finger on the one thing that matters. Civilisation is a conspiracy . . . Modern life is the silent compact of comfortable folk to keep up pretences. And it will succeed till the day comes when there is another compact to strip them bare.'[31]

Not quite all men are so agreed, however, and it is those extra-social intelligences which constitute the villain in Buchan's work: Lumley, Castor, Medina, D'Ingraville, The Black Stone group, all are deeply hostile to established society and all have plans for its overthrow.

> . . . the absent Skipper had become to them no longer a colleague but a master. They were people whose plans lay well inside the pale of what we call civilisation. They had reputations to lose, ambitions which demanded some respect for the conventions, comfortable lives which they were not inclined to sacrifice. But they had become yoked to one who cared for

none of these things, a man from the outlands who had long ago discarded their world.[32]

The reason behind the insistence on universal observance of the compact is as clear as it was in Kipling's case: anyone outside it, like D'Ingraville who came 'from the outlands', was a potential danger, and all the more so if organised. The Buchan heroes spend most of their time striving to prevent just this, fighting to prevent the fulfilment of Lumley's vision which has revealed so clearly their society's vulnerability:

. . . I read now and then in the papers that some eminent scientist has made a great discovery. He reads a paper before some Academy of Science, and there are leading articles on it, and his photograph adorns the magazines. That kind of man is not the danger. He is a bit of the machine, a party to the compact. It is the men who stand outside it that are to be reckoned with, the artists in discovery who will never use their knowledge till they can use it with full effect.[33]

And as in Kipling and Conrad, the destruction of one's own society, with its attendant anarchy and chaos, means the destruction of the self. Buchan's world is still solipsist: integrity of the self is still being sought in terms of its physical environment. As the men in Conrad's *An Outpost of Progress* came to realise, identity can only be maintained with the help of a familiar environment, human and natural, which one can understand. Hence the danger of the unfamiliar. When the captured agent Ivery was suddenly placed in a milieu which was utterly alien to him he understood the meaning of this. 'He was in a hard, unfamiliar world, in the grip of something which he feared and didn't understand, in the charge of men who were in no way amenable to his persuasiveness.'[34] Leithen's acceptance that, '. . . life is a prosaic thing and if you are to have marvels in it you should take them in your stride . . .'[35] also recognises the danger and paraphrases Kipling in *Beyond the Pale*. Many of the villainous antagonists in these novels express their dangerousness precisely through the medium of their catalytic strangeness and unfamiliarity; they are outside the circle and therefore are seen to threaten it. Thus we have the 'mysterious' Hilda von Einem who was not simply to be described in Blenkiron's terms as 'mad and bad':

I did not think they were the proper terms, for they belonged to the narrow world of our common experience. This was something beyond and above it, as a cyclone or an earthquake is outside the decent routine of nature.[36]

Hannay's words may come near to describing Hilda: they certainly serve one of the many painful reminders that Buchan is, for the most part, completely lacking in any subtlety of organisation or expression. When he adds to this an owlish *naïveté* the consequences can be disastrously risible. Stumm's eccentric and insidious threat to solidarity, for instance, is symbolised in his homosexuality, the narrator recoiling in horror and alarm from a prospect so full of menace:

. . . there had never been a woman's hand in that place. It was the room of a man who had a passion for frippery, who had a perverted taste for soft delicate things. It was the complement to his bluff brutality. I began to see the queer other side to my host, that evil side which gossip had spoken of as not unknown in the German army. The room seemed a horribly unwholesome place, and I was more than ever afraid of Stumm.[37]

Awareness of a civilisation 'compact', then, posits awareness of the anti-civilisation, anti-self forces which constitute a permanent threat. The anarchic primitive, reminding us so forcibly of the man-made nature of the concept, is, as in Conrad, a particular anathema. Unfortunately, the expression of this idea too frequently suffers from being couched in what can only be described as the classical Buchan idiom:

As I looked on, I had a sharp impression of the change which five years had brought. This was not, like a pre-war ball, part of the ceremonial of an assured and orderly world. These people were dancing as savages danced — to get rid of or to engender excitement. Apollo had been ousted by Dionysos. The nigger in the band, who came forward now and then and sang some gibberish, was the true master of ceremonies. . . .[38]

A more delicate touch is required, however, if the heart of darkness is to be made manifest in Chelsea. The idea fares a little better later in the same story, which is, as a whole, very much concerned with the reaction of the primitive on the civilised. Janni and Leithen are staring in fascination at the pagan scene on the Dancing Floor:

The place was no more the Valley of the Shadow of Life, but Life itself — a surge of daemonic energy out of the deeps of the past. It was wild and yet ordered, savage and yet sacramental, the home of an ancient knowledge which shattered for me the modern world and left me gasping like a caveman before his mysteries. The magic smote on my brain, though I struggled against it. The passionless moonlight and the passionate torches — that, I think, was the final miracle — a marrying of the eternal cycle of nature with fantasies of man.

The effect on Janni was overwhelming. He lay and gibbered prayers with eyes as terrified as a deer's, and I realised that I need not look for help in that quarter. But I scarcely thought of him, for my trouble was with myself. Most people would call me a solid fellow, with a hard head and a close-textured mind, but if they had seen me then they would have changed their view. I was struggling with something which I had never known before, a mixture of fear, abasement and a crazy desire to worship. Yes — to worship.[39]

While one would not wish to push the analogy very far it is obvious that Leithen's thought has distinct affinities with Marlow's.

After the Great War in particular, it seemed to Buchan that civilisation became increasingly vulnerable to this enemy within. You could no longer 'take the clear psychology of most civilised human beings for granted. Something was welling up from primeval deeps to muddy it.'[40] And with all this there arises in him a growing desire, half romantic and half ascetic, for a more extraneous self-fulfilment: a growing realisation that the fullest and most enduring integrity would not be found by excluding the non-self but in communion with it. Describing the spiritual nostalgia of the Turks and Arabs he wrote,

They want to live face to face with God without a screen of ritual and images and priestcraft. They want to prune life of its foolish fringes and get back to the noble bareness of the desert and the empty sky that cast their spell over them — these, and the hot, strong, antiseptic sunlight which burns up all rot and decay. . . . It isn't inhuman. It's the humanity of one part of the human race. It isn't ours. It isn't as good as ours, but it's jolly good all the same. There are times when it grips me so hard that I'm inclined to forswear the gods of my fathers![41]

There is intense personal feeling in this, and the theme is repeated elsewhere. When he says that 'it isn't as good as ours' we get the impression that the reference is to a purely utilitarian good.

Within the terms of the compact, however, one finds identity and stability and an anodyne for self-destructive thoughts.[42] This

could not be more clearly expressed than in *The Half-Hearted*;
indeed, it is what this novel of empire is about.

A man must have that direct practical virtue which forgets itself and
sees only its work. Parsons will tell you that all virtue is self-sacrifice,
and they are right, though not in the way they mean. It may all seem a
tissue of contradictions. You must not pitch on too fanciful a goal, nor
on the other hand, must you think on yourself. And it is a contradiction
which only resolves itself in practice, one of those anomalies on which
the world is built up.[43]

This is a clear and Kiplingesque statement of creed: the sacrifice of
the self to work and duty where the goal is never remote from
actual life and 'formulas and shallow little ideals' never become
gods: where the sacrifice can be kept clear of self-conscious introspection which would defeat the whole plan since it creates 'the
egotist whose eye is always filled with his own figure, who investi-
gates his motives, and hesitates and finicks, till Death knocks him
on the head and there is an end of him.'[44]

Civilisation and the reality of actuality is a carefully fostered
illusion, impermanent and without intrinsic value; materially one
dwells within it, spiritually one is wholly detached. Puritanically,
Buchan despises the world in which he makes his soul. At the
beginning of a very much later work, *A Prince of the Captivity*,
published in 1929, he quotes 'The Emperor Akbar's inscription
at Fatehpur-Sikri':

Thus said Jesus upon whom be peace. The world is a bridge; pass
over it but build no house upon it.

And later in that book Mr. Scrope expounds Duty as

'a thing both terrible and sweet, transcending life and death, a bridge
over the abyss to immortality. But it requires the service of all of a man's
being, and no half-gods must cumber its altar . . . "He that findeth his
life shall lose it" . . . That is not enough', he added, 'He that findeth his
soul shall lose it — that is the greater commandment.'[45]

It is something much greater than life which one finds and loses,
it is the self-made and self-sustained integrity of soul, of moral
being.

At times this self-dedication is so strenuously insisted on that
it almost amounts to a death-wish.

A new kind of peace fell upon him. It was not the peace of the fakir who has renounced everything for the high road and the begging-bowl, but something more absolute still, for Adam did not ask for a hope of Heaven. Even Eilean Ban dropped out of his picture. He was content to lay himself under the eternal plough . . . He took to prayer, which was a kind of communing with his own soul . . . And finally there came a night when he dedicated himself humbly yet exultingly to whatever uttermost service might be asked, and rose from his knees with the certainty that his vow had been accepted.[46]

Immortality has no character suggested whatsoever: there is not the faintest hint of bliss everlasting; it is simply the unknown.

3

Buchan, then, is acutely concerned with the relationship of self and non-self. Conradian images of littleness in the face of Immensity abound, but with Buchan there is always the tendency towards an abject surrender to the non-self which he seeks increasingly to identify with God:

He had forgotten the author, but bit by bit he managed to build up one quatrain, and it seemed to run something like this:

'Come ill, come well, the cross, the crown,
    The rainbow or the thunder —
I fling my soul and body down,
    For God to plough them under.'

There was a strange fascination in the idea . . . He had always drawn comfort from the thought that, while it was a man's duty to strive to the uttermost, the result was determined by mightier things than man's will. He had believed most devoutly in God, though he would have been puzzled to define his creed. Suddenly there came over him a sense of the microscopic littleness and the gossamer fragility of human life. Everything lay in the hands of God, though men fussed and struggled and made a parade of freedom. Might not there be a more potent strength in utter surrender?'[47]

For Buchan the awareness of the individual's fragility produced an intensification of desire for an assimilation so complete that all doubts and conflicts would be resolved, and the fragment of troubled consciousness consumed in a sublime passivity. It is this great yearning for communion which gives so much of his work its mystic character, and increasingly he involves it in a theological pattern. Even then, however, a real equilibrium has not been reached. Man, for some time, remains merely 'an atom in infinite space' casting around him a little way into the vastness a brief, warm glow. But space — the non-self — according to Father Duplessis at least, is God.

'Do you never feel crushed by this vastness?' he asked. 'This country is out-size.'

'No,' was the answer, 'for I live in a little world. I am always busy among little things. I skin a moose, or build a boat, or hammer a house together, or treat a patient, or cobble my boots or patch my coat — all little things. And then I have the offices of the Church, in a blessedly small space, for our chapel is a midget.'

'But outside all that?' said Leithen, 'you have an empty world and an empty sky.'

'Not empty,' said Father Duplessis smiling, 'for it is filled with God. I cannot say, like Pascal, "le silence éternel de ces espaces infinis m'effraie." There is no silence here, for when I straighten my back and go out of doors the world is full of voices. When I was in my Picardy country there were little fields like a parterre, and crowded roads. There, indeed, I knew loneliness — but not here, where man is nothing and God is all.'[48]

And Leithen by the end of the book realises this, and in doing so recognises the bridge which will connect the self to the non-self, which is space, which is God.

Before analysing the connective, however, it is worth recalling the young man's answer in the confident defence by Hannay and his confrères of their solipsist world, as they suppress with the most nonchalant exertion of imperial sinews the slightest threat to their carefully arranged society. The unfamiliar and the remote within the actual world had to be mastered for the sake of making one's soul — in either the Puritan or the Kiplingesque sense: thus Sandy's astonishing prowess in the art of disguise, penetrating (and thereby destroying) the mystery of Turkish gipsies and South American *vaqueros* alike. For the same reason we have that far-flung knowingness which at times reads like a parody of the strain found both in Kipling and, to a less extent, in Conrad.

'Where did you find out this story?' I asked.

'I got the first hint in an inn on the Achensee in Tyrol. That set me enquiring, and I collected my other clues in a fur-shop in the Galician quarter of Buda, in a Strangers' Club in Vienna, and in a little bookshop off the Racknitzstrasse in Leipsig. I completed my evidence ten days ago in Paris.'[49]

To return, however, to the connective between God — as the non-self has become — and man. Briefly stated, it is humanity. Although in the earlier books we find a considerable amount of lip-service paid to humanity, it is rarely, if ever, more than this. The self-sacrifice that we hear about in *The Half-Hearted* is, we are told, not the sort the parson means. And this is precisely true. Lewie's self-sacrifice in the foothills of the Himalayas is for an extremely selfish ideal, and is the logical conclusion to his ideal of service. That is, the self, for its own good, for a sense of its own competence, must be fused in the job, the service: the completest fusion will demand the completest physical self-sacrifice. In death he smugly perfects the integrity of his moral existence.

Having made their souls, a phrase used frequently by Buchan, his heroes selfishly continue to behave with something very near to arrogance towards humanity. The dashing action itself is self-assertion rather than self-sacrifice. Nothing is to be allowed to threaten society, or, through it, the integrity of the self: and death in such service is, to repeat, merely the perfection of integrity. In political terms this is, of course, a philosophy of stagnation which will, by and large, petrify society in the state it has reached: hence we get the rigidly stratified and rigidly defended social organisation of the Buchan novel and its sometimes nauseating class-consciousness.

The Half-Hearted was published in 1900 and for over twenty years this thinking is the foundation for his writings. But it becomes increasingly obvious that the price, clearly anticipated in the enunciation of the creed in this book, is proving too much. The action in the later novels is sustained now with less of the earlier wholeheartedness, and the gusto of the brave young man's world is sadly diminished by a pervasive despondency and a gradually accelerating withdrawal of confidence.

At this point we might give some brief attention to the McCunn novels, for it is with the first of these — *Huntingtower* which appeared in 1922 — that a shift in emphasis becomes obvious. In the earlier novels, and, though to a less extent, even in many of the later,

Buchan invested the aristocracy with the middle-class virtues of efficiency and competence (thereby largely creating the image of the British Colonial Governor and Administrator as seemingly casual and unprofessional, yet beneath it all amazingly informed and wholly efficient). His was the ideal of a secularised Puritanism, an ideal of personal character and conduct. But for Buchan these had appeared best described in the idea of aristocracy. His stoicism in itself demanded an austere nobility among the doers — a quality which he obviously failed to associate with the middle-class. But with the passing of the phase of Great Action in the aftermath of the war, the innate validity which the middle-class ideal held for him was almost bound to reassert itself and does so in the centrality which Dickson McCunn, 'a retired provision merchant', holds in three of the later novels. We still feel that he achieves this position in spite of his trade, but his presence is no mere accident or whim. Saskia says of him,

> He is the *petit bourgeois*, the *épicier*, the class which the world ridicules. He is unbelievable. The others with good fortune I might find elsewhere — in Russia perhaps. But not Dickson.

and Alesha replies,

> No ... You will not find him in Russia. He is what they call the middle-class, which we who were foolish used to laugh at. But he is the stuff which above all others makes a great people. He will endure when aristocracies crack and proletariats crumble. In our own land we have never known him, but till we create him our land will not be a nation.[50]

This does not mean that aristocracy was rejected in favour of the once-despised middle-class;[51] it does mean, however, that his stoicism is beginning to weaken. Even the irrepressible Sir Archie suffers a change of tone and a surprising lapse in confidence:

> I don't mind runnin' some kinds of risks — I've had a few in my time — but this is so infernally outlandish and I — I don't quite believe in it. That is to say, I believe in it right enough when I look at you or listen to McCunn, but as soon as my eyes are off you I begin to doubt again. I'm gettin' old and I've a stake in the country, and I daresay I'm gettin' a bit of a prig — anyway I don't want to make a jackass of myself. ...[52]

The whole book is troubled by the fluctuation of McCunn's interest back and forth from a rather naïve romanticism to a quasi-pessimistic realism. So much, too, is — rather wistfully — achieved by youth: and if we take up next the last of the McCunn trilogy we find that the hopes and achievement of youth form the main theme. Quite apart from comments like Archie's,

> They're tired of having the old 'uns call the tune and want to play a sprig themselves. I don't blame 'em, for the old 'uns have made a pretty mess of it.[53]

we find Janet affirming after the victory of Juventus [sic],

> Yes, youth is the force in the world today, for it isn't tired and it can hope.[54]

The change can also be seen in *The Three Hostages*, published in 1924, where another world — the ruminative life of Fosse Manor — is raised in antithesis to the world of action. And it does not merely intrude in a few insignificant asides: it is there in great detail, making its existence colour the whole of the story, offering an alternative value. *The Blanket of the Dark*, published seven years later, could be taken as another example: Peter after his vision of Immortality renounces entirely the world of action and high politics and disappears into the world 'of which there has never been a chronicle', the heaths and forests of old England:

> Somewhere in Bernwood or Savernake or Charnwood or Sherwood he may have found a home, or in the wild Welsh marshes, or north among the heather of the dales. Or he may have been a wanderer, taking for his domicile the whole of the dim country whose border is the edge of the highroad and rim of the tillage and the last stone walls of the garths. The blanket of the dark might lift for England, but no light will ever reveal those ancient recesses.[55]

The book which starts with the quotation 'Where is Bohun, where is Mowbray, where is Mortimer?' ends with 'Gone in name, but not perhaps in blood. Somewhere those high strains are in the commonalty of England, for it is the commonalty that endures.'[56]
The growing malaise which afflicts formerly resolute characters is reflected in Hannay's self-appraisal in *The Island of Sheep*, referred to earlier, in his son's indifference to old public school ideals, in Sandy Arbuthnot's increasing fits of abstraction in *The Courts of the Morning*, in Sir Edward Leithen's 'accidie'. And this

uneasiness is always found in the context of man's relationship to his environment. Gradually we witness the evolution of a new attitude to humanity. When Castor, the megalomaniac international financier, says,

For twenty years I have watched a world which I despised as futile, and pulled the strings of its folly. Some of those years were occupied by war. I took no apparent part in the war, for I had no fatherland, but I caught fish in its troubled waters. I evolved a philosophy, but I have never lied to myself, and I knew that I cared for that creed only because it flattered my egotism. I understood humanity well enough to play on its foibles. I thought that it was all foibles, save for one or two people like myself in each generation. I wanted to adjust the world so that it would be in the hands of this select few. Oh, I was supremely confident. I believed in the intellect, and mine told me that I was right. I even cultivated a dislike of the things and the people that were opposed to my creed. But there was no passion in my dislike — there is no passion in contempt, just as there is no fear.[57]

— we have an important sign, and a temptation to indulge in a further comparison. For twenty years Buchan as a writer *did* stand aside aloof and detached; he *did* in a certain sense — which I have tried to show — despise the world as futile in these years: he *did* evolve a philosophy calculatingly and without illusions, caring for it only because it flattered his egotism: he *was* supremely confident in the power of the intellect. And, notably, there was no passion in his cool, intellectual distaste: there is, as Castor says, 'no passion in contempt'. Contempt denies involvement, passion implies it. Yet Castor was to become involved and to die for ideas of involvement which were at the outset utterly alien to him.

An interesting comparison, though not, of course, in terms of literary achievement, could be made between Castor and Heyst in Conrad's *Victory*; even the biographical details — together with their implications — bear a marked resemblance:

I was educated by my father, who was an embittered genius. I inherited very young a great fortune . . . I was born in Austria, and therefore had no real country. Even before the war Austria was a conglomerate, not a people . . . I was brought up to despise the world, but I did not learn the lesson fully, for I excepted myself.[58]

Ultimately he has to face the world he has despised and to die as a result of his involvement. Castor's realisation of his community

M

with the world around him was, like Heyst's, facilitated by a woman's love — again the symbol of involvement. I don't suggest that the analogy is to be carried further: Jones shows the impossibility of standing apart, but he also shows the destructiveness of commitment. Castor, who is also the type of dangerous capitalist dealt with in *A Lodge in the Wilderness*, is characteristically made to show the destructive force harnessed; although commitment may still mean destruction, it is death with a purpose, cauterising and meaningful. Buchan is still pursuing the argument that there is safety in the solidity of numbers. An antidote is still sought to the Jones/Life-force and it is still to be found in the Grand Alliance. There is, however, an emergent appreciation of what the alliance means in human terms: the picture is becoming noticeably less abstract.

4

With *Sick Heart River* the transition is complete and we return to what is, in fact, the parson's meaning — spurned at the time — of self-sacrifice.

Buchan's development had much in common with Professor Teufelsdrockh's journey towards the Everlasting Yea. Of the earlier stage the latter's interpreter writes:

What Stoicism soever our wanderer, in his individual acts and motions, may affect, it is clear that there is a hot fever of anarchy and misery raging within; coruscations of which flash out. . . .[59]

Of these we are given an example:

Is there no God, then; but at best an absentee God, sitting idle, ever since the first Sabbath, at the outside of his universe, and seeing it go? Has the word duty no meaning?[60]

This goes a considerable way towards summing up the earlier Buchan. As *Sick Heart River* shows, he had then more or less accepted God as an absentee and Duty as good in itself — largely since at least it sustained identity.

A certain inarticulate Self-consciousness dwells dimly in us; which only our Works can render articulate and decisively discernible. Our Works are the mirror wherein the spirit first sees its natural lineaments. Hence,

too, the folly of that impossible Precept, Know thyself; till it be translated
into this partially possible one, Know what thou canst work at.[61]

Work is not only an ethical duty but a psychological necessity.
This last quotation illustrates Buchan's attitude to duty, work and
competence, at the same time as, by itself, it reiterates Kipling's
conclusion. Buchan, however, could never have made an end there:
for him the self was constantly seeking fulfilment in a transcendental
communion. Even when God was at his furthest there was still
dimly present to him, as to the Professor, something of the 'Infinite
nature of Duty':

living without God in the world, of God's light I was not utterly bereft;
if my as yet unsealed eyes, with their unspeakable longing, could nowhere
see Him, nevertheless in my heart He was present.[62]

Yet Buchan's earlier remoteness and unreality, his essential indifference to his characters, his fundamental isolation, are well
represented in Teufelsdrockh's prevailing mood:

The men and women around me, even speaking with me, were but
Figures; I had practically forgotten that they were alive, that they were
not merely automatic. In the midst of their crowded streets and assemb-
lages I walked solitary.[63]

The Centre of Indifference is reached in the first part of the signi-
ficantly-named *Sick Heart River*. For the first time, in this book,
Buchan faces life fully. Hitherto a tight-lipped fortitude and a burst
of activity had been a match for his frequent, symptomatic fits of
'accidie': now at last he has permitted himself a clearer vision.

'I have no extreme respect for human life,' we find characters
saying in various places, and this is of a piece with his earlier stoicism
and self-abstractions. Again and again we find the Buchan character
egotistically turning away from humanity to make his or somebody
else's soul in some non-human environment.[64] For his consciousness is not just of the isolation of the self, but of an essential demand
for fulfilment in the non-self:

The sad, elemental world was his, the fury and the tenderness of
nature, the peace of the wilds which the old folk had called the Breathing
of God.[65]

This clearly marks him off from Kipling and Conrad. To them the
self was the one reality, if an uncertain one, and a relative degree of

fulfilment in its world of actuality was all that one could hope for: all that the non-self offered was chaos and disintegration. There had, however, been moments even for Buchan, as *The Half-Hearted* shows, when doubt had threatened to dissipate the core of moral integrity, and the solution had been to immerse himself like Kipling and Conrad in 'the world of compromises which is the world of action'. But Buchan's fundamentally religious nature would neither allow him to accept the logical existentialist conclusion to his moment of awareness, nor to see any innate validity in the world of action itself. The result was his very frequent admission of accidie and his increasing determination to achieve the only meaningful self-fulfilment in communion with the Absolute. So he seeks to come face to face with God in the emptiness of the desert or in the towering majesty of an Alpine nature.

This is, of course, the religion of a Puritan, and R. H. Tawney in describing the latter describes Buchan in all but the latest stages:

Those who seek God in isolation from their fellow-men, unless trebly armed for the perils of the quest, are apt to find not God, but a devil, whose countenance bears an embarrassing resemblance to their own. The moral self-sufficiency of the Puritan nerved his will, but it corroded his sense of social solidarity. For, if each individual's destiny hangs on a private transaction between himself and his Maker, what room is left for human intervention? A servant of Jehovah more than of Christ, he revered God as a Judge rather than loved him as a Father, and was moved less by compassion for his erring brethren, than by impatient indignation at the blindness of vessels of wrath who 'sinned their mercies'. A spiritual aristocrat, who sacrificed fraternity to liberty, he drew from his idealisation of personal responsibility a theory of individual rights, which, secularised and generalised, was to be among the most potent the world has ever known.[66]

Though foreshadowed in *A Prince of the Captivity*, first published in 1933, it is not until the publication of *Sick Heart River* eight years later that the full realisation of his error 'broke in on him like a sunrise'. Like Teufelsdrockh he sees at last that the world is not to be despised and neglected and that God will not be reached in isolation. At the beginning of his last novel we find Buchan reiterating that, believing firmly in God, he had 'no undue reverence for man'. By the end of the book, however, he has sacrificed everything reverentially for the sake of a few unattractive specimens of humanity and pronounced his Everlasting Yea.

For a start Leithen heads for the frozen arctic wastes of northern Canada in his pursuit of Galliard, but all he gets from these vast spaces is a sense of desolation. It had been easy to detect a Divine Spirit, and to sublimate the self, in the grandeur, awe and authority of Alpine peaks, or in the idea of a desert pure and immense, but here it was very different:

> The mountains were shapeless, mere unfinished bits of earth; the forest of pine and spruce had neither form nor colour; the river, choked with logs and jetsam, had none of the beauty of running water. In coming into the wilderness he had found not the majesty of Nature, but the trivial, the infinitely small — an illiterate half-breed, a rabble of degenerate Indians, a priest with the mind of a child. The pettiness culminated in the chapel, which was as garish as a Noah's Ark from a cheap toy-shop . . .[67]

God must surely be elsewhere, for how could he possibly be this — the petty and the mean? What sort of fulfilment could this meagre vision offer? And gradually we see the direction of his developing thought. Father Duplessis had affirmed God's equation with space, which Leithen had questioned: now he comes to recognise this. At the point of death, with his world contracting, 'the majesty of God filled his universe. He was coming face to face with his religion.' It seemed to him then that he had always rather vaguely assumed God's existence, but his creed had remained aloof from his life. Now he perceived its truth: God's presence, he realised, pervaded the universe. This is comfort, but it is still impersonal, Spartan and remote: then a spark flickers in the bleak darkness:

> Now he suddenly saw the valley of the Sick Heart as a marvellous thing. This gash in the earth, full of cold, pure sunlight, was a secret devised by the great Artificer and revealed to him and to him only. There was no place for life in it — there could not be — but neither was there room for death. This peace was beyond living and dying. He had a sudden vision of it under a summer sun — green lawns, green forests, a blue singing stream, and cliffs of serrated darkness. A classic loveliness, Tempe, Phaeacic. But no bird wing or bird song, no ripple of fish, no beast in the thicket — a silence rather of the world as God first created it, before He permitted the coarse welter of life.[68]

Through the vision he had been given direct evidence of God's hand in all this, it was no longer 'an empty world and an empty sky' as he had earlier suggested to Father Duplessis: the Father had been right, it *was* filled with God. The world had seemed a desert of space here where 'the hand of God had blotted out life for millions of miles and made a great tract of the inconsiderable ball which was the earth, like the infinite interstellar spaces which had never heard of man'.[69] But suddenly God had revealed to him, in the midst of this desert, ideal Beauty, 'a classic loveliness, Tempe, Phaeacic'.

The next stage in the transition comes in his recognition of the quickening spirit in God's mercy and consideration. Before this his main thought still had been that

under the shadow he must not quail but keep his head high, not in revolt or in defiance but because He, who had made him in His image, expected such courage. 'Though thou slay me, yet will I trust in Thee.'[70]

But now this profound fatalism was given a warmth and richness which deepened and transformed it.

Now there suddenly broke in on him like a sunrise a sense of God's mercy . . .[71]

Man had not been left to fight his battle with only a thin-lipped fortitude, austere and bleak; a gift of immeasurable strength and richness had been vouchsafed to him in God's mercy and love.

The penultimate stage is divine love translated into human terms: and the recognition that only through the human community can this love be returned and fulfilment achieved. The approach to this stage is carefully and subtly prepared. The warmth in the appreciation of God's great gift is to thaw the frozen egotism of his erstwhile 'faith' and this in turn will reveal that his course can no longer lie among frozen, majestic ideals of conduct and service. Hitherto his juxtaposition of man and a varyingly spatial nature dimly backed up by an invisible and unfelt God, always resulted in the reduction of man to insignificance. In such a context a stiff fortitude, a brave acceptance of divine ordination seemed the only quality which meant anything. One could face life and death courageously because that was expected of one by the unsensed Creator, 'because an effort was demanded, something which could stir the imagination and steel the heart'. And in facing up to them one made one's self and soul. But this preoccupation with one's own salvation becomes, inescapably, exclusive and utterly 'selfish'. The world may be a worthless abstract, and all talk about humanity a glib and cynical façade to conceal this fact, but the world of fragmentary humanity struggling blindly and so often hopelessly with the forces of life and death is not.

Gradually Leithen finds himself involved. He first realises this when he sees himself forced into the leadership of the band who would save the Hares, forced to give decisions 'on a thing wholly outside his world'. In the making of his own soul a noble if bleak ideal had been matched — necessarily — by noble action and noble achievement: all this was to be refuted.

All his life he had been mixed up in great affairs. He had had his share in 'moulding a state's decrees' and 'shaping the whisper of a throne'. He had left England when Europe was a powder magazine and every patriot was bound to put himself at the disposal of his distracted land. Well, he had cast all that behind him — rightly, for he had to fight his own grim battle. In that battle he seemed to have won a truce, perhaps even a victory, and now he was being asked to stake all his winnings on a trivial cause — the *malaise* of human kites and crows roosting at the end of the earth.[72]

He was being forced away from the grandeur of this austere and selfish creed with the distasteful realisation that 'it was not a surrender to the celestial will that was required of him, but a decision on small mundane questions'.[73] There could be no going back; the 'sudden realisation of mercy behind the rigour of nature', which had just come to him making him 'warm towards common humanity' mocked the arrogance of his self-reliance and clearly spelt out involvement. One could no longer stand apart, but must accept fairly and squarely the fullest immersion.

They were facing the challenge of the North, which a man must accept and repel or submit to servitude. Lew and Johnny and their kind did not face that challenge; they avoided it by walking humbly; they conciliated it by ingenious subterfuges; its blows were avoided and not squarely met, and they paid the price; for every now and then they fell under its terrors.[74]

One had to wrestle with life if one were searching for a genuine integrity; one could, of course, evade it neatly while seeming to deal with it. Lew and Johnny do this — and so, for instance, does Captain Mitchell in *Nostromo* — and are the lesser characters, the more vulnerable, incomplete beings as a result. Total immersion may, as Stein pointed out in *Lord Jim*, bring destruction, and Leithen is, in fact, destroyed; but, in a fuller sense than either Lord Jim or Heyst, in the article of death he secures his victory.

'You see, I have made my peace with the North, faced up to it, defied it, and so won its blessing. Consider, my dear. The most vital forces of the world are in the North, in the men of the North, but only when they have annexed it. It kills those who run away from it.'
'I see,' she said after a long pause. 'I know what you mean. I think I feel it . . . But the Sick Heart River! Wasn't that a queer fancy?' Galliard laughed.
'It was the old habit of human nature to turn to magic. Lew Frizel wanted a short cut out of his perplexities. So did I, and I came under the spell of his madness. First I came here. Then I went to the Ghost River. Then I heard Lew's story. I was looking for magic, you see. We both had sick hearts. But it was no good. The North will always call your bluff.'
'And Leithen? He went there, didn't he?'
'Yes, and brought Lew away. Leithen didn't have a sick heart. He was facing the North with clear eyes. He would always have won out.'
'But he died!'
'That was victory — absolute victory . . .' [75]

The North is, of course, synonymous with life – for this we have Father Duplessis's comment on Leithen as evidence:

He fell into a *malaise* which, it is my belief, was at bottom the same as the Hares' affliction, and which seems to be endemic in the North. It may be defined as fear of the North, or perhaps more accurately as fear of Life. In the North man, to live, has to fight every hour against hostile forces; if his spirit fails and his effort slackens he perishes. [76]

The final stage is that of true self-sacrifice and the ultimate in love which gives up life for the sake of another, and it closes with Father Duplessis's benediction:

'celui qui perdra sa vie pour l'amour de moi, la retrouvera'.

Leithen, whose God had remained something aloof from his life, at last recognised that his stoicism had been abject but without true humility. When had the change begun? At Sick Heart River, when he had a vision of the beauty which might be concealed in the desert? Then, that evening in the snow-pit had come the realisation of the tenderness behind the iron front of Nature, and after that had come thankfulness for plain human affection. The North had not frozen him, but had melted the ice in his heart. God was not only all-mighty but all-loving. His old happinesses seemed to link in with his new mood of thankfulness. The stream of life which had flowed so pleasantly had eternity in its waters. He felt himself safe in the hands of a power that was both God and friend . . . He had been inhuman, Leithen told himself, with the dreary fortitude of a sick animal. Now whatever befell him he was once again in love with his fellows. The cold infernal North magnified instead of dwarfing humanity. What a marvel was this clot of vivified dust! . . . The universe seemed to spread itself before him in immense distances lit and dominated by a divine spark which was man. An inconsiderable planet, a speck in the infinite stellar spaces; most of it salt water; the bulk of the land rock and desert and austral and boreal ice; interspersed mud, the detritus of aeons, with a thin coverlet of grass and trees — that vegetable world on which every living thing was in the last resort a parasite! Man, precariously perched on this rotating scrap-heap, yet so much master of it that he could mould it to his transient uses, and, while struggling to live, could entertain thoughts and dreams beyond the bounds of time and space! Man so weak and yet so great, the chief handiwork of the Power that had hung the stars in the firmament! [77]

Communion between the self and non-self has at last been achieved. The universe — space — humanity — is in God, and individual man, his image, the recipient of his mercy and love, can reach him through love for his fellow-men. No longer is he dwarfed into insignificance, minute and alone, and no longer does he have to attempt an arrogant and absurd self-reliance. To spend his time laboriously protecting the integrity of the self in splendid isolation was utterly selfish and instead of leading to any real fulfilment threw him continually back upon his own inadequacy. All such self-protective concern had to be abandoned in the interest of others: only then could real integrity be achieved, and an enduring bridge between the self and non-self built. 'He that findeth his life shall lose it, but he that loseth life shall find it,' Mr. Scrope had quoted in *A Prince of the Captivity*, but he had added that that was not enough; the greater commandment was 'He that findeth his soul shall lose it . . .' This is exactly how it has turned out: Leithen, his soul made, his self secure, renounces everything to do with the egotistical self and its protection in order to serve humanity. Greater sacrifice could not be made. Father Duplessis sums up:

> He had been frozen by hard stoicism which sprang partly from his upbringing and partly from temperament. He was a strong man with an austere command of himself, and when he had to face death he divested himself of all that could palliate the suffering, and stood up to it with a stark resolution which was more Roman than Christian. What I witnessed was the thawing of the ice.
>
> He had always bowed himself before the awful majesty of God. Now his experience was that of the Church in the thirteenth century, when they found in the Blessed Virgin a gentle mediatrix between mortal and divine. Or perhaps I should put it thus: that he discovered that tenderness and compassion which Our Lord came into the world to preach, and, in sympathy with others, he lost all care for himself. His noble, frosty egoism was merged in something nobler. He had meant to die in the cold cathedral of the North, ceasing to live in a world which had no care for life. Now he welcomed the humblest human environment, for he had come to love his kind, indeed, to love everything that God had made.[78]

His lack of respect for human life has vanished with the thaw, and in its place has come genuine community.

At the very least, *Sick Heart River* is a correlative of the search which pervades all Buchan's work for a creed which will bring absolute self-fulfilment: and with the orderliness characteristic of all his novels this, his last, announces a solution. *The Half-Hearted*, almost his first novel, had attempted an answer which, once reached, was resolutely — too resolutely — applied: but it was a compromise and brought no peace — indeed it almost enjoined a continual Kiplingesque battle. The dissatisfaction grew and was evinced in various ways; and the movement was a constant yearning towards something that would warm and make intelligible a universe which seemed only to encourage a bleak self-reliance, and to offer nothing but the prospect of death with the wind in one's teeth. His occasional flights into a mystical idealism have their origins here. In the short story *Fountainblue*, for instance, Maitland quotes the motto of his house, 'Parvu ceu haut bois conduyrai m'amie' — 'Through the high wood I will conduct my love', and sees it as an encouragement to carry untarnished to the end an austere and beautiful dream. His little ambitions had been but shreds and echoes and shadows of this supreme reality.

Similarly, his love for Clara had been

but another such simulacrum: for what he had sought was no foolish laughing girl, but the Immortal Shepherdess, who, singing the old songs of youth, drives her flocks to the hill in the first dewy dawn of the world.[79]

His true environment he discovers is the 'sad elemental world' and his real search had been for Ideal Beauty and Ideal Love. There is a similar example in *The Blanket of the Dark*, where Peter's vision of Divine Love in the form of the Virgin Mary is preceded by his recollection of St. Augustine's words, 'Nondum amabam et amare amabam; quaerebam quid amarem, amans amare' — 'I did not yet love, but I sought something to love for I was in love with love.' And, content with this earnest of immortality he renounces the greatness which the world is holding out to him. *A Prince of the Captivity* shows him in search of a leader who will connect the actual and the ideal, only to be brought up short against the question 'You wish to be a kingmaker, but what if there are no kings?' It is, however, left to *Sick Heart River* to reconcile all these themes and bring the search to a triumphant close.

5

It is into this development that Buchan's imperialism fits with a rightness which amounts almost to inevitability. The only thing which could redeem imperialism, Conrad had said, was an idea behind it — 'not a sentimental pretence but an idea; and an unselfish belief in the idea . . .' For Buchan the imperial idea meant just this: and it was represented in the total of service and sacrifice, duty and trust, clear purpose and exemplary conduct, demanded of and willingly given by the true servant of empire. For him it was an idea which wakened all that was best in man and curbed all that was worst, reminding him of his own higher nature: an idea which united man to man in a great fellowship which was more than the sum of individual effort: an idea which would have behind it a great catholic tradition in thought and feeling, in art and conduct, of which no one part, but the empire itself, would be the appointed guardian.

Too simple? Naïve? Impossibly idealist? It might or might not be all of these, but certainly, as we see from the larger context of his work, neither superficial, fake nor bogus. In fact, Buchan tried to make of the imperial idea what Calvin had tried to make of his religion:

> The essence of the system was . . . the attempt to crystallise a moral ideal in the daily life of a visible society, which should be at once a Church and a State.[80]

It was to be his great link between the Actual and the Ideal.

There is the superficies to be disposed of to start with: for instance, the carefully cultivated insularity of his upper class. 'What an extraordinary young woman' Mrs. Lamington whispers to Leithen. 'Is she a little mad or only foreign?' [81] This must be seen, too, simply as the characterising expression of Buchan's upper class — a much better example of which is to be found in *Huntingtower*:

> 'You were a friend of Captain Kennedy?'
> 'His oldest, we were at the same private school, and he was at m'tutors, and we were never much separated till he went abroad to cram for the Diplomatic and I started east to shoot things.' [82]

But this is only skin-deep: in fact, the Briton's ability to understand and 'get on with' the foreigner is insisted upon most emphatically in a very typical Hannay speech:

> We call ourselves insular, but the truth is that we are the only race on earth that can produce men capable of getting inside the skin of remote peoples. Perhaps the Scots are better than the English but we're all a thousand per cent better than anyone else.[83]

The overweening racialism in this does not do much to diminish the real basis of insularity, but it does at any rate posit an attempt at understanding, whatever the reasons behind it, and it does disclaim the 'mad or foreign' type of comment.

However, in *A Lodge in the Wilderness*, orderly as ever, he presents under a very thin fictive disguise a complete appraisal of imperialism. As the previous paragraph suggests, all his thinking on the subject was coloured by a degree of racialism which resulted, at best, in a none-too-humble paternalism:

I knew then the meaning of the white man's duty. He has to take all risks, recking nothing of his life or his fortunes, and well content to find his reward in the fulfilment of his task. That is the difference between white and black, the gift of responsibility, the power of being in a little way a king; and so long as we know this and practise it, we will rule not in Africa alone but wherever there are dark men who live only for the day and their own bellies. Moreover, the work made me pitiful and kindly. I learned much of the untold grievances of the natives, and saw something of their strange, twisted reasoning. Before we had got Laputa's army back to their kraals, with food enough to tide them over the spring sowing, Aitken and I had got sounder policy in our heads than you will find in the towns, where men sit in offices and see the world through a mist of papers.[84]

— and at worst into a thorough-going *Herrenvolk* conception of an aristocracy of blood:

I define Imperialism as the closer organic connection under one Crown of a number of autonomous nations of the same blood, who can spare something of their vitality for the administration of vast tracts inhabited by lower races, — a racial aristocracy considered in their relation to the subject peoples, a democracy in their relation to each other.[85]

It is paternalism, too, which ought to have a capital P, for lurking behind it all — not only in the expression but in the form of the expression also — is a staggering identification with the Deity:

And in that hour I saw my work, and, I think, too, the ideal of our race. If we cannot create a new heaven, we can create a new earth. 'The wilderness and the solitary place shall be glad for us; the desert shall rejoice and blossom as the rose.'[86]

The quotation does, however, suggest another ingredient in his paternalism — a Carlylean activism bent on productive effort. And this is where it connects with Puritanism and the practical ideal of competence. Not only did imperialism make familiar what had been vague, unknown and therefore potentially dangerous — a further pegging down and pegging out of space — but it brought with it the need to assimilate all this thoroughly, the need to master it with one's competence which cannot admit any diminution, to inscribe one's pattern on the dust and to do it not casually and crudely, but with clarity and precision as befitted both the Elect of God and the representatives of this great controlling and salvation-bringing force.

It is to be expected, then, in a man who had certainly reached the very zenith of competence, that we should find a great deal of concern with the practical realisms of imperialism.

The great administrative questions of the future will be tropical questions. The Tropics will be the training-ground of our great officials. It is high time, therefore, that we tried to get at some scientific understanding of our responsibilities. If expert knowledge and not a mere handful of moral platitudes is to be our guide, we must take steps to systematise and develop that knowledge.

We are not without precedents. Both France and Germany have set the example in founding schools of what they call 'colonial science'. And four centuries ago our own Hakluyt urged something of the same kind. The risk is that we allow ourselves to be misled by the case of India, where we have made a great success by a kind of accident. We send out raw boys to that service, and in a year or two they are efficient administrators. Yes, but the same rule will not hold everywhere. India is a long-settled country, which runs by herself. We control, amend here and there, give her the benefit of our protection, but we do not interfere. The social machine in its essentials is independent of us. It is quite a different matter in lands where the fabric of civilisation has to be built up from the beginning. There you have no rules to go by, except your own wits; and knowledge is the only dividing line between success and failure. We must take up the business very seriously, and equip ourselves resolutely for the work . . . I want to see imperial colleges established where young men will be taught tropical medicine, and surveying, and natural history and ethnology, where, in a word, the long experience of the Empire will be concentrated into precepts.[87]

There is similar close thinking and 'competence' in this plan for State-organised emigration within the empire — State-organised because it is only under these conditions that you can have it scientifically organised and supervised. Emigration is the least easy art in the world. It needs careful selection, long preparation of the land and people for each other, and it wants at the back of it all the authority of the State.[88]

And the participation of the state is not sought for any coercive function, but to ensure that the scale is large enough to make the whole plan worth while, to provide the machinery for 'framing its schemes on the surest and most scientific grounds', to act as mediator with colonial Governments, and to subsidise transport.

The human element — the imperial servant — must, then, be of the greatest practical experience and competence. Lewie had been told in *The Half-Hearted* that 'the great things of the world have all been done by men who didn't stop to reflect on them', and later reproved for not bringing himself down 'to the world of compromises which is the world of action', thus losing 'the practical touch'. A near parallel can be found in *A Lodge in the Wilderness* where Horace Walpole's dictum,

No great country was ever saved by its good men, because good men will not go the lengths that are necessary.[89]

is quoted with approval. Having accepted the value of the thing he strives for there must be no distrust or lack of resolute action.[90] Those who fail to see this are represented by Mr. Luke Simeon who

surrendered his fellowship at King's to 'labour' as he says, among the masses. He is eminent at Browning halls and university settlements, and has done much, I believe, to civilise the East End by the distribution of indistinct reproductions of Giotto and Botticelli. He is a pale, earnest, well-meaning, and rather silly young man, who should have remained in the church of his clerical forefathers. He attacks Imperialism as the 'worship of force'. It represents, he says, that tendency of a decadent age which may be observed in the Roman ladies who took their lovers from the prize-ring. Up to a point I agree with him. The worship of brute force, of mere conscienceless power, is the most certain sign of degeneration. His fallacy is that he really condemns force altogether, whether exercised for a beneficent purpose or not, and he hides his bias under the assumption that Imperialism means power without ideals or conscience.[91]

Perhaps it is the knowledge of the cost of the compromise to the man of intellect and sensitivity which makes him so hard on those who are not among the 'doers': his diatribe on Mr. Simeon continues,

He has a temperamental shrinking from certain of the hard realities of life, and he flatters his weakness by investing it with a moral halo. He lives in a little world of artistic and literary trifling, and he has consequently no perspective, so that he will quote you a bad artist on some point of foreign policy and a minor poet on some problem of economics. His shallow aesthetic soul is revolted by three-fourths of life, so he dubs it evil and rejects it. He is not a young man whom it is worth taking pains to convert, but his stuff has its vogue, and he has disciples.[92]

As for the subject races themselves, Buchan affords an almost classical example of the 'humane' paternalist:

But Aitken did more than mine diamonds, for he had not forgotten the lesson we had learned together in the work of resettlement. He laid down a big fund for the education and amelioration of the native races, and the first fruit of it was the establishment at Blaauwildebeestefontein itself of a great native training college. It was no factory for making missionaries and black teachers, but an institution for giving the Kaffirs the kind of training which fits them to be good citizens of the state. There you will find every kind of technical workshop, and the finest experimental farms, where the blacks are taught modern agriculture . . . There are playing-fields and baths and reading rooms and libraries just as in a school at home.[93]

Almost unbelievably he makes this even more explicit in *A Lodge in the Wilderness* adjuring imperial educationists to confine themselves to subjects which will turn the native into a prosperous citizen and devout Christian. If they preached sound hygiene, the Atonement and the Fatherhood of God — and possibly handicrafts — they were doing all that could be desired. In time they might even succeed in getting these 'strange, sullen, childish, dark-skinned people' to 'take their place in our complex system – low down, of course — but still indubitably within it'.[94]

This is the creed which gets an entertainingly 'popular' expression in a remark like that of Hannay in *Mr. Standfast*:

. . . to my joy, one night there was a great buck nigger who had a lot to say about 'Africa for the Africans'. I had a few words with him in Sesutu afterwards and rather spoiled his visit.[95]

But what *is* imperialism, how is it to be interpreted? Certainly not by a snap generalisation. 'If I could define Imperialism satisfactorily in a sentence I should be very suspicious of its truth.'[96] First the thing it is not, the impurities in the idea:

It will be remembered that some little while ago the creed which is commonly called Imperialism was tossed down into the arena of politics to be wrangled over by parties and grossly mauled in the quarrel. With the fall of the Government which had sanctioned such tactics there came one of those waves of reaction which now and then break in upon our national steadfastness. The name of 'Empire' stank in the nostrils of the electorate. Those who used it fell like ninepins; in the huge majority which the new Ministry acquired there were many who openly blasphemed it; and the few who still cherished the faith thought it wise to don temporarily the garb of indifference. Carey viewed the change with philosophic calm. He trusted the instincts of his race, and was not sorry that the dross should be purged and the spirit purified by misfortune.[97]

and later

Every vulgar feeling in the whole treasury of our national vulgarity has been enlisted in its support. Small wonder that England is a little sick of the very name of Empire.[98]

Then Mrs. Deloraine makes an admission in which she describes how there could be a note in jingoism capable of arousing feeling and intellectual awareness in one who was quite insusceptible to its 'vulgar' appeal.

I remember that when I was a young girl the very name Empire was a hateful thing to me. All the old orderly life which I loved seemed to be threatened by these barbarians who talked in a strange jargon, half mercantile, half Jingo. Their Palace of Art seemed to be constructed on the lines of a New York sky-scraper, and their music was the thumping of a brass band. And yet even then I seemed to hear behind the shouting a new note which haunted me in spite of my prejudice. As I grew older I came to live less in the past, and looked more to the realities of the world around me. Art came to be less a thing of dainty memories and delicate echoes, and more and more something solemn and tragic, and yet instinct with immortal humour, the voice of God speaking through the clamour of His creations. And then I felt the need of a wider horizon, a hope which should not be the perquisite of the few but the treasure of the humble. And suddenly I saw that I had been blind and deaf to a new world of which simple folk had long ago entered into possession.[99]

One might object that this is merely to make a dual carriageway of the road to Mandalay: it certainly describes rather well what Kipling in retrospect considered his practical 'superficial' purpose.

However, there is no doubt that the jingoism of 'conscienceless power', of the sort which fails to recognise that the white man has a burden indeed, is wholly repugnant to Buchan,

But size has its own disease and we may easily fall into the vice of looking upon it as something worthy in itself, however alien it may remain to our culture. Whether we call the disease 'Jingoism' or 'grandeur' or 'self-complacency', its root is the same. It means that we regard

N

our empire as a mere possession, as the vulgar rich regard their bank accounts — a matter to boast of, and not an added duty. All the braggart glorification we sometimes hear means a shallow and frivolous understanding of what empire involves. No serious man dare boast of the millions of square miles which his people rule, when he remembers that each mile has its own problem, and that on him and his fellow lies the burden of solution.

Jingoism, then, is not a crude Imperialism; it is Imperialism's stark opposite . . . it has no kinship with the ideal of an empire moving with one impulse towards a richer destiny . . . The glory of England is not the mileage of her territory but the state into which she is welding it.[100]

But it is hard to see this jingoism as the 'stark opposite' of Buchan's imperialism: there is between the two an emotional affinity which Mrs. Deloraine's remark brought out. Only, the one was vulgar, in the narrowest and widest sense of the word, cerebrally muscular, uninformed, and unintelligent, while the other was intelligent, sensitive, intellectual and intellectualised, and interpreted through the media of certain historical ideals. With this last particularly in mind it is not difficult to account for the stern regard to duty, the paternalism, the emphasis on efficiency, purpose and success, and the suggestion of a divine mission.

Buchan, of course, goes further, spiritualising and idealising the whole concept of imperialism far beyond what one would have expected with even the fullest allowances for the influence of his mentors at Brasenose. When Mrs. Deloraine defines imperialism as an 'enlarged sense of the beauty and mystery of the world' or when Miss Haystoun pronounces in Emersonian terms a vision of absolute truth in the ideal,[101] we are dealing with pure Buchan. Characteristically, the idealist in Buchan is ungenerous towards the idealism of others. In a surprisingly impercipient passage on socialism and imperialism, Carey (the organiser of the seminar, whose 'amazing energy annihilated space' and whose affinities with Rhodes are very obvious) concludes summarily with the pronouncement,

The one is a method, a particular theory of administration, the other is an ideal, a gospel of a fuller national life.[102]

Buchan has been searching for an ideal of social organisation and has found it in the British Empire, therefore one must expect that the core of its appeal will not be in any material justification. Here as elsewhere he seeks an ideal which will satisfy man's profound need for a social compact ('man cannot advance except through organised action'), which will at once unite him in strength and security with a great universal brotherhood, guaranteed, almost literally, to subdue the earth, give him a *modus vivendi* and a purpose for the expenditure of his energy: the whole to be founded on a metaphysic of self-fulfilment endowed with the strength and mystique of a religion. That this explanation of Buchan's imperialism as a link between the actuality of the self and the ideal of its fulfilment is not in the least fanciful is proved by two separate pieces of evidence: the first refers to Empire as religion and the second to the rationale that a quantitative basis is essential for qualitative development.

Although Lord Launceston reminds the distinguished party assembled in the lodge of the dangers of exalting imperialism to too high a plane and seeking in a political ideal 'that which belongs only to what, in the widest sense of the word, we call religion', it is Lord Appin who has the last and rather different word. (The quotation is a long one which must be given in full for it contains the complete statement of what was at this time Buchan's creed.)

We do not profess to teach a religion, but, if we are not theologians, we are in a sense ecclesiastics. The state, remember, has now taken the place of the mediæval church. Once we had popes and bishops supervising the lives of their flock and making themselves sponsors for their spiritual well-being. But their pride crumbled, because they fell into that very error against which Lord Launceston has been warning us, and sought to imprison the longings of the human spirit within the narrow walls of creed and ritual. Religion has triumphantly proved itself stronger than ecclesiasticism, and to-day we see a revolt — perhaps an unwise revolt — against all that savours of formality. And yet man cannot advance except through organised action, and if this Church is destroyed under one guise he will revive it under another. The Church in the Middle Ages had three great attributes. In the first place it was a brotherhood, a body of men linked together by a common faith. Again, it was inspired by an ideal which was professedly spiritual, a creed where success or failure was defined by other than material standards. Lastly, it was surrounded by an alien and hostile world, so that its members were drawn close to each other, and filled with a zeal which, according to our view of history, we label missionary or intolerant. That old church can never be re-established, for we have travelled too far from the sanctions which gave it strength. But we can no more do without a church than without a religion. Only we have learned nowadays that the true and lasting work for which such an organisation is adapted is rather political than doctrinal, and that the Seal of the Fisherman is better affixed to state decrees than to edicts against conscience. I maintain that our view of empire gives that empire something of the character of a church. We are a brotherhood banded together in a common quest. Our union, if less mystic than that which Augustine preached, has yet in it something not wholly human, not merely the sum of individual effort. In the midst of all our failures the work advances, for the plan is greater than the builders. Above all, we must achieve our desires in face of a stubborn and alien world. All around us are the frontiers of barbarism — I use the word as the Greeks used it. It is this environment which will perfect our brotherhood and give us something of the old crusading fervour. And if we have this clear purpose, not untouched with emotion, our empire will be another, and more truly Catholic, church. Then — to use Plato's phrase — the quest of truth will not lack the warmth of desire.[103]

At the end of the book the identity is made explicit:

'It is a religion', he said, 'to me, and I think to others. If you quarrel with the word, I can only say that what any man desires with his whole heart, what wakens all that is best in him and curbs all that is worst, is a religion, whatever else the term may mean. . . . If my religion is not to include my politics, then I am content to have none, for to me the one as much as the other is an attempt to subdue the material world of our common sight into harmony with an unseen world of spirit.'[104]

Comment is scarcely necessary here: political and religious institutions merge and the ideal of social organisation is complete.

The second piece of evidence is found in the assertion that 'you cannot find true spiritual progress unless you provide adequate material conditions'. A definition of spiritual development is obviously needed: it is

the broadening and deepening of the mind till it regards the world in its true perspective, and the strengthening of the character so that the will is a tempered and unerring weapon in the charge of a man's soul. And this end is to be achieved only by the exercise of the mind upon the largest possible manifold of experience, and by the conflict of character with the alien forces of the world. I am talking, remember, not of the saint and recluse, but of the citizen. What is true of the individual development is no less true of the state's. A nation becomes great in the most sublimated sense of the word by its ability to present its citizens with a sphere of action wherein their civic responsibilities may be fulfilled. A microcosm, however perfect, will never be a true arena for civic virtue.[105]

He goes on to explain this in terms which interestingly ante-date Spengler by several years:

> I do not for a moment deny that for a new colony intensive activity may be the path of wisdom. But in all old and highly developed lands there comes a time when, without spacial extension, all that is possible is a barren rearrangement, a shuffling of the cards. Just as we cannot describe a mere analysis and readjustment of a few dogmas as mental progress, so I call any preoccupation with what after all must be the formal aspect of our own affairs — their emendation without the introduction of fresh elements, — I call that national stagnation.[106]

This 'philosophical conception', then, is 'the sine qua non of Imperialism',[107] and in the summing-up at the end of the book it is finally defined as

> ... the recognition of the value of material greatness for spiritual development, the belief that since ideals can only be realised under conditions of space and time, it is right and proper to attend to these conditions.[108]

It is all here in these last four important quotations: imperialism, in literary terms an inheritor of Romanticism, reveals man, insignificant *sub specie aeternitatis*, but in himself strong, dynamic and undauntable, striving to the last to come to terms with the vastness of his environment, finding himself in 'the conflict of character with the alien world'. Here is the vision completed:

> All my days the epic of our future has sung itself in my ears, but as I grow into late middle age I think less of the pomp and pageantry and more of the grave austerity at the heart of it. I can foresee an empire where each part shall live to the full its own life and develop an autochthonous culture. But behind it all there will be the great catholic tradition in thought and feeling in art and conduct, of which no one part, but the empire itself, is the appointed guardian. In that confraternity of peoples the new lands will redress the balance of the old, and will gain in return an inheritance of transmitted wisdom. Men will not starve in crowded islands when there are virgin spaces waiting for them, and young nations will not be adventurers in far lands, but children of a great household carrying the fire from the ancestral hearth. Our art will be quickened by a breath from a simpler and cleaner world, and the fibre of our sons will be strung to vigour by the glimpse of more spacious horizons. And our English race will vindicate to mankind that doctrine which is the noblest

of its traditions — that liberty is possible only under the dominion of order and law, and that unity is not incompatible with the amplest freedom. We of the old countries shall give and receive. Our Trojan manhood, our Trojan Lares and Penates will be there, but so too will Latium and the ancient Ausonian rites.[109]

In *Sick Heart River* the reconciliation between the self and non-self was achieved once it was realised that the non-self, or space, was God, and that God had not left man unprovided in his battle with life. The genuinely Christian humility of Leithen's sacrifice is the final renunciation of the earlier arrogant and selfish defiance of the universe and reflects Buchan's humility in seeking a solution which is entirely personal and individual. Certainly others, if they choose, may follow the same path and may likewise find salvation, but there is no insistence that they should: Leithen, by himself has sought and found his own answer for himself. All along we are acutely aware that this is one man's struggle for communion, one man's honest and unrelenting battle to come to terms with his own particular destiny.

In *A Lodge in the Wilderness* (1906) Buchan is still in his Roman days, still speaking from behind the mask, still seeking a public solution and a Grand Alliance. The search is for an ideal of social organisation, which will incorporate man satisfactorily in his environment. The answer, given the time, is inevitable: ideals can be realised only under conditions of space and time and here in Empire is a concept which, as he has most amply demonstrated, appears wholly to fill the role, physically and metaphysically both. In *Sick Heart River* the reconciliation of man and space is found in God; in *A Lodge in the Wilderness* it is Empire. There is not much difference at first sight. Yet the Catholic Church of Empire is remote from the God of *Sick Heart River* for the latter is a God of mercy and love, while the imperial God is Hebraic, demanding service and creating arrogance, and his Church too dependent on a precarious balance between space and time. The emphasis will fall on self-assertion and religious muscularity: 'This is my opinion and since it is God's truth, the world *shall* accept it,'[110] exclaims a character in *A Lodge in the Wilderness*. Out of its own mouthpiece it condemns itself:

No man can be religious who is not a fighter, who does not know the odds which the world sets against him, who has not suffered and struggled and tried the temper of the human spirit against the rigour of nature. Religion is not a comfortable thing of easy prayers and ready thanksgivings, but something as fierce and stubborn and consuming as life itself. How else is it to wither the hosts of the enemy?[111]

That is the God of *The Half-Hearted*: it is emphatically not the God of *Sick Heart River*. The space between is the distance travelled by John Buchan in search of a solution for his problem, and his final answer is the measure of his progress.

NOTES

1. *A Lodge in the Wilderness* (n.d.), p. 213–14.
2. *Sick Heart River* (1941), p. 58.
3. *A Lodge in the Wilderness*, p. 175.
4. *The Half-Hearted* (1922), p. 208.
5. *The Gap in the Curtain* (1932), p. 30–31.
6. *Greenmantle* (1956), p. 25.
7. *Mr. Standfast* (1956), p. 33.
8. Ibid., p. 39.
9. Ibid., p. 28.
10. *The Island of Sheep* (1960), p. 106.
11. *The Half-Hearted*, pp. 210–11. A largely Kantian philosophy of the Understanding is clearly enunciated as a thoroughly pragmatic philosophy of Compromise in *A Lodge in the Wilderness*, pp. 214–18.
12. *Mr. Standfast*, p. 33.
13. *The Half-Hearted*, p. 208.
14. Ibid., p. 216.
15. Ibid., pp. 376–7.
16. *The Blanket of the Dark* (1952), p. 255.
17. *The Half-Hearted*, p. 375.
18. Ibid., p. 275.
19. Ibid., p. 213.
20. *Greenmantle*, p. 21.
21. *The Blanket of the Dark*, pp. 93–94.
22. *Mr. Standfast*, p. 21.
23. *The Island of Sheep*, pp. 19–20.
24. *The Dancing Floor* (1951), p. 65.
25. *Huntingtower* (1958), p. 177.
26. *Courts of the Morning* (1929), pp. 197–8. Cf. 'His strength and also

his weakness is that he has no illusions. For one thing, he does not possess the illusion which ordinary people call a creed' (p. 106).

27. *The Courts of the Morning*, pp. 111–12.

28. *The Power House* (1922), p. 216.

29. Ibid., pp. 218–20.

30. *The Three Hostages* (1955), p. 61.

31. *The Power House*, p. 214.

32. *The Island of Sheep*, p. 195.

33. *The Power-House*, p. 216.

34. *Mr. Standfast*, p. 316.

35. *The Dancing Floor*, p. 98.

36. *Greenmantle*, p. 174.

37. Ibid., p. 82.

38. *The Dancing Floor*, p. 79.

39. Ibid, pp. 227–8.

40. *The Three Hostages* (1924), p. 14.

41. *Greenmantle*, pp. 183–4.

42. Cf. Sandy, who 'Unless he is tied to duties which need every atom of his powers . . . will begin to torment himself with questions', (*The Courts of the Morning*, p. 326).

43. *The Half-Hearted*, pp. 208–9

44. Ibid., p. 209.

45. *A Prince of the Captivity* (1933), p. 48.

46. Ibid., p. 35.

47. Ibid., p. 34.

48. *Sick Heart River*, pp. 103–4.

49. *The Thirty-Nine Steps* (1922), p. 20.

50. *Huntingtower*, pp. 313–14.

51. We might recall the characteristic incident on board ship in *Prester John* (1910) where the First Class easily beat the Second, but had a hard tussle with the steerage.

52. *Huntingtower*, p. 272.

53. *The House of the Four Winds* [1956, (first published in 1935)] p. 99. The third is *Castle Gay*, published in 1930.

54. *The House of the Four Winds*, p. 337.

55. *The Blanket of the Dark*, p. 375.

56. Ibid., p. 377.

57. *The Courts of the Morning*, p. 258.

58. Ibid., p. 258.

59. Thomas Carlyle, *Sartor Resartus*, p. 128.

60. Ibid., pp. 129–30.

61. Ibid., p. 132.

62. Thomas Carlyle, *Sartor Resartus*, p. 128.

63. Ibid., pp. 129–30.

64. The best example is probably Creevey in *A Prince of the Captivity*.

65. *The Watcher by the Threshold* (1951), p. 256.

66. R. H. Tawney, *Religion and the Rise of Capitalism*, p. 229.

67. *Sick Heart River*, p. 113.

68. Ibid., p. 184.

69. Ibid., p. 174.

70. Ibid., p. 173.

71. Ibid., p. 203.

72. Ibid., p. 252.

73. Ibid., p. 253.

74. Ibid., p. 293.

75. Ibid., pp. 316–17.

76. Ibid., p. 308.

77. Ibid., pp. 293–5.

78. Ibid., pp. 309–10.

79. *The Watcher by the Threshold*, p. 256.

80. R. H. Tawney, *Religion and the Rise of Capitalism*, p. 123.

81. *The Dancing Floor*, p. 90.

82. *Huntingtower*, p. 213.

83. *Greenmantle*, p. 29.

84. *Prester John*, pp. 293–4.

85. *A Lodge in the Wilderness*, p. 28. It is only fair to point out, however, that this is said by Ebenezer Wakefield whose voice is not dominant in the house-party.

86. *A Lodge in the Wilderness*, p. 32.

87. Ibid., pp. 115–16.

88. Ibid., pp. 157–8.

89. Ibid., p. 51.

90. Buchan in *The House of the Four Winds* makes a typical modification — or at any rate vulgarisation — of Conrad: 'It's the idea that wins every time — the idea with brains and guts behind it' (p. 337).

91. *A Lodge in the Wilderness*, pp. 59–60.

92. Ibid., p. 60.

93. *Prester John*, pp. 299–300.

94. *A Lodge in the Wilderness*, p. 140.

95. *Mr. Standfast*, p. 40. Despite this piece of evidence Buchan was not entirely humourless on the subject: see his parody of bad colonial verse in *A Lodge in the Wilderness*, p. 64.

96. *A Lodge in the Wilderness*, pp. 141–2.

97. Ibid., p. 14.

98. *A Lodge in the Wilderness*, p. 27.

99. Ibid., pp. 196–7.

100. Ibid., pp. 227–8.

101. Ibid., p. 29. 'It means a renunciation of old forms and conventions and the clear eyed facing of a new world in the knowledge that when the half-gods go the true gods must come.'

102. Ibid., p. 148.

103. Ibid., pp. 208–9.

104. Ibid., p. 245.

105. Ibid., p. 225. It is, of course, tempting to speculate about Hegelian influences here.

106. Ibid., p. 225.

107. Ibid., p. 235.

108. Ibid., p. 235.

109. Ibid., p. 244.

110. Ibid., p. 237.

111. Ibid., p. 245.

Epilogue

THE late-nineteenth-century imperial idea had no innate dynamic or character of its own: no one sat down in Whitehall and said 'Let's have an empire'. It was found to exist as the physical product of one defensive political decision after another as the country's statesmen interpreted the international situation; and a product moreover, which, until the Chamberlain era at least, was considered to have little but extrinsic value. All too often *post hoc* has been confused with *propter hoc* and men's reactions to the facts of empire assumed to be its cause.

An interesting parallel suggests itself in the conclusions of this study. Not even in Kipling is the imperial idea in itself seen to provide the basic inspiration. It is *not* essentially creative: Kipling is not writing in order to express the idea of empire. Given the idea, he reacted in the way any artist would — by finding in it a means through which to express his own artistic vision. The mistakes that have been made about him from Buchanan to Edmund Wilson almost wholly arise from a failure to apprehend the precise role of the imperial idea in his work. Awareness of man's estrangement and his compulsive need to armour himself against its effects, creates the dramatic tension in Kipling. His articulation of this tension within the imperial idea provides the latter with a dual level and a significance profound enough to add a whole new dimension to his work. To concentrate purely on the political level means a failure to appreciate that out of the imperial idea has been forged an outstanding contribution to the symbolism of self-salvation.

A refusal to see Kipling as a sort of Sibylline mask through which the imperial idea gives tongue is not meant to deny Kipling's support for the idea in political terms. In doing so, however, he was frequently, and to a large extent deliberately, concealing his tracks. If those which he allowed to remain in view were seen by some to lead straight to an imperial Delphos, it can only appear as a rather ironic piece of poetic retribution.

For Conrad, the imperial idea, while it exposes human avarice at its most naked and squalid, is, fundamentally, a symbol of man's isolation and his utter failure to communicate with his fellows. No solutions are offered by means of it, except in so far as service to an ideal must always, in his eyes, strengthen individual integrity. And this sums up both the affinity and the gap between him and Kipling, clearly indicating the greater writer and the reason for his greatness.

Buchan, even more distinctly than Kipling, sets out to find salvation. But, from the basis of a firmly religious temper, he searched for it beyond the self, and approached the imperial idea with far more of the altruism of Conrad's ideal than Kipling ever possessed. It seemed to him that the idea could furnish a great chain of communion which would link man and his world of actuality with the Divine Will. Conrad, in recommending the virtue of bowing down before, and sacrificing to, an ideal, did not have a God; Buchan had, and his ultimate discovery was that he was a God of mercy and love who could be reached, not through an aloof abstraction from the world but through personal service and sacrifice to humanity. The imperial idea was for him simply a moment in his progress towards this realisation.

A study of the nature of the idea in these three writers reveals that in every case it is an expression of the individual's response to the fact of his own isolation. Kipling and Buchan, particularly, when they called men to imperialism called them to their salvation.

Haggard's work offers an extremely informative contrast. Writing from a tradition which had its dynamic in a radically different idea of nature, he gives to empire a function which illustrates his concern with the ambiguity of man's place and purpose in a universe seemingly characterised by chance and change. Action is still being directed towards the elucidation of the mystery and the establishment of the Great End: it is action, moreover, through aeons of time, for only through this gradual evolution, impenetrable to the particular moment, is there any hope that meaning in nature can be verified.

It is this conviction which leads Haggard to despise the foolish snobbery of cultural exclusiveness, to see culture and morality instead, as affairs of latitude, and to recognise that distinctions between one race and another — where these are more real than apparent — are the sport of history, temporal not moral. Empire offers a highly appropriate field for such comparisons while at the same time evoking, in its ultimate transience, the magnitude of the historical process.

Allowing for this necessary and fundamental distinction in the evolutionary mode by which meaning is established for these authors, one important affinity between Haggard and the others deserves emphasis. For, however much Haggard suspected a lack of providential design, his revolt against the notion of a totally mechanistic view of reality, so contemptuous of the human spirit, could never have been suppressed. Describing the advance of fatalism in the aftermath of Darwin's submissions, Jacques Barzun writes:

Evolution . . . was an absolute. Behind all changes and actual things it operated as a cause. Darwinism yielded its basic law and its name, when viewed historically, was Progress. All events had physical origins; physical origins were discoverable by science; and the method of science alone could, by revealing the nature of things, make the mechanical sequences of things wholly benevolent to man. Fatalism and progress were as closely linked as the Heavenly Twins and like them invincible.

Their victory, however, required the banishment of all anthropomorphic ideas, and since mind was the most anthropomorphic thing in man, it must be driven from the field, first in the form of God or Teleology, then in the form of consciousness or purpose.[1]

Haggard, however uncertain of the alternative, strenuously resisted such a development and in so doing identified himself with the anti-positivism of the other imperial writers discussed here.

For these others, action, as this study has shown, is inspired by illusion and myth and justified in terms of self-consciousness. In no sense is it fundamentally political or positivistic. It is this attribute which roots these writers very firmly in that epoch of great mental ferment which closed the nineteenth century and opened the twentieth. Though I am unable to agree with Mr. Annan's conclusions and have reservations over his comparison of Kipling with Durkheim, his placing of Kipling in the context of the anti-positivists makes a valuable contribution.

The most distinguished of the social thinkers so classified were to be found on the Continent, positivism remaining well entrenched in England throughout the entire century. Most of them — Freud, Durkheim, Mosca, Bergson, Weber, Troeltsch, Benda — were, like the subjects of this study, born between 1855 and 1875. Sorel and Pareto, though a few years older, were very much part of the same constellation. Their achievement had been to expose the inadequacy of the eighteenth century's faith in the 'objectively verifiable' when it came to examining and explaining human conduct.

... they found themselves inserting between the eternal data and the final intellectual product an intermediate stage of reflection on their own awareness of these data. The result was an enormous heightening of intellectual self-consciousness ... 'Seeing through' — probing in depth — these are the hall-marks of early twentieth-century thinking.[2]

No longer could man's actions be seen as determined by some universal law.

Psychological process had replaced external reality as the most pressing topic for investigation. It was no longer what existed that seemed most important: it was what men thought existed.[3]

It is not sufficiently meaningful, therefore, to link Kipling with the continental sociologists merely because his conclusions show a marked affinity with Durkheim's theory of groups: this would establish neither Kipling's vision nor Durkheim's anti-positivism. The fundamental level at which Kipling, Conrad and Buchan connect with the continental sociologists is to be indicated more precisely in the special recognition shared by all of the highly subjective and non-rational basis from which society was articulated. Professor Hughes describes these intellectual innovators as being 'obsessed, almost intoxicated, with a rediscovery of the nonlogical, the uncivilised, the inexplicable', and his remarks could well apply to these three authors. The point of departure for *both* sociologist and writer was the same — having advanced the disparity between 'external reality and the internal appreciation of that reality' (the phrase is Hughes's) they were compelled to an acute awareness of the sovereign powers of the individual consciousness to create its own world with reference to none but purely subjective criteria. And it was a short step to the recognition of that 'world' as the only ultimate reality.

One of the most celebrated of the anti-positivists, Benedetto Croce, gave his summing up of the development in these succinct terms (the italics are his):

We no longer believe . . . , like the Greeks in happiness of life on earth; we no longer believe, like the Christians, in happiness in an other-worldly life; we no longer believe like the optimistic philosophers of the last century, in a happy future for the human race . . . We no longer believe in anything of that, and *what we have alone retained is the consciousness of ourselves, and the need to make that consciousness ever clearer and more evident . . .*[4]

Another, William James, put it even more tersely:

Our own reality, that sense of our own life which we at every moment possess is the ultimate of ultimates for our belief.[5]

Even Durkheim, perhaps the most reluctant of all to abandon the old positivist methods and standpoints, finally subsumed the same conclusion with his admission in *Formes élémentaires* that society existed only in the minds of individuals.

In the hands of the imaginative writers these insights led, as this study has shown, to the sharpest delineation of the individual's isolation, to the consciousness of selfhood and the perils of moral disintegration.

Between the response of these three writers whose work is most intimately — indeed organically — concerned with the idea of empire and that of the politician there is a curious parallel. For the latter the empire could also be a symbol of isolation. Those who shared the faith of men like Cobden and Gladstone in the capacity of their ideas and ideals to penetrate along with their commerce, found their position rapidly eroded in the last quarter of the century. Confident of the rightness of these ideals but unable to convert or convince others, they came to the conclusion that action rather than argument would alone protect their interests. So the 'imperial' politician himself retired to a Sinaic aloofness. But, to recall one of R. H. Tawney's observations, those who seek God in isolation tend to find, instead, a devil cast in their own image: certainly, the knowledge of God's support did remarkably little to diminish His servants' sense of isolation: their strength still remained the brittle inner strength of self-reliance. Authority, discipline, fidelity, devotion, fortitude and self-sacrifice constitute the ideal imperial servant whether he is making his soul in the fiction of Kipling, Buchan or Conrad, or in the ranks of the pro-consuls.

To fight for the right, to abhor the imperfect, the unjust or the mean, to swerve neither to the right hand nor to the left, to care nothing for flattery or applause or odium or abuse . . . never to let your enthusiasm be soured or your courage grow dim . . .

These words could have come from Orde or, in their more sober moments, from any of the Buchan heroes; they were, in fact, Lord Curzon's farewell to India.

The imperial idea revealed, to both the politician and the writer, man's isolation. At the same time it also suggested ways of making one's soul in the light of this realisation — a light which nineteenth-century political and intellectual developments had focused upon the individual more sharply than ever before.

One might add that as the imperial fervour diminished in the aftermath of the Boer War the relationship between the imperial idea and the imaginative writer took on a new and very different form. For Kipling, Conrad and Buchan the crisis of empire had also been their own personal crisis: alienation, the violation of integrity and the loss of self-consciousness. It is, therefore, not surprising that the tensions of these writers' moral awareness are found to be in remarkable sympathy with the tensions of the imperial idea. For them, a war of aggrandisement predicating an unceasing antagonism between self and nonself was a condition of existence: a war which was, in one sense, as much a war of oppression as any imperial campaign, with full and continuing self-consciousness as its objective.

In this context it is interesting to recall a remark made by one of these later writers, George Orwell. In 'Shooting an Elephant' he writes:

I perceived in this moment that when the white man turns tyrant it is his own freedom he destroys. He becomes a sort of hollow, posing dummy, the conventional figure of a sahib. For it is the condition of his rule that he shall spend his life in trying to impress the 'natives', and so in every crisis he has got to do what 'the natives' expect of him. He wears a mask, and his face grows to fit it.

There is an apt comment in this: ritual and 'form' provide an identity, a uniform which will house and preserve the otherwise unprotected consciousness. Conrad, though well aware of the advantages of ritual and form as his intense attachment to the sea-man's world clearly informs us, despised their offer of a way out. Kipling, on the other hand, put a desperate trust in just such shields and masks, for the sort of freedom Orwell talks about was, to him, pure anarchy. The character Flory in another Orwell book, *Burmese Days*, recognises with bitterness that he had become 'a creature of the despotism, a pukka sahib, tied tighter than a monk or a savage by an unbreakable system of taboos'; but Kipling's sympathy for the milieu was largely derived from this very fact — that it prescribed his place firmly, so offering him a mask and a function and, therefore, a guarantee of being.

What the 'imperial' writings of men like Orwell and Joyce Cary show is that for them the significance of the relationship works the other way round. Their point of view is that of the 'oppressed'. As these quotations would indicate, Orwell had an abhorrence for what destroys the individual's freedom while for Cary, too, freedom by which the individual creates and develops is of central concern in his colonial stories and elsewhere.

Obviously this subject offers scope for much further enquiry, but perhaps enough has been said here to suggest that if we are to describe any of these writers in the idiom of the Beerbohm cartoons as the banjo-bards of Empire, we must at once revise our notions of the range and sophistication of an unduly neglected instrument.

NOTES

1. Jacques Barzun, *Darwin, Marx and Wagner*, pp. 351–2.
2. Stuart Hughes, *Consciousness and Society* (1959), p. 16.
3. Ibid., p. 66.
4. H. S. Hughes, op. cit., p. 428.
5. William James, *The Principles of Psychology*, vol. 2, p. 297.

Select Bibliography

This bibliography includes only those works which have been of specific assistance in the writing of this book.

General and Chapters 1 and 3

Dates given here are of editions to which reference is made in the text.

W. H. AUDEN, *The Enchaféd Flood*, 1951.

JACQUES BARZUN, *Darwin, Marx and Wagner*, 1942.

F. W. BATESON, *English Poetry: A Critical Introduction*, 1950.

ANTHONY BEAL, *D. H. Lawrence: Selected Literary Criticism*, 1955.

GEORGE BENNETT, *The Concept of Empire: Burke to Attlee 1774–1947* (British Political Tradition, no. 6), 1953.

W. S. BLUNT, *My Diaries*, 1932.

C. A. BODELSEN, *Studies in Mid-Victorian Imperialism*, 1960.

FRIEDRICH BRIE, *Imperialistische Strömungen in der Englischen Literatur*, Halle, 1928.

ASA BRIGGS, *Victorian People*, 1954.

J. H. BUCKLEY, *William Ernest Henley: A Study in the 'counter-decadence' of the nineties*, Princeton, 1945.
The Victorian Temper: A Study in Literary Culture, 1952.

O. BURDETT, *The Beardsley Period: An Essay in Perspective*, 1925.

J. B. BURY, *The Idea of Progress: An Enquiry into its Origin and Growth*, 1920.

THOMAS CARLYLE, *Critical and Miscellaneous Essays.*

(Collected 1838).
Heroes and Hero-Worship.*
Latter-Day Pamphlets.†
Past and Present.‡
Sartor Resartus.§
(Centenary Edition, 1896–1901)

C. E. CARRINGTON, *The British Overseas: Exploits of a Nation of Shopkeepers*, Cambridge, 1950.

JOYCE CARY, *Mister Johnson*, 1952.

* First published 1841.   † First published 1850.   ‡ First published 1843.   § First published 1833–4.

W. S. CHURCHILL, *The River War*, 1899.
  The Story of the Malakand Field Force, 1904.
ALFRED COBBAN, *Edmund Burke and the Revolt against the Eighteenth Century*, 1929.
FREDERICK COPLESTON, *A History of Philosophy*, 1946.
G. CROLY, *The Englishman's Polar Star!!* Preston, 1828.
BERNARD DARWIN, *The English Public School*, 1929.
CHARLES DARWIN, *On the Origin of Species*, 1902.
FRANCIS DARWIN, *The Life and Letters of Charles Darwin*, 1887.
FRANCIS DARWIN and A. C. SEWARD, *More Letters of Charles Darwin*, 1903.
CHARLES DILKE, *Greater Britain* (4th edn., 1869).
E. EDWARDES, *Memorials of the Life and Letters of Sir Herbert Edwardes*, 1886.
R. C. K. ENSOR, *England 1870–1914*, Oxford, 1936.
A. C. EWING, *The Idealist Tradition*, Illinois, 1957.
J. G. FICHTE, *The Vocation of the Scholar*,
  The Nature of the Scholar,
  The Vocation of Man, etc., in *The Popular Works of Johann Gottlieb Fichte* (trans. William Smith), 1889.
E. M. FORSTER, *A Passage to India* (1924).
H. NORTHROP FRYE (ed.), *Romanticism Reconsidered*, 1963.
G. P. GOOCH (*et al.*), *The Heart of Empire*, 1901.
H. B. GRAY, *Public Schools and the Empire*, 1913.
GRAHAM GREENE (ed.), *The Old School*, 1934.
J. C. GREENE, *The Death of Adam*, New York, 1961.
PHYLLIS GROSSKURTH, *John Addington Symonds. A Biography*, 1964.
RICHARD HAKLUYT, *Discourses on Western Planting*, Hakluyt Society Publications (2nd ser.), no. lxvii, 1935.
ÉLIE HALÉVY, *A History of the English People in The Nineteenth Century*, vols. 4 and 5, 1951.
C. F. HARROLD, *Carlyle and German Thought 1819–1834* (Yale Studies in English, 82), New Haven, Conn., 1934.
G. W. F. HEGEL, *Lectures on the Philosophy of History*, 1857.
  Reason in History, New York, 1953.
L. T. HOBHOUSE, *Democracy and Reaction*, 1904.
J. A. HOBSON, *The Psychology of Jingoism*, 1901.
JOHN HOLLOWAY, *The Victorian Sage*, 1953.
W. E. HOUGHTON, *The Victorian Frame of Mind 1830–1870*, New Haven, Conn., 1957.
S. HOWE, *Novels of Empire*, New York, 1949.
H. S. HUGHES, *Consciousness and Society*, 1959.

RICHARD HUMPHREY, *Georges Sorel. Prophet Without Honour*, New Haven, Conn., 1951.

HOLBROOK JACKSON, *The Eighteen Nineties*, Penguin edn., 1950.

WILLIAM JAMES, *The Meaning of Truth*, New York, 1909.
Pragmatism, 1907.
The Principles of Psychology, 1910.

IMMANUEL KANT, *Critique of Pure Reason* (trans. Norman Kemp Smith), 1929.
Critique of Practical Reason (trans. Abbot), 1883.

HANS KELSEN, *The Foundations of Democracy* (pub. as Part II of *Ethics*, vol. lxvi. Oct. 1955).

RAYNE KRUGER, *Good-bye Dolly Gray: The Story of the Boer War*, 1959.

W. L. LANGER, *The Diplomacy of Imperialism*, New York and London, 1935.

W. E. LECKY, *History of the Rise and Influence of Rationalism in Europe (1865)*, New York, 1903.

V. I. LENIN, *Marx–Engels–Marxism*, n.d.

A. O. LOVEJOY, *Essays in the History of Ideas*, Baltimore, 1948.

PERCY LUBBOCK (ed.), *The Letters of Henry James*, 1920.

E. C. MACK, *Public Schools and British Opinion since 1860*, 1941.

J. S. MILL, *Letters* (ed. Hugh Elliot), 1910.

ALFRED MILNER, *The Nation and the Empire*, 1913.

P. T. MOON, *Imperialism and World Politics*, New York, 1953.

GEORGE MOORE, *Avowals*, New York, 1926.

IRIS MURDOCH, *Sartre. Romantic Rationalist*, 1961.

EMERY NEFF, *Carlyle and Mill. An Introduction to Victorian Thought*, New York, 1926.

JAWAHARLAL NEHRU, *Autobiography*, 1936.

DAVID NEWSOME, *Godliness and Good Learning*, 1961.

ROLAND OLIVER, *The Missionary Factor in East Africa*, 1952.

GEORGE ORWELL, *Selected Essays*, 1957.
Burmese Days, 1949.
Keep the Aspidistra Flying, 1954.
A Clergyman's Daughter, 1935.
Homage to Catalonia, 1951.

STOW PERSONS (ed.), *Evolutionary Thought in America*, New Haven, Conn., 1950.

ERNEST RENAN, *Histoire du Peuple d'Israël*, Paris, 1893.

RONALD ROBINSON and JOHN GALLAGHER, *Africa and the Victorians: the official mind of Imperialism*, 1961.

H. V. ROUTH, *Towards the Twentieth Century*, Cambridge, 1937.

JOHN RUSKIN, *Works* vols. 18 and 20 (ed. E. J. Cook and A. Wedderburn), 1903–12.

BERTRAND RUSSELL, *Freedom and Organisation*, 1945.
Portraits from Memory, 1956.

G. H. SABINE, *A History of Political Theory*, 1951.

JEAN-PAUL SARTRE, *L'Existentialisme est un Humanisme*, Paris (Les Éditions Nagel), 1951.

J. A. SCHUMPETER, *Imperialism and Social Classes*, Oxford, 1951.

J. R. SEELEY, *The Expansion of England*, 1883.

BERNARD SHAW, *Fabianism and the Empire*, 1900.

D. C. SOMERVELL, *English Thought in the Nineteenth Century*, 1940.

GEORGES SOREL, *Reflections on Violence* (trans. T. E. Hulme and J. Roth), Illinois, 1950.
L'Ancienne et la nouvelle Métaphysique (D'Aristote à Marx), Paris, 1935.

JAMES FITZJAMES STEPHEN, *Liberty, Equality, Fraternity*, 1874.

LESLIE STEPHEN, *The English Utilitarians*, 1900.

J. A. SYMONDS, *Essays Speculative and Suggestive*, 1890.

R. H. TAWNEY, *Religion and the Rise of Capitalism*, 1961.

DAVID THOMSON, *England in the Nineteenth Century*, The Pelican History of England, vol. 8, 1950.

A. P. THORNTON, *The Imperial Idea and its Enemies: a study in British power*, 1959.

W. Y. TINDALL, *Forces in Modern British Literature*, New York, 1947.

LIONEL TRILLING, *Matthew Arnold*, 1956.

ROBERT TUCKER, *Philosophy and Myth in Karl Marx*, Cambridge, 1961.

BEATRICE WEBB, *Our Partnership*, 1948.

J. A. WILLIAMSON, *A Short History of British Expansion*, 1941–3.
The Age of Drake, 1938.

ESMÉ WINGFIELD-STRATFORD, *The Victorian Tragedy*, 1930.
The Victorian Sunset, 1932.
The Victorian Aftermath, 1933.
The Unfolding Pattern of British Life, 1953.

G. M. YOUNG, *Victorian England: Portrait of an Age*, 1949.

G. YOUNGHUSBAND, *A Soldier's Memories*, 1917.

Chapter 2

The following index is of works specifically referred to in Chapter 2. The date given here is that of the work's first appearance either in serial form or as a book.

Allan and the Ice-Gods, 1927.
Allan Quatermain, 1887.
Allan's Wife (including *Long Odds*, 1886, and *A Tale of Three Lions*, 1887), 1889.
Ayesha, 1904–5.
Child of Storm, 1913.
Finished, 1917.
Ghost Kings, The, 1907–8.
Jess, 1885.
King Solomon's Mines, 1885.
Marie, 1911–12.
Nada the Lily, 1892.
She, 1886–7.
Stella Fregelius, 1902–3.
Way of the Spirit, The, 1906.
Witch's Head, The, 1884.

Books about Rider Haggard referred to in Chapter 2.

MORTON COHEN, *Rider Haggard. His Life and Work*, 1960.
— *Rudyard Kipling to Rider Haggard. The Record of a Friendship*, 1965.
LILIAS RIDER HAGGARD, *The Cloak that I left*, 1951.

Chapter 4

The following index is of works specifically referred to in Chapter 4. Date of first publication is given along with the title of the volume in the Sussex Edition in which short stories alluded to can be found.

Collected Works of Rudyard Kipling. Sussex Edition, 1937–9.
Address at Stationers' Hall, 1925 (*A Book of Words*).
Army of a Dream, The, 1904 (*Traffics and Discoveries*).
Art of Fiction, The, 1926 (*A Book of Words*).
As Easy as ABC, 1912 (*A Diversity of Creatures*).
At the End of the Passage, 1890 (*Life's Handicap*).
At Howli Thana, 1888 (*Soldiers Three*).
At the Pit's Mouth, 1888 (*Wee Willie Winkie*).
Beyond the Pale, 1888 (*Plain Tales from the Hills*).
Black Jack, 1888 (*Soldiers Three*).
Bridge-Builders, The, 1893 (*The Day's Work*).

Captains Courageous, 1896–7.

Children of the Zodiac, The, 1891 (*Many Inventions*).

City of Dreadful Night, The, 1885 (*Life's Handicap*).

Conference of the Powers, A, 1890 (*Many Inventions*).

Conversion of Aurelian McGoggin, The, 1887 (*Plain Tales from the Hills*).

Courting of Dinah Shadd, The, 1890 (*Life's Handicap*).

Deal in Cotton, A, 1907 (*Actions and Reactions*).

Disturber of Traffic, The, 1891 (*Many Inventions*).

Dray Wara Yow Dee, 1888 (*Soldiers Three*).

Drums of the Fore and Aft, The, 1888 (*Wee Willie Winkie*).

Education of Otis Yeere, The, 1888 (*Wee Willie Winkie*).

England and the English, 1920 (*A Book of Words*).

Enlightenments of Pagett, M.P., The, 1890 (*Many Inventions*).

Eye of Allah, The, 1926 (*Debits and Credits*).

Finest Story in the World, The, 1891 (*Many Inventions*).

Gardener, The, 1925 (*Debits and Credits*).

Gemini, 1888 (*Soldiers Three*).

Georgie Porgie, 1888 (*Life's Handicap*).

God from the Machine, The, 1888 (*Soldiers Three*).

Head of the District, The 1890 (*Life's Handicap*).

His Chance in Life, 1887 (*Plain Tales from the Hills*).

Independence, 1923 (*A Book of Words*).

'In the Interests of the Brethren', 1918 (*Debits and Credits*).

In the Same Boat, 1911 (*A Diversity of Creatures*).

Judgment of Dungara, The, 1888 (*Soldiers Three*).

Just So Stories, 1902.

Kidnapped, 1887 (*Plain Tales from the Hills*).

Kim, 1901.

Letters of Travel, 1920.

Light that Failed, The, 1890.

Limitations of Pambé Serang, The, 1889 (*Life's Handicap*).

Lispeth, 1886 (*Plain Tales from the Hills*).

Little Tobrah, 1888 (*Life's Handicap*).

Madness of Private Ortheris, The, 1888 (*Plain Tales from the Hills*).

Madonna of the Trenches, A, 1924 (*Debits and Credits*).

Mark of the Beast, The, 1890 (*Life's Handicap*).

Mary Postgate, 1915 (*A Diversity of Creatures*).

Matter of Fact, A, 1892 (*Many Inventions*).

Mother Hive, The, 1908 (*Actions and Reactions*).

Mowgli's Brothers, 1894 (*The Jungle Book*).

Mrs. Bathurst, 1904 (*Traffics and Discoveries*).

Mutiny of the Mavericks, The, 1891 (*Life's Handicap*).
On the City Wall, 1888 (*Soldiers Three*).
On the Gate, 1926 (*Debits and Credits*).
On Greenhow Hill, 1890 (*Life's Handicap*).
One View of the Question, 1890 (*Many Inventions*).
Only a Subaltern, 1888 (*Wee Willie Winkie*).
Phantom 'Rickshaw, The, 1885 (*Wee Willie Winkie*).
Puck of Pook's Hill, 1906
Record of Badalia Herodsfoot, The, 1890 (*Many Inventions*).
Sahib's War, A, 1901 (*Traffics and Discoveries*).
Sea Constables, 1915 (*Debits and Credits*).
Solid Muldoon, The, 1888 (*Soldiers Three*).
Something of Myself, 1937.
Stalky and Co., 1899.
'They', 1904 (*Traffics and Discoveries*).
'Tiger! Tiger!', 1894 (*The Jungle Book*).
To be Filed for Reference, 1888 (*Plain Tales from the Hills*).
Tod's Amendment, 1887 (*Plain Tales from the Hills*).
Values in Life, 1920 (*A Book of Words*).
Walking Delegate, A, 1894 (*The Day's Work*).
Wish House, The, 1924 (*Debits and Credits*).
With the Main Guard, 1888 (*Soldiers Three*).
Without Benefit of Clergy, 1890 (*Life's Handicap*).
Woman in his Life, The, 1928 (*Limits and Renewals*).
Wressley of the Foreign Office, 1887 (*Plain Tales from the Hills*).

Books and essays about Kipling referred to in Chapter 4.

N. G. ANNAN, 'Kipling's Place in the History of Ideas', in *Victorian Studies*, June 1960.

G. C. BERESFORD, *School-days with Kipling*, 1936.

C. HILTON BROWN, *Rudyard Kipling*, 1945.

C. E. CARRINGTON, *Rudyard Kipling. His Life and Work*, 1955.

BONAMY DOBRÉE, 'Kipling', in *The Lamp and the Lute*, Oxford, 1929.

ROBERT GRAVES, 'Rudyard Kipling', in *The Common Asphodel*, 1949.

RICHARD LEGALLIENNE, *Rudyard Kipling*, 1900.

ANDREW RUTHERFORD (ed.), *The Mind and Art of Rudyard Kipling*, 1964.

DIXON SCOTT, 'The Meekness of Rudyard Kipling', in *Men of Letters*, 1916.

E. B. SHANKS, *Rudyard Kipling: A study in literature and political ideas*, 1940.

J. M. S. TOMPKINS, *The Art of Rudyard Kipling*, 1949.

LIONEL TRILLING, 'Rudyard Kipling', in *The Liberal Imagination*, 1961.

EDMUND WILSON, 'The Kipling that Nobody Read', in *The Wound and the Bow*, 1961.

A. W. YEATS, *Rudyard Kipling. A Bibliographical Catalogue*, Toronto, 1959.

Chapter 5

The following index is of works specifically referred to in Chapter 5. The date given here is that of the work's first appearance either in serial form or as a book.

Collected Works, The Medallion Edition, 1925–8 (the Uniform Edition has the same pagination).

Almayer's Folly, 1895.

Arrow of Gold, The, 1918–20.

Chance, 1912.

Heart of Darkness (published along with *Youth* and *The End of the Tether*), 1902.

Lord Jim, 1899–1900.

Mirror of the Sea, The, 1906.

Nigger of the Narcissus, The, 1897.

Nostromo, 1904.

Notes on Life and Letters, 1921.

Outcast of the Islands, An, 1908–9.

Personal Record, A, 1908–9.

Rescue, The, 1919.

Rover, The, 1923.

Secret Agent, The, 1906–7.

Set of Six, A, 1908.

Shadow Line, The, 1916–17.

Tales of Hearsay, 1925.

Tales of Unrest (including *Karain; A Memory, An Outpost of Progress, The Return*), 1898.

'Twixt Land and Sea — Tales (including *The Secret Sharer*), 1912.

Typhoon, 1902.

Under Western Eyes, 1910–11.

Victory, 1915.

Within the Tides (including 'The Planter of Malata'), 1915.

*Books and essays about Conrad which have influenced the composition of
    Chapter 5.*

JOCELYN BAINES, *Joseph Conrad. A Critical Biography*, 1960.
M. C. BRADBROOK, *Joseph Conrad. Poland's English Genius*, Cambridge,
    1941.
RICHARD CURLE, *Joseph Conrad and his Characters*, 1957.
ALBERT GUERARD, *Conrad the Novelist*, 1958.
DOUGLAS HEWITT, *Conrad. A Reassessment*, Cambridge, 1952.
F. R. LEAVIS, 'Joseph Conrad', in *The Great Tradition*, 1948.
ROBERT PENN WARREN, 'The Great Mirage,' in *Selected Essays*, New
    York, 1958.
V. S. PRITCHETT, 'A Pole in the Far East,' in *The Living Novel*, 1946.

Chapter 6

The following index is of works specifically referred to in Chapter 6.
The date given is that of the work's first publication.

Blanket of the Dark, The, 1931.
Castle Gay, 1930.
Courts of the Morning, The, 1929.
Dancing Floor, The, 1926.
Gap in the Curtain, The, 1932.
Greenmantle, 1916.
Half-Hearted, The, 1900.
House of the Four Winds, The, 1935.
Huntingtower, 1922.
Island of Sheep, The, 1936.
Lodge in the Wilderness, A, 1906.
Memory-Hold-the Door, 1940.
Moon Endureth, The, 1912.
Mr. Standfast, 1919.
Power House, The, 1916.
Prester John, 1910.
Prince of the Captivity, A, 1939.
Sick Heart River, 1941.
Thirty-Nine Steps, The, 1915.
Three Hostages, The, 1924.
Watcher by the Threshold, The, 1902.

Index